W Wilson

A Summer Ramble in the Himalayas

With Sporting Adventures in the Vale of Cashmere

W Wilson

A Summer Ramble in the Himalayas
With Sporting Adventures in the Vale of Cashmere

ISBN/EAN: 9783337179328

Printed in Europe, USA, Canada, Australia, Japan

Cover: Foto ©Andreas Hilbeck / pixelio.de

More available books at **www.hansebooks.com**

A SUMMER RAMBLE

IN

THE HIMALAYAS.

WITH

Sporting Adventures in the Vale of Cashmere.

EDITED BY

"MOUNTAINEER."

LONDON
HURST AND BLACKETT, PUBLISHERS
SUCCESSORS TO HENRY COLBURN
13 GREAT MARLBOROUGH STREET

INTRODUCTION.

As this volume is published without the Author's name, and as the Editor appears only under his *nom de plume* of "Mountaineer," the reader may fairly expect some little information regarding it. The original manuscript consisted of the Author's rough notes, and these were made over by him to the Editor, by whom they were thrown into a connected narrative form. In Chapter III. the Author speaks of falling in with "Wilson's Camp," and in Chapter VII. he refers to "a series of articles in the *Indian Sporting Review*, entitled "Game of the Himalayas," by *Mountaineer*. Mountaineer is a name familiar to all Indian sportsmen of the last twenty years, as identical with that of Mr. Wilson, of Mussoorie, our present Author's well-valued companion during much of his ramble.

Mountaineer carries with him to the chase, not only all those qualities essential to success, but many which render him something more than a sportsman: he is fond of natural history, alive to the beauties of Nature, inquisitive as to the habits and customs of the people to whom his wanderings introduce him; and the descriptive faculty is developed in all his writings. It will be seen that two chapters in the present volume, giving an account of the Gurwhal country, are entirely from his pen.

It only remains to add, that the " Summer Ramble" being entrusted to my hands for publication by Mr. Wilson, I gladly avail myself of the opportunity to offer to the Public a volume which, I believe, will not be found dull in any single page, but interesting in many; and which will, undoubtedly, have the charm of novelty for the great majority of European readers.

JAMES HUME.

Reform Club, Pall Mall.
June, 1860.

A SUMMER RAMBLE

IN

THE HIMALAYAS.

CHAPTER I.

I STARTED from Meerut, in the north-western provinces of British India, bound for a summer's excursion in the Himalayan mountains, to enjoy some of the shooting for which they are so celebrated, and to try the effect of their cool and bracing climate in palliating the ravages which sundry hot seasons in the enervating one of the plains had committed on a once tolerable constitution.

In the primitive fashion of palanquin and bearers, which is, as yet, in India the only means of speedy travelling on any but the grand trunk roads, I left Meerut for Mussoorie, one of the hill sanatariums. The distance is one hundred and ten miles, and the journey generally occupies thirty-six hours, including stoppages for refreshment at the different dāk bungalows. From Mozufernugger, about twenty-four miles out of Meerut, the snowy mountains could, in the clear light of the early morning, be distinctly seen, and here, at the distance of one hundred and twenty miles, I had the first view of these "habitations of the Deity," as the Hindoo deems them, though in clear weather they are often visible from Meerut. The road was very good to Saharunpore, being thus far on the route to the large military station of Umballa; but from thence it was extremely dusty, and full of deep ruts, which ought not to be the case, considering that it leads to a place which in summer contains more European residents than any station in Upper India. The pass through or over the Sewalic hills, which bound the pretty valley of the Dhoon, was, from Mohun to near the crest of the low range, a distance of six miles, the bed of a mountain-torrent, strewn thickly over with stones and boulders of all sizes, which must make it at all times rather rough work for wheeled carriages, and in the rains almost impassable. The slight descent into the Dhoon was comparatively good road. The whole way from Keree to beyond Shorepore, on the approach to, and passage through this low range of hills, some twenty-four miles, is through dense jungle, in some places nearly impenetrable, from the high rank grass which nearly buries the trees. Deer, and jungle and pea-fowl, frequently cross the path before the traveller, and once or twice a year, as if to prove they still exist near, a tiger or wild elephant disturbs the tranquil passage of one more unfortunate, or fortunate if he is of the sterner sex, and likes the excitement, than the rest. Half way across the Dhoon, I was put down at the neat little town of **Deyrah**, at a very nice hotel kept by an Englishman, where I was most comfortably housed for a few days. The European portion of this little station is, without exception, the most cheerful place of the kind I have seen in India. The houses, each enclosed in a garden or well-wooded compound, and the green lanes bordered with hedges of roses or other shrubs or trees, give a home-like appearance which no other station possesses. But for the natives passing and repassing, I could often have fancied myself in some village of merry England. Deyrah is the winter residence of the invalid officers and others who have made Mussoorie a permanent home, the climate in the cold weather being thought more agreeable than that of the hill station. It is the cantonment for one of the Goorkha regiments in the Company's service, has a magistrate and collector, with the title of superintendent of the Dhoon, an assistant magistrate, and in winter a clergyman. It has a church, a mission house and school belonging to the American missionaries, a race course, and two hotels. The climate at this season (March) appeared to me delightful, with a freshness and purity I had not felt for years, and quite wanting even in the coldest weather in the plains. This feeling was not generally shared in by the residents, for I heard frequent complaints about its beginning to get too warm, and many had already left for Mussoorie, and nearly all were preparing to do so.

The Dhoon of Deyrah is a little valley at the foot of the great Himalayan range, between the Ganges and the Jumna rivers. It is separated from the plains by the Sewalie hills, before mentioned, a low, thickly wooded range, rising about 1500 or 2000 feet above the general level, and very rugged and broken. The valley is about sixty miles long and fourteen broad. By far the greater portion is dense forest, but several canals for irrigation having been recently made, a much larger portion will shortly be under cultivation. With the markets at Deyrah and Mussoorie so near at hand, where grain is generally dearer than in the plains, it appears to offer great advantages to an agricultural population. The great drawback, I believe, is that the cattle suffer severely in the rainy season, and die in great numbers. This will most probably wear off as the land is cleared, as there is little doubt it is caused by the great extent of jungle, and the malaria arising from its decomposition at the close of the rains. From October to July the Dhoon is healthy in every part, and in the cold weather its climate is perfect, but the autumnal months in the uncleared parts are most fatal. At this period it would be almost certain death to encamp in the forest for a week. The town of Deyrah and its environs, and generally all the cleared portion of the valley, is exempt from this fatal malaria, and at all times healthy. The

Dhoon forests have for years supplied nearly the whole of Upper India with timber for building purposes, and until lately the remotest corners of the Punjaub. No one, however, having thought fit to look after the preservation of the young trees, the supply is now nearly exhausted, while a little supervision and forethought on the part of Government would have secured a continuation of it for centuries. Now, when too late, something is being done, but it is very strange the waste should have been allowed to go on so long under the very noses of the successive superintendents, and stranger still, the revenue derivable from these extensive forests should have been entirely thrown away. The forests in India are the property of Government, but here, though timber was becoming more valuable every year, any person, until a short time ago, was allowed to cut down wherever and whatever he liked. The consequence was, that, instead of cutting up some of the large trees into small timbers, all the young ones have been destroyed for that purpose. Game, as might be expected, is abundant throughout the valley. Tigers, leopards, elephants, several kinds of deer, and wild pigs, are found in the forests; and of smaller game there are peafowl, pheasants, jungle fowl, partridges, quail, snipe, floriken, and hares. Tiger shooting is followed in March and April, but from the vast extent of forest is not so successful as might be expected, from the number of feline animals the country is known to contain. First-rate fishing may be had in the Jumna and other streams, mahseer being caught from ten to a hundred pounds' weight.

A tea plantation and manufactory, a few miles out of Deyrah, forms one of its principal lions. It is an experiment of Government, and has succeeded very well. Several thousand acres of land are now planted with tea trees, and a considerable quantity of first-rate tea is made every year. The whole is under a European superintendent, and some Chinese manufacturers have been imported from the Celestial Empire to make the tea. A private enterprise of the same nature is also in satisfactory progress. A few miles in another direction is the Kalunga hill, on which stood the fort of that name, where General Gillespie was killed. Nothing now remains of it but here and there the half-buried fragment of the foundation of a wall, and the site is covered with jungle.

The drive to Rajpore at the foot of the hill, six miles, in a buggy from the hotel, and the pony ride from thence to Mussoorie, on a bright spring morning, was something in itself worth a journey from the plains. From Rajpore, a large thriving village, with two hotels, the ascent is about seven miles, the first half a steady pull in zigzags along the hill side, in some places far too steep for comfortable riding; the other half a little diversified, with here and there a few score yards of level ground, a great relief to both man and beast. The whole was through forest, nowhere very dense, which changed in character as we ascended. The lower part was covered with dwarf trees and bushes, intermingled with gigantic creepers. Before we got half way up, pines, oak, and rhododendron gradually made their appearance, and are the principal trees on the Mussoorie range. The oaks of the Himalayas are evergreens, and on the lower ranges, with a few exceptions, all the forest trees are the same. The rhododendron must not be confounded with the bush rhododendron of our English gardens, which in the Himalayas is confined to the limits of forest near the snow. Here it is a large forest tree, and nothing can be conceived more beautiful than a hill side covered with these trees in full blossom, each tree a mass of rich crimson flowers.

I almost envy the man who has yet to enjoy his first ride up the Mussoorie hill. To the most indifferent it cannot but be interesting. The lateral valley on the left, with its villages and green fields cut in terraces along the hill sides, the varied hue of the forest patches, the ridge above dotted with white mansions, the park-like Dhoon valley below, its encircling range of low wooded hills, and the shadowy plains beyond, gave at each fresh turn a succession of views so novel, and so widely different from the flat plains of India, that the journey seemed too soon over. Bands of porters were transporting baggage up-hill, some sturdy hill-men from the interior, with their loads strapped to their backs; others, many of them of the gentler sex, appeared to be from the plains, and carried their loads on their heads. Some carried single loads others two, four, or half-a-dozen together; and to one large box, which I was told contained a pianoforte, twenty-four men were attached. Mules, donkeys, and ponies, chiefly loaded with grain, were intermingled with the throng, and though the road was seldom more than nine feet wide, with often a dangerous precipice on one hand, there was no confusion, and accidents are of rare occurrence. Many years ago, a gentleman and his pony fell off the road, both being killed; but this was the only mishap of the kind any one appeared to remember as connected with the ascent of the hill. The porters, on hearing my pony behind them, sidled to the edge of the road, and I remarked, almost invariably to the ravine side. The only difficult thing to pass was the piano, which, where I overtook it, took up the entire breadth of the road, and I had to ride behind it some distance till we reached a wider part, ere I could pass. Most of the hill-men greeted me with a broad grin, and the least jocose remark I made to them as I passed seemed to cause infinite merriment. Two annas and a half, or about four pence, is the regulated hire for a single load, or for every porter when more than one are required to a load. The loads are not weighed, and some are more and some less, but fifty-six pounds is considered the average, and four pence the hire, which is certainly not too much for carrying that weight seven miles of steep ascent. Some years previous to my visit, the whole of the hill-porters, as well as most of the hill-men employed in Mussoorie, ran away from a very laughable cause, though it was scarcely a laughing matter to the residents, who were put to great inconvenience. A report got circulated amongst them, that some of the Europeans were catching any unfortunate native they could find alone, and taking him to a secluded house, extracting the oil from his body by hanging him up by the heels before a large fire. How this strange report originated could never be discovered, but it was most implicitly believed in, and nothing could persuade the ignorant puharies of its utter improbability. Many left their places without waiting to receive their wages, so great was their fear; and in my progress through the hills I found the strange idea still entertained, and was several times asked for what purpose the oil of puharies was required. I have not the least doubt that to this day thousands in the hills firmly believe in the ridiculous report.

I had received an invitation to spend the few days I remained at Mussoorie with a captain of the Company's army, whom I met with at Meerut, on his way up for the hot season; and I easily found my way to his house, every one seeming to know where every one else resides ere they have been up a day. It was on the southern side of the hill, consequently had no view of the snowy range which I was rather impatient to see, but it embraced a very fine one of the Dhoon and the distant plains. Daybreak was recommended as the best time to see the north side to advantage, so I deferred that pleasure, my host offering to accompany me on the morrow to Landour, from whence a more extensive view could be had than from Mussoorie. In the evening we took a stroll on the Mall, a piece of road in the centre of Mussoorie, which has been made quite level, and as wide as possible for about a mile, and forms the public promenade. Being so early in the season, there were but few people on the hill, and we were certainly not incommoded by the throng. The air was sharp, and I had to move about briskly to keep myself comfortably warm, though clothed as one would be on a cold day in England. The Mall faces the south, and is sheltered from the cold north winds by a craggy hill, which rises some 500 feet above it, called the Camel's Back, and round which your walk or ride may be continued on a narrower, but still level and good road.

One might wander over a considerable portion of the globe, and penetrate into many remote corners in search of the picturesque, without finding an equal to the view, which, in clear weather, the residents of Landour may gaze on every morning of their lives. It was indeed well worthy of the burst of admiration which broke from my lips as, before sunrise next morning, we rounded the shoulder of the hill and stood on the north side of the Landour ridge, and I saw for the first time, rising before me in all its majestic sublimity, the long unbroken line of snowy mountains. To have as extensive a view as possible, we ascended to the top of a little hill from which both the snowy range and the plains were visible. No words can do justice to what was now before us. One half the horizon was bounded by an unbroken wall of snow, surmounted by fantastic peaks of every conceivable form, rising clear and high above the vast wave like wooded ranges that stretched before us to its base. Directly in our front it appeared to be about forty miles off, the outline clearly and sharply defined against the sky, and the smooth rock in places too perpendicular for the snow to lie plainly visible. Receding into distance on either hand it was more indistinct, particularly to the west, where a dim shadowy vapour blended snow and sky together. From some of the highest peaks light clouds seemed to rise, drifting slowly away in the direction of the wind, but disappearing soon after leaving the peak from which they rose. This is a common phenomenon, and I then imagined it was a vapour drawn from the snow by the action of the atmosphere, but I afterwards found its origin to be this. The snow in some places becomes frozen into particles as fine as dust, and is then whirled into the air by the first gust of wind, at a distance appearing like a light cloud. I had pictured to myself ranges rising one above another till the last was topped with snow, but the intervening ranges seemed nearly all of the same height as the one on which we stood, while, enthroned in its own lonely grandeur, the snowy one rose majestically as if from the summit of the most distant. The scene may not have the awfully grand appearance that some present, when one has penetrated into the recesses of the snowy mountains themselves, and standing at their feet gazes on the vast spectre-like masses rising directly overhead; but there is something so striking in its calm and still repose when seen from this distance, that the first view of the snowy range from the Landour ridge will impress many minds with more lasting feelings of admiration than closer views. As the sun rose the whole lost much of its vivid clearness, a shroud-like vapour gradually stealing over the scene, so that in many places the before sharp outline of the snowy peaks against the sky, could no longer be traced. Turning our faces the other way, the valley of the Dhoon lay at our feet, encircled by the low range of wooded hills, the dark aspect of which was broken here and there by bright yellow spots, the sites of landslips, which sparkled like beds of gold in the sunlight. The valley appeared nearly all in a state of nature, either dense forest or grass jungle, — the reclaimed portion round the town of Deyrah, on each side of the road from Rajpore, and here and there round isolated villages, looked small indeed in comparison with the whole. The rich green tint of the spring crops of corn in the cultivated parts was at this distance very striking, and contrasted well with the brown sombre hue of the grass jungle, and the dark shades of the forest. Beyond the hills that enclosed the valley, the plains of India stretched far out into the distance, the horizon so remote that the division of earth and sky could nowhere be distinctly made out. Two silver threads meandering through the maze showed the courses of the Ganges and Jumna, and small silver specks the lakes and swamps. Who could gaze on such a scene, the ideal of sublimity on one hand, and of calm and repose on the other, and not exclaim, "What a glorious creation!"

A week passed away ere my preparations were completed, in which time I became tolerably well acquainted with the sanatarium. Few visitors had as yet arrived, so there was little society; but I found the time pass very pleasantly. What with getting things ready, and riding about to see the place, every hour of the day was agreeably occupied. Mussoorie is on the first range of hills, which here rises abruptly 5000 feet above the plains, or rather the Dhoon, to which it runs parallel. The eastern portion, called Landour, is the military or cantonment part, and is nearly a thousand feet higher than the rest. It contains five or six barracks for the sick and convalescent soldiers of the European regiments stationed in the north-western provinces, a fine hospital, a church, and is besides just as well studded with private mansions as Mussoorie. Landour is but a distinctive local name, the entire station being generally termed Mussoorie; while in Government documents "the hills north of Deyrah" is the most common appellation. The houses are built on or near the crest of the ridge, and extend ten or twelve miles along it. Most are on the southern slope, or on the ridge itself, there being but few on the bleak northern side. The hill itself is steep and rugged, and there are few places where one can walk comfortably off the made roads. There are still a good many trees about the place, chiefly oaks and rhododendron; but a great many have been cut down for firewood, and all would ere this have disappeared, but for an order not to fell any more within a certain distance. The houses are built much in the same fashion as in the plains, with a verandah on one or more sides, and with one or two exceptions, are all single-storied. Most of the old ones are thatched; but a great many, built of late years, have flat pucka roofs. There is of course no attempt at regularity, each being erected where its owner could get a plot of ground naturally level enough to build on, or which could be made so without too much outlay. There are very few sites which have not required some artificial levelling, and on many this must have cost nearly as much as the erection of the house itself. Nearly all the houses belong to officers in the civil or military service, and yield a very fair return for the capital invested in them. From 60*l.* to 120*l.* is the usual rent of a house for the six months it is occupied, and some were pointed out to me as renting for 100*l.* which certainly were not intrinsically worth more than double that sum, being very old ones, built of unburnt mud bricks, and only made habitable by a yearly renewal of plaster and whitewash; but their desirable situation secured tenants every year, when much better at lower rents remained unoccupied. The owners have, however, foolishly continued building new houses year after year, so that there are now too many for the usual number of visitors, and consequently some must remain without tenants. The cost of building a house, which in a decent situation will rent for 100*l*., is now about 800*l*.; but in the infancy of the station, when material was much cheaper, it was proportionably less. Very few of the owners of estates at Mussoorie being on the spot, most are in charge of agents, who receive for their supervision five per cent. on the rent, and ten per cent. on all the outlay for repairs.

The roads are numerous and good, and railed off on the ravine side, which is very needful, as some of them border on fearful precipices. The Mall or promenade has been before mentioned. It, and indeed all the public roads, are kept in the best order, and so well gravelled that a few hours are sufficient to dry them after the heaviest showers. Being open to the west the Mall has the advantage of the setting sun, and affords a very nice evening's walk or ride. In the season it is a busy scene, on fine evenings all the residents, both of Mussoorie and Landour, repairing to it. The ladies generally eat the air (this is the translation of the Hindoostanee words) in jampauns, a kind of chair swung on poles, carried by four men at a time, the gentlemen who escort them riding or walking alongside. The bearers, or jampaunees, are hillmen from the interior, and a set of six or eight is an indispensable part of the hill establishment for every lady, and those of the other sex who are too ill to walk or ride. During the day they are employed cutting wood or grass, running errands, or doing anything they are set to, about five o'clock dressing themselves for the evening. Their fair employers turn them out in all sorts of impossible livery; grey turned up with black; blue, white, or tartan, with some other contrasting colour; but the favourite, or, perhaps, I should say that used by quiet easy-going people, who don't want to be conspicuous, is black turned up with red or yellow. The dress is always a kind of full-skirted blouse, with a broad border round the edges, and belt to match; and the various bright colours, when the Mall is crowded, have a gay and lively effect. Some ladies prefer equestrian exercise, undaunted by the drawbacks to it on the hills, and canter backwards and forwards from one end of the Mall to the other. Some portion of the evening's exercise is by many devoted to walking, which, however, is not practised to that extent one would expect it to be in such a bracing climate, and as a change from the universal riding or driving in the plains. The public roads, except the one up the hill from Rajpore, and those about the cantonment, which were made and kept up by Government, were, until lately, made and kept in repair solely at the expense of the householders, a yearly percentage on the value of each house being collected for the purpose. A new road to Rajpore having been projected, application was made to Government for some assistance, and the Akbaree revenue (the value of licences to sell spirituous liquors) of the station allotted for the purpose. With the road fund thus increased, many roads were greatly improved, and the new one rapidly progressed with. It is to be on a very gentle incline the whole way, so as to admit of wheeled carriages, which, indeed, is the only thing that could justify the outlay of such a large sum of money as it must cost. Unless made fit for wheeled carriages, it will be quite useless, as for ordinary purposes, the mere going up or down the hill, it would be scarcely ever used either by Europeans or natives, being unavoidably much longer than the old one. The money expended on it would, under present circumstances, have been much better laid out in improving the old, or making a better road through the Sewalie hills into the Dhoon, though it is very probable a carriage road from Rajpore to Mussoorie may some time or other be of infinite importance to the station. A dearth of porters at Rajpore for any length of time, would, without such a road, put the residents in a queer fix, as nearly everything for the supply of the station is brought from below.

For a place where a slip off the road would often

be attended with certain destruction or serious injury, and where riding is so universal, accidents are of rare occurrence; indeed, it is wonderful more do not happen, particularly when it is remembered that at the beginning of each season the inhabitants are nearly all fresh arrivals, many perhaps never having been on a hill before. Two places were pointed out to me where accidents had lately occurred. One was to a gentleman who, while walking on the road near his house, was met by one of his dogs, which leaping up against him, probably to be caressed, knocked him over, and he died a few hours afterwards from the effects of the fall. The spot did not look at all dangerous, nor was the hill very steep, for I walked up and down it without difficulty, and no one would have thought a fall in such a place could be attended with such a serious result. Another was to a gentleman and lady who were riding together; their horses became restive and both slipped off the road. One pony was killed on the spot, the other had to be shot where it lay; but, strange to say, the riders escaped with little injury.

The bazaar, which is common to Mussoorie and Landour, is the dividing boundary of the two places, and is under the surveillance of the military authorities. Supplies are very little dearer than in the plains, and every article likely to be required may be had either here or at one of the European merchants' shops, of which there are three, besides millinery and clothing establishments. The Mussoorie brewery is an old speculation, set on foot by a Mr. Bohlie in the infancy of the station, and now under the superintendence of an energetic cidevant trainer of youth; successful he has been in both these widely differing occupations. Do-the-boys hall, while kept up, rarely contained less than one hundred of the rising generation, and now you will sometimes hear people say they would as soon drink his beer as English. The latter, however, sells at nine rupees, or eighteen shillings, a dozen, and his at four rupees; and this, I imagine, tickles the palate as much as the flavour of the beer. It is used chiefly in the canteens of the European regiments stationed in the north-west.

The other public buildings and establishments are two churches, three boys' and three girls' schools, a club-house, hotel, billiard room, library, and a masonic lodge, besides a Government botanical garden. The club-house is the largest building in the place. It was intended for an hotel, and is said to have cost the first proprietor nearly a lakh of rupees, or 10,000*l.* It was purchased from him by a few gentlemen of capital, and made into a club; afterwards mortgaged by them to the Bank, and has, I hear, been lately sold for 35,000 rupees, or 3500*l.* The North-West Bank of India was commenced by the same capitalists at this little station as the Mussoorie Bank. With the change of name the locality was also changed, the head-quarters being removed to Calcutta, and Mussoorie sinking into an agency.

The climate of Mussoorie is at all times very salubrious, and there is no doubt it is the healthiest of our hill sanatariums. It is very rare for a person arriving in tolerable health to get sickness of any kind while on the hill, and some hundreds leave it at the close of every year in renewed health and vigour, many of whom would have sunk under their diseases in the plains. It was a great mistake on the part of Government not choosing it, or a spot near, as the station for the European regiments quartered in the hills, instead of those near Simla, where fevers and dysentery are sometimes as prevalent as in the plains. In spring it is delightful; in March the difficulty is to keep warm enough, and in May and June, though the sun is rather powerful, one may keep out all day without inconvenience, and the mornings and evenings are all that could be desired. The rainy season, from the middle of June to the middle of September, is not so pleasant, though it still continues healthy. The mornings are often fine, but soon after sunrise the clouds roll up from the Dhoon and envelop the hill in a damp fog, in all stages, from mist to downright rain, for the rest of the day. It often gets fine again about sunset, in time to allow of the evening's out-door exercise, and there is sometimes a break of several days' or a week's fine weather at a time; but this is only a chance, and two days out of three it either rains or there is a thick fog, which walks into every corner of your house, and is often so dense that you cannot see twenty yards through it. October and November are the finest months in the year. It is not too warm in the sun, and the mornings and evenings are again delicious. There is seldom now a cloud to be seen in the heavens. Frost comes in November, and the winter is cold, but still very pleasant till the first fall of snow, which seldom comes till late in December. Few people, however, remain up in the cold weather. The severity of winter varies considerably. Some seasons there may be no snow at all, or only a few inches, and in others several feet; some seasons but one, and in others half-a-dozen different falls. The snow seldom extends more than half way down the hill, but twice in the last twenty years it has snowed to the very foot of the hill, and over a considerable part of the Dhoon.

In the rainy season a charming spectacle is often presented in the early morning from Mussoorie. Dense white clouds lie over and perfectly shut the Dhoon from sight, and you look down on these as on a sea of vapour, all around you being perfectly clear. Presently the clouds begin to move, and breaks appear, through which portions of the Dhoon are seen like islands in a distant lake. The effect is most beautiful, but very transitory, for the clouds soon roll up the hill, and you are enveloped in them the rest of the day. Another singular spectacle, which some people call a glory, is of not uncommon occurrence in the rainy season. You are walking up or down a little ridge, and your shadow is thrown on a bank-side opposite, forty or fifty yards distant. The sun is shining through a thin watery cloud, in which you are enveloped, and round your shadow is an arch of from five to nine small rainbows, the inner one perfectly resplendent, and the outer gradually decreasing in lustre as they increase in size.

It must not be supposed that only sick people visit Mussoorie. Two thirds, perhaps, are on medical certificate, but the rest are officers on general leave, who visit Mussoorie and the other hill stations for the sake of the climate, and to escape for a season the heat and discomfort of the plains. A great many of these, particularly amongst those of a sporting turn, spend the whole or a portion of their leave travelling in the interior, and the number has greatly increased since Cashmere has been added to the places they may visit.

The season visitors come up in April and leave in October. The every-day life, if not particularly exciting, is pleasant enough. Those determined to make the most of the invigorating climate rise with the sun, and take a walk or ride on some of the good roads. On their return the rest are up, and then comes breakfast. Each spends the day as fancy directs, just as idle people do everywhere else, and very few at Mussoorie have anything to do but to kill time the best way they can. In the evening comes the walk or ride on the Mall, which lasts till dark; and as late hours are not the fashion, except perhaps at the club, where cards or billiards keep some up till the small hours, the domestic fire-side closes the day. This is varied by a few balls, private evening parties, archery meetings, picnics, theatricals, a run for a few days to Deyrah for the races, and the season is over.

CHAPTER II.

THE day came at length when I was to bid adieu for a time to civilised life. Travellers in India, either on hill or plain, seldom do what is called "roughing it," and I must confess I am one of those who think it useless to dispense with creature comforts when there is no occasion for doing so, though quite ready to fraternise for a time with savages, or rough it in the most primitive fashion when necessary, or when anything can be gained thereby. Limiting my baggage to what I thought compatible with comfort, I found I had twenty-five Cooly loads. It was thus distributed. Three men carried two small tents, one for myself and one for the baggage and servants, with the poles, pegs, &c. Two carried my bedstead and bedding; four my clothes, books, and tent furniture. Two were loaded with ammunition, arsenical soap, &c., for preserving skins; four with supplies for the inward man, tea, coffee, sugar, biscuits, preserved meats, &c.; one with bacon and ham, another with potatoes, and three with drinkables. The rest had the indescribable loads which, do what you will, your servants contrive to make up. Besides the men who carried the loads, I engaged two who called themselves shikaries, or orderlies, to carry my guns. Myself, a chuprassie, and two of my household servants, cook and man-of-all-work, completed the party.

The route I had sketched out for myself was first to visit the source of the Ganges, and from thence cross, viâ Koonawur, Spiti, and Ladak, to Cashmere; this to be varied or changed as circumstances might dictate. Though intending to hold intercourse with Mussoorie, or other hill stations, if practicable, I had left nothing to chance, and was fully supplied for the six or seven months I intended remaining out. Starting all the traps early in the morning, I remained to partake of breakfast with my hospitable entertainer, who then rode out with me to the outskirts of the station, where, bidding him good-bye, I was fairly launched on the ocean of adventure.

The road led for several miles along the Landour ridge, the Dhoon and the plains forming the view on one hand, and the snowy range, partially enveloped in clouds, on the other. My companions, the two orderlies, walked behind me, exchanging a few words now and then. For some time I was too much occupied with my own reflections to notice them, but at length we made an attempt at conversation. I flattered myself on being a good, or at least a tolerable hand at the colloquial, but we managed very indifferently at first. Many of their words were new to me, and some of mine evidently not understood by them; their way of putting them together, also, was different from mine, and I had often to make them repeat sentences over and over again ere I fully made out the meaning.

Suddenly leaving the road, along the ridge, we turned down a ravine, and the road, which had hitherto been tolerably good, it being the highway to Teree, became a mere track, and very rough, giving a good idea of what was before me. The dried leaves made it very slippery, and I was jerked about like a drunken man, besides getting twice intimately acquainted with the hard ground. Every time I made a slight stumble my companions gave a grunt, and told me to take care, and when I fell, expressed as much concern as if some dreadful calamity had occurred, besides offering to lead me by the hand. My shoes, which I had chosen as just the things for hill travelling, being stout half-boots, like English shooting-boots, were, they said, quite unfitted for the purpose, and the cause of my stumbling so much. This was rather disgusting, for I prided myself on being a good walker. On reaching a little rivulet at the foot of the steep hill we had come down, I halted to rest a little, and the men had a smoke out of a rather primitive pipe. With a small stick they made a hole in the ground, some inches deep, widening it a little at the top. A span from this they made another, slanting to the bottom of the first. Into the former they dropped a small ball of grass rolled up, and over it the tobacco. Putting their closed hand over the orifice of the other, they inhaled the smoke through it. What various methods are pursued in imbibing the narcotic weed! This I found to be universal in the hills when no hookah was at hand; but generally a small hollow reed, to serve as a pipe stem, is inserted in an upright position in the mouth of the slanting hole. If the ground will not admit of a pipe of this kind being made, a leaf from the nearest tree is rolled up like a sugar-paper, the little ball of grass and the tobacco dropped in, and the smoke inhaled through one side of the closed hand, the leaf being held in the other. This method never seemed to give the amount of satisfaction a pipe in the ground or the hookah did; and on enquiring the reason, I was told the smoke came out very hot. The hill-men smoke something like the Spaniards, seldom taking more than a single whiff at a time, so that one pipe of tobacco serves half-a-dozen smokers. After a few preliminary draws, one hearty pull is taken, the smoke being inhaled through the lungs, and the pipe is then passed to the next individual. During my travels I several times remarked this manner of smoking to have an extraordinary effect, and the first time I was somewhat alarmed for the consequences. A man, after taking a hearty pull at his hookah, was seized with a violent trembling, as if in a paralytic fit, and gradually sank to the ground, totally devoid of consciousness, while the face and muscles seemed to denote a state of intense suffering. This lasted several seconds (in some cases it continues several minutes), when he slowly recovered, to be soundly rated by his companions. He had been too greedy, and taken too much smoke into his lungs, which, if the tobacco is at all strong, has always this effect; and I was told of one man, who, while sitting by the fire, and unfortunately alone, fell into it while in this state of insensibility after smoking, and before he recovered sufficiently to get out, was burnt so badly that he died shortly from the effects. Wilson, who often smokes in the puharie fashion, told me he had once or twice unwittingly taken too hard a pull, and described the sensation. At first a numbness is felt in the hands and fingers, the breathing is suspended, a feeling of sinking and giddiness almost agonising comes on, which, if sufficient smoke has been inhaled, subsides into perfect insensibility. On recovering, an icy chill and creeping of the flesh is felt throughout the frame, and it is several minutes before perfect consciousness and use of all the faculties is restored.

I found the camp pitched on some flats in the oak forest, near a small village, and having delayed a good deal on the way, it was dusk when we reached it. In some coppices near the road-side the dogs (I had brought two favourite spaniels) put up some pheasants, and eager to commence shooting, I had spent some time in their pursuit. I succeeded in bagging two, both shot in trees, into which they flew when flushed by the dogs. They were of the species called at Mussoorie kalleege, or black pheasants, and were common in the patches of jungle and little wooded ravines on the road-side till I got near the snow. I had walked about fourteen miles, and been six hours on the road. It was hardly to be expected everything should be quite smooth the first evening, but the cook had made a good dinner, and the novelty of the scene, the wild-looking puharies seated round their fires, with the anticipation of what was to come, made the hours, till bed-time, pass quickly enough. There is always a little confusion in a camp at first; some things are misplaced and cannot be found, while to get at others half the baggage has to be unpacked; but everything soon falls into perfect regularity, and ere many days had elapsed, mine was pitched and broken up in a few minutes. I had been fortunate, too, in getting a good lot of men; many of them had been with Wilson, and some had accompanied him and Colonel Markham, one of the most successful and enthusiastic of hill-sportsmen, in all their excursions. This is a great thing in a trip in the hills, for a bad lot of men, besides grumbling about the camp, are often getting into quarrels with the villagers, are a constant source of irritation and annoyance, and in shooting of little or no real service.

Next day, soon after starting, we found ourselves in the Oglia valley, which runs parallel to the Mussoorie range of hills, and divides it from the next range. It was well cultivated, as well as

* Shooting in the Himalayas, London, 1854

a great portion of the hills on each side, on which numerous villages could be seen. Large herds of cows and milch buffaloes were grazing near the small stream that ran through the valley, and the inhabitants of both sexes busy tilling the fields. It seemed the most thriving place I met with in the hills, probably owing to its vicinity to Mussoorie, where a ready and profitable market is found for its products of every kind. The day's march took us to the head of this valley, after a walk of fourteen miles. I had exchanged my stout half-boots for a pair of soft buff leather ones, in which I got on much better. There was little to interest in the scenery, as walking along the bottom of the narrow valley the view was very confined. On our right, where the hill-side faced the north, it was clothed with forest, oak being the principal tree; while the left, facing the south, was everywhere almost destitute of trees, and where not cultivated, covered with grass. This is a general characteristic of the Himalayas, particularly the lower and middle ranges. The south and east faces are generally destitute of forest, while the opposite are everywhere thickly wooded. When speaking of the hills, it is customary to say, "the higher, middle, and lower ranges;" but this should not lead to the inference that the chief ranges run parallel to the plains. As a little thought will at once suggest, the main ridges run in just the opposite direction, or from the great backbone of snow to the plains. The long spurs, jutting out at right angles from these, give the appearance of a succession of distinct ranges running parallel to the plains.

From the crest of the ridge at the head of the Oglia valley, which we crossed early in the morning, a view of the snowy range still more grand than that from Landour was presented. The eye seemed to look down on and over the intervening hills as on a sea of mountain ridges, the great wall of snow towering above still more clearly and distinctly defined. I endeavoured to transfer the scene to paper, but failed entirely in giving its imposing look. The view is too extensive for a picture. Descending from this ridge, on the fourth day from leaving Mussoorie we reached the Ganges, flowing in a well-cultivated valley, here upwards of a mile wide, the hills on each side rising about 6000 feet above its level, and in most places with a moderate slope. From many parts of the road, while coming down the long descent, a good and extensive view of the opposite hill-side was presented, and as it will give a good idea of the lower Himalayas generally, I will endeavour to describe it. The angle of inclination was so varied that a line stretched from top to bottom of the hill in any part would pass over ground of all degrees of acclivity, from the nearly perpendicular to the nearly level, the whole from base to summit being about 35°. A good deal of the lower part was cultivated, the villages and fields extending about half way up. The view embraced about eight miles of the hill-side in breadth, and from base to summit was, as nearly as I could judge, about six, so that twenty-four square miles of the cultivated portion was seen. In this I counted eight villages of from six to twenty houses each, and about one eighth of the land seemed under present cultivation, and from appearance nearly one half had been so at some former period. The rest of the lower half was composed of patches of various kinds of jungle, from scrubby brushwood to large trees, grassy slopes and knolls, and bluff rocky projections, with here and there a grove of pine trees. The upper part was more wooded, strips of dark-looking oak and rhododendron forest, groves of pine trees, patches of low jungle, grassy slopes, and ledges of rock, to within a mile of the hill-top, from whence was one dense and continuous forest of oaks, broken only here and there by a projecting mass of rock or a small open glade. The whole hill-side was a succession of small lateral ridges, ravines, and slopes, running from top to bottom, so that, though as a whole it faced southerly, many portions faced nearly east and west. I could see no water, but my men said there were small streams in most of the ravines, and springs in many places. The summit of this hill was about 8000 feet, and the valley at its base about 3000 feet, above the level of the sea.

The Ganges was nearly at its lowest level, a half pellucid stream, averaging about forty yards in width, and where running strong, apparently not more than five or six feet deep, but in many places it lay in deep pools, where the current was but just perceptible. Though insignificant now, the dry bed showed it to be a formidable stream when full, the high-water mark being at least fifteen feet above the present surface of the river. It begins to rise about the latter end of March, and is full in July, when it becomes a muddy, boisterous, and very rapid torrent. In the rainy season all the tributary streams from the middle ranges add a little to its volume, but the vast increase is chiefly caused by the melting of the snow in the higher regions. Such is its velocity at this time that the water retains its icy coldness in the close and hot lower valleys for almost its entire course through the hills. The atmosphere near the water partakes of the cold, and on a hot day in summer, the change, when standing without its influence and stepping to the water's edge, is something like what might be expected in stepping from the equator to the poles.

My camp being pitched early, and the men saying there were lots of large fish in the river, I put my rod together to while away the evening, and, after long trying in vain with a variety of flies, at last succeeded in hooking one with the minnow. With a good deal of trouble, after breaking my shins, and at the extreme hazard of doing the same to my neck while running over the immense boulders on the bank, I landed a mahseer of twelve or fourteen pounds. The astonishment of the puharies, who evidently had never seen a large fish caught in this manner before, was really laughable, and the fish at one time giving a leap right out of the water, their excitement became intense. I had soon all the camp and several villagers from the fields near the river as spectators. When all was over I was congratulated by I don't know how many different individuals, and all pressed forward to see the tackle and spoil. The gut at the end of the line was the great object of attraction, and the simple puharies could not comprehend how so slight a string could hold so large a fish, almost strong enough, I heard one of them remark, to pull a man into the river.

The next six marches were along the banks of the Ganges, and without much ascent or descent. In some places the valley was open, with villages and cultivation on both sides of the river, both in the valley and up the hill-sides. In others the hills rose steep and rugged from the water's edge, and were left to nature, or as pasturage for cattle. What strikes one very forcibly in this part of the hills, and through the whole of Gurwhal, is the great quantity of land which has at some former period been under cultivation to what is so at the present day. You continually meet with hill-sides, the whole or a greater portion of which have been cut into terraced fields with evidently no inconsiderable amount of labour, the walled faces of many of the fields being from six to twelve feet high; but these fields are now entirely waste, and overgrown in many places with jungle and forest. The inhabitants will point out spots now left to nature where once stood large and flourishing villages, and, to judge from appearances, the hills must at one time have contained more than double the present population. The people themselves say the decrease took place during the time the Goorkhas had possession of the country, those ruthless conquerors murdering or sending to their own country as slaves men and boys on the most frivolous pretences, and taking the best looking of the softer sex into their own households. As the Goorkhas, however, only held the country some six years, it is difficult to suppose this the sole cause of the extraordinary decrease of population; and besides, the growth of trees on some of this deserted territory, and the total disappearance of villages, the sites of which are pointed out, while scarce the vestige of a building is left, point to a more distant period. Whatever may have been the primary cause, the rule of the present rajah, which has extended over nearly half a century, has rather increased than diminished the evil. Though on the whole he treats his subjects with more lenience than most native sovereigns, like the generality, he troubles himself very little about the improvement of his country, and his supineness has been fatal to any increase of population. The villages are still the same dirty and consequently unhealthy places they always were, and though there has been no outward drain, no pestilence or famine, or any other special cause, the mortality seems to have kept pace with the new births. There has, it is true, been a little emigration, but so trifling as to be hardly worth notice. The rajah never travels through the country to observe its real state, and see that the orders he gives are carried out, and his subordinates, possessed of, or at least exercising, almost unlimited authority the short time they are in office, and being paid by a per-centage on their collections, are so oppressive that some families have been driven to emigrate into the British territories; and the emigration would be more general but for the passionate love of home inherent in the puharies, as in most inhabitants of a mountain country.

The scenery was not very varied, and, but for an occasional glimpse of a distant peak or a portion of the snowy mountains through some opening, the look of the hills for the whole six marches would have been extremely monotonous. The road was generally along the bottom of the valley, and here and there, where the hills rose steep and abrupt from the river, a little distance up their slopes. The general characteristic was that of passing through a narrow defile, with hills, not particularly rugged or steep, on each side, rising from 3000 to 5000 feet above, a view now and then up some lateral valley, showing that these were but the bluff ends of long spurs that ran back to a main ridge running parallel with the defile. For the first four marches pine was the prevailing forest tree on both sides, many of the hills being entirely covered with it, while oaks and other trees, common to the lower and middle Himalayas, filled the hollows and ravines; but, wherever a distant hill or a portion of the main ridge on each side could be seen, dark-looking oak forest was the general characteristic of the wooded portions. As we got further into the hills the whole detail seemed to acquire enlarged proportions. Each hill looked as if moulded on a more gigantic scale, and the main ridges on each side towered to the height of 10,000 or 12,000 feet, the crests being in many places above the limits of forest, and showing the commencement of the grassy regions. In the forest the change was very striking; on the right bank it was in scattered patches as before, and pine the most common tree; but on the left miles and miles of hill and valley presented one unbroken mass of foliage, the individual trees partaking of the general development, and being much larger than in the lower hills. Oak was the prevailing tree, but intermingled with many others now first making their appearance, amongst which the spiry tops of the dark-looking morenda and rye pines were most conspicuous. The river was gradually but almost imperceptibly diminishing in size, but was more rapid, and the deep, quiet, glassy pools which made it so beautiful lower down were now no more. In the six marches I had made up the Ganges, I had ascended, according to the barometer, 2000 feet, which would give the river a fall of nearly 40 feet per mile, not a great deal in such hills. The next 30 miles to the Gangootree temple the fall is upwards of 100 feet per mile, and from thence to the glacier from which the river flows, about 16 miles, the fall must be at least 200 feet per mile.

The camp was always pitched near a village, and this and my seldom leaving the road may account for so little game being met with. I saw a few kalleege pheasants and black partridges every day, but the only animals I had yet seen were three goral, and these having been disturbed, there was no chance of getting a shot. Unless properly sought after, game will appear to a traveller in the Himalayas very scarce; and had it not been for the dogs, I should probably not have seen half a dozen birds in this part of my journey. The Himalayas are undoubtedly tolerably well stocked with game, but it is a great fallacy to suppose that every person who makes a few months' excursion into the interior must, if such be the case, necessarily meet with it if he goes through the districts where it is to be found. One might as well judge of the best shooting counties in England by the number of birds he saw while riding on the turnpike road through it. The roads in the hills, though they be the veriest tracks imaginable, are still the roads of the country, over which people are continually passing, and the wild animals in the vicinity are doubtless aware of the fact. Again, when walking on a path perhaps not more than a foot wide, with scenery of the wildest description on all sides, and **no sign of** human habitation near, it is easy to imagine oneself in the wilds of nature, and to be surprised that no wild animals **are** seen; not reflecting that every day some members of the human family, everywhere the objects **of** their dread, **are** passing the same spot, which must naturally prevent their making it a general resort. In the hills, as almost everywhere else, large game must be sought for in places less frequently disturbed than the nooks and corners near the paths, however likely they may appear; and I can easily imagine a person travelling for months **in** the hills, and through wild parts of **the** country **too,** and seeing scarcely **a** single wild animal.

At one spot I passed a lot of people, children and adults of both sexes, washing the sand of the Ganges for gold, and I spent a few hours watching the process, which was simple enough. A mat, made of reeds, about the thickness of one's finger, placed parallel with each other, was placed over a shallow wooden trough; on this the sand and earth scraped up from amongst the rocks and large stones of the dry part of the river's bed was put by small basketfuls at a time, a woman seated alongside stirring the mass with one hand, while she poured water over **it** from a small wooden ladle with the other. The fine sand was thus washed **through the** reed mat into the trough, while the pebble and stones were pitched off into the **river, as** each fresh **basketful** was brought. When the wooden trough was nearly full, the mat was taken off, and the trough placed in a slightly slanting position. The sand was then moved about with one hand and water poured over it from the other, in such a manner that the lighter particles were washed away while the heavier remained. When it had all gone but a few handfuls, this was put into a small wooden tray open at two sides, which was held and moved about in one hand, and water again poured on it from the other, but now very gently. After about ten minutes of this, during which nearly all the sand was washed away, the process of washing was finished. The result of one washing was about a teaspoonful of fine reddish sand, in which I could see about a dozen small particles of gold, the largest not bigger than a grain of coarse gunpowder and very thin, and others so minute as to be but just perceptible. The proceeds of the day's washing is taken to the bivouac, and separated from the sand by amalgamation with quicksilver. There were several families of washers, the men and children collecting the sand and the women washing it. A family of five or six people, I was told, seldom get more than a shilling's worth of gold in a day, and sometimes much less; but if a little more art was introduced into the process, each family might wash ten times the quantity of sand, and thus make a decent livelihood. The sands of some of the minor streams are more productive than those of the large rivers, and in one particularly, where another party was washing, the gold appeared so abundant as to lead one to imagine the stream must in some part of its course flow through a highly auriferous region.

At one village I delayed the camp half the day to witness an extraordinary performance, which deserves describing in detail. It consisted of a man sliding down a rope nearly half a mile in length, and is called in local parlance a "burt." The rope extended from an eminence on the hill side above the village, over a ravine and down to a green knoll in the fields below, and was drawn as tight as several hundred men with their united strength could effect. They had just finished stretching it when we arrived, and I could scarcely believe a man was actually going to slide down it, the feat appeared so utterly impracticable with any chance of safety. Imagine a rope extended from the top of a rock at least 500 feet high, to a pole some 2000 feet from its base, and some idea may be formed of the undertaking. A great concourse of people of both sexes were assembled, all in their holiday garb, and the man who was to slide was swinging round at the end of a long plank fixed on an upright pole as a pivot. Every few moments he called some person amongst the crowd by name, and swinging round several times to the individual's honour, received from him a trifling gratuity. He no sooner noticed me than I was included in this category, and being told it was in no way a religious ceremony, I gave him a rupee. When this was over, he was escorted to the eminence above, amidst the loud lamentations of his family, and the discordant music of the village band. With the glass I saw him placed on a kind of saddle on the rope, two individuals busied fastening something to his legs, which I saw afterwards were bags filled with earth. The spectators, amongst whom I stood, were assembled in groups near the pole to which the lower end of the rope was attached, all intently watching for the descent. Presently he was let go, and came down several hundred yards with terrible velocity, a stream of smoke following in his wake. As he approached us, the incline being gradually diminished, his career was less rapid, and became slower and slower towards the end, where the rope being sufficiently near the ground he was taken down, amidst the shouts and congratulations of the villagers. The ride, which was over in a few moments, did not appear to have at all distressed him. I afterwards learnt the following particulars regarding this strange custom.

The men who slide are of a particular caste and make it a profession, going from place to place as their services may be required. There are not many of them, perhaps only a single family in a large district, the ceremony only taking place at long intervals in particular villages, where it has been observed from time immemorial. The total neglect of it in these would, in the belief of the inhabitants, subject them to a failure of their crops, and to prevent this is the only reason alleged for its observance. When a village community have decided on celebrating the ceremony, **they send for a " bada,"** as the sliders are called, **who comes** with his family and resides in the village while making the rope. This occupies him two or three months, the villagers themselves cutting the grass of which **it is** made. This **grass,** which grows abundantly on the lower hills, **whole** slopes being covered with **it,** is cut when dry and made **into rope** and string for ordinary purposes **without** undergoing any preparation whatever. These **are** tolerably strong at **first,** but constant exposure to the dry atmosphere soon renders them rather fragile, a defect which **is at** once remedied by a few moments' immersion in cold water. **The** rude suspension bridges over the rivers in this part of the country are constructed of ropes **made** from this grass. The bada's rope is made of one piece in three strands, and coiled up, as it is made, in one end of the shed the man occupies. It is very neatly and evenly twisted, and about **the** thickness of one's wrist. While employed making it the man and his family are supplied with food by the villagers, and in the evenings amuse them with songs and dances **of** a most indecent kind. Himself, his wife, and perhaps his mother **or** daughter, join in these dances, in which the most obscene and revolting expressions and actions are used and witnessed without disgust or shame by old and young of both sexes. **When** the rope is nearly made, a day is fixed for the ceremony, and as it approaches the man is closely watched, lest he should abscond if his resolution happens to fail. When all is ready, the people assemble from the surrounding villages, generally the evening before the day the ceremony is to take place, the songs and dances being then continued throughout the night. In the morning the rope is carried in coils by a string of men to the nearest stream, where it is well damped, and from thence in the same manner to the place fixed upon, which is generally the same every time the ceremony takes place. While this is doing the bada is employed as before described, swinging on the pole and collecting what he can from the bystanders. He then takes leave of his family, and is immediately conducted to the starting post. Here two poles are firmly fixed upright in the ground, with a cross-piece at the top to which the rope is attached; sometimes the trunk of a tree serves the purpose. At the lower end the rope is fastened to a single pole, after being tightened as much as possible. The length varies at different villages according to the nature of the ground. In some it is 300 or 400 yards, in others upwards of half a mile, and is often carried over a deep valley or ravine. From its great length it naturally, even when pulled as tight as possible, forms a great curve; but as the upper station is always many hundred feet above the lower, the incline from the top, for one half its length, is so great that the impetus it gives carries the man forward along the small portion which remains horizontal. The man sits on a small wooden saddle, grooved underneath to fit the **rope, and bags** of sand or earth are fastened to his legs **to keep him** balanced, and this is all the artificial support **he** has. **To** prevent him coming with too much force against the lower pole, blankets are wound loosely round the rope for some distance **before** it, and these help to stop him **gradually.** When he is seated in his saddle and all ready, he himself **gives** the signal to let go, and this being done, he shoots down at first, as might be expected from the angle of incline, with meteor-like velocity, which gradually relaxes **as** he approaches his goal. The rapid friction would doubtless set the saddle on fire **were** it not for the rope being **so** well saturated **with** water. Accidents **are not** unfrequent. **If** the **rope** breaks during the ride, which is sometimes **the** case, the unfortunate performer **is of** course **killed** on the spot. Sometimes, notwithstanding the **blankets** wound round **the** rope to prevent it, the concussion at the lower pole is so great, that he is thrown from his seat and receives serious injury, **but** no fear seems to be entertained **of his** tumbling **off** the rope during **the** ride. When he finishes **his** ride in safety, the villagers take him down, and he then receives the stipulated reward for his perilous adventure, and departs **to** his home at pleasure. **If** he is killed, a catastrophe which is considered a most unlucky omen for the village, it **is** altogether withheld, and his family get nothing. The reward varies from 50 to 200 rupees, according to the size of the village; besides which he gets a few more from the spectators. This, and every ceremony or festival where both sexes congregate, is wound up with singing and dancing.

Having been told that there was some very good shooting at Bengallee, instead of encamping at the usual place by the river, I went up to the village, and next day to the Kunnowlie hill, considered the best tahr ground in this part of the country. Having been out now ten days and not fired a single shot at an animal, I was impatient enough to see some of the sport of which I had heard so much, and which I had been enjoying in anticipation ever since leaving Mussoorie. Let me try to describe the scene of my first attempt at deer stalking in the Himalayas. How vividly is it now presented to my mind as memory flies back over the past and conjures up the scenes of my sporting triumphs and disappointments! There are few events of one's past life, the minute details of which are remembered better than remarkable sporting adventures. Years and years roll by, but the very bushes, trees, rocks, or whatever may have been the characteristic features of the scene, the whole details of the event from first to last, rise up again so distinctly that it appears but yesterday, and every true sportsman will bear me out in saying, there are few of our recollections more pleasant to dwell upon.

The Kunnowlie hill is a spur jutting from the high ridge between the Ganges and Jumna, not far from where that ridge itself joins the mass of snowy mountains between **the sources of the two rivers**. The south face, which is first **reached on** approaching from Bengallee, is a steep hill-side, about four miles from base to summit, the greater portion grassy slopes and rough craggy ground, with a few isolated patches of thick oak forest. As it recedes towards the main ridge, the forest in the lower part becomes continuous and dense; the upper a succession of rocks and undulating slopes. The east face, which runs down **to the** Ganges, **is** more thickly wooded as far as forest extends, and the open ground **is** more **steep and** rugged; the furthest half being **in** most places inaccessible to human footsteps, but affording a safe retreat to the tahr when disturbed. The base **of the** hill is about 5000 feet in elevation, and the crest near 12,000. Almost every kind of mountain-climbing **and** walking is experienced in a good day's ramble over it; from the gentle hill, "green and of mild declivity," to the almost perpendicular rock, of which I once heard a waggish person remark, " You must cling on with hands, feet, **and** eyelids."

My camp was pitched in a patch of oak forest, about half-way up the hill, and the spot seemed to have been chosen by many parties of former years, as broken bottles, pieces of paper, and other et-ceteras testified. The evening of our arrival I went out, accompanied by the two orderlies and a villager, who had promised to find the tahr. After a couple of hours' walk we saw a herd of females, but they either saw or winded us, and went away long ere we got within range. There were a good many moonall pheasants, and I could not resist the temptation of potting a fine male, which was perched most invitingly on a rock, and offering a splendid rifle-shot at about one hundred yards. The ball cut it nearly in two, and the shot seemed to give great satisfaction to the men, one of whom immediately remarked that "we should kill a lot of game this trip." I thought this was inferred from something about the bird or the shot being considered a lucky omen, but it was only because he saw I could hit something. If the tales some of the orderlies and shikaries tell be true, many of the people who attempt to shoot in the hills make but a sorry exhibition of themselves as marksmen. When shikaries engage for a trip, their first great anxiety is, whether master can hit anything or not; and the next, whether he can walk, meaning whether he can climb about the rocks, and walk over steep and dangerous places. One day I was walking with my orderlies down the banks of a little rivulet in one of the valleys near the snow, and during the day they had been telling me tales about the different gentlemen they had been with. "Here," said one of them, "twelve shots were fired at a snow-bear by three gentlemen I was with some years ago, as it went up that bank," pointing to the slope not more than sixty yards off, "and not one of the bullets hit." Some of these shikaries and orderlies are intelligent men, and capital hunters, and a novice cannot do better at first, till he becomes acquainted with the habits of the animals, than put himself entirely under their guidance. Many of them, if not what we should call good, are sure shots, for they will seldom fire till they get a dead pot within eighty yards. More than a hundred they consider a long shot, and they would not dream of firing at two hundred yards.

In the morning, about three miles from camp, we discovered three male tahr feeding on one of the grassy slopes, and succeeded in stalking within eighty yards, but either from over-excitement, or from being rather blown walking up the hill, I missed as good a shot as anyone could desire, at an animal as big as a fallow-deer, and standing broadside towards me. At the report of the rifle they bounded off, and the second barrel also missed. My smooth gun was put into my hand immediately, but though the beasts stood once or twice to look at us, they had got too far for anything but a good rifle, and it was also discharged without effect. Though with very small horns, the tahr had a far more noble appearance than I expected from the description I had heard of them, and this served to increase my eagerness to bag one. We sought about till near noon without seeing any more, and then, after breakfasting, sat and rested till evening, when we found a lot of females, and I knocked over my first, having stalked to within sixty yards under the guidance of the villager, and getting such a nice pot-shot, it was almost impossible to miss. I had a leg roasted, and found it, if not very good, at least eatable; and the soup other portions made was excellent.

The same ground was hunted over next day, but nothing seen till evening, when, instead of tahr, I was delighted at seeing a large black bear. It was in a little ravine amongst some small bushes, and appeared busily employed scratching up the ground and turning over the stones, and moreover was in a very favourable place to stalk. I was soon within sixty yards of it, and taking a deliberate aim, with the rifle resting over a rock, had the satisfaction of seeing it roll over. It was soon, however, on its legs again, and off down the ravine, uttering several loud grunts, and the second barrel only served to accelerate its speed. I was rather crest-fallen, afraid I had lost it, but my attendants, the two orderlies and the villager, assured me we should soon find it, and the blood sprinkled plentifully on its track seemed to show their surmise would prove correct. We followed nearly a mile, and the drops of blood becoming fewer as we proceeded, my hopes gradually began to evaporate, though almost sure the beast was hit right in the shoulder. Once or twice we lost the track altogether, and had some difficulty in finding it again; but at length, to my great delight, it led to the entrance of a small cave, in which it was evident our chase was ensconced. How to get the brute out was now the question, and it seemed rather difficult to solve, for all the noise we could make, and a shot fired into the hole, brought no response, while no one was bold enough to venture into the cave. I had, a few days before, in one of the villages we passed through, seen a man with his face terribly mangled by a bear, and the recollection of this did not tend to make me ambitious of attacking a wounded one in a dark cave. I was thinking of trying smoke, when one of the men, who was peering about the mass of rock, said he could see the bear through a small crevice. On looking, at first I could see nothing, but at length made out a mass of black fur, at which I fired, though it was impossible to form any idea to what part of the animal it belonged, but I expected it would either kill or cause the beast to bolt out, in which case I had the second barrel to deliver at a few paces. All remained quiet, and when the smoke cleared away, on looking again through the crevice, there was the black fur still in the same place. He must be dead, I exclaimed; and cutting a long stick, we poked at the fur for some time, till certain of the fact. With some difficulty we managed to drag him out, and I had the pleasure of turning over the first bear I had ever shot. He must have been dead some time, for the jaws were fixed and rigid. The first ball had, as I thought, hit him right in the shoulder, and ought to have killed him dead, or at least prevented him coming such a distance, but the bruin tribe are very tenacious of life, and the best shot can never calculate on dropping one like a rabbit.

Our camp was now moved to the east face of the hill, and the same evening we found seven male tahr. They walked out of a patch of oak forest while we were looking from a ridge over the hillside below. Creeping down behind another little ridge that ran past the place where they were, on reaching their level and looking cautiously over, there they were, unsuspectingly browsing on the grass, and one within fifty yards. I was careful this time, and having walked down hill in the stalk was not at all blown, and he rolled over to the shot, while I was so intent on seeing whether he got up again, that I let the chance of a second shot at one of the others slip by. The fallen one rolled over and over down the hill till brought up against a large stone in the ravine a hundred yards below, yet he was not dead when we got to him, but making violent efforts to get on his legs again, so I thought it best to give him another bullet.

We remained two more days at this camp and twice saw male tahr, but I did not succeed in getting another shot, and found they were not quite so easy to stalk as I at first thought. No country can possibly be conceived better adapted for stalking than the Himalayas, as the ground is so broken, it is almost impossible for an animal to get where there is not some way of approaching within shot unperceived; but the animals are so wary that scores besides myself, many of whom may have been considered first-rate sportsmen in the plains, make but a sorry figure in their first attempts at deer-stalking in the hills. The failure generally takes place at the most exciting moment, when one is just getting within shot. The animals either see or hear you, or get the wind, and when, after a hard fag, you look over the rock or ridge you intended to shoot from, you have the mortification to find they have vanished, or perhaps are just in time to see a few of the last bounding over the rocks. Not unfrequently one stalks up well to the place, and after all lets some of the sharp-eyed animals see him as he peeps over the rock or ridge, and they are off before he can get a shot. It is some time, too, before a fresh comer gets into the way of seeing animals as quickly as he ought. There are so many different little objects to strike the eye, small bushes, clusters of brown fern, pieces of rock, decayed or burnt trunks of trees, and other things, all isolated as it were, and demanding each a separate look, that an animal may sometimes stand fully exposed to view within easy gun-shot for some time before being seen. A little experience improves one wonderfully in this, as well as in discovering animals at a great distance. The latter is, however, I think, more a natural than an acquired art, and depends on the strength and powers of the eye.

The last day I shot over this hill, while walking through the oak forest, a large animal, in appearance something between a cow and a jackass, which the shikaree said was a serow, suddenly jumped up, but was out of sight amongst the bushes before I could get hold of the rifle, which one of the men was carrying. Had I been prepared, I might have had a very good running shot. On my way back to Bengallee, where I had left my heavy baggage, I got a couple of woodcocks and a cheer pheasant, and had a long shot at a goral. This ended my first fair attempt at shooting in the Himalayas. I thought I had done indifferently, but my men and the villager assured me that very few sahibs, and many had tried the hill, in fact some one or other almost every year, succeeded in making so good a bag, a bear, and a male and female tahr.

CHAPTER III.

The weather had up to this time been very fine; but it commenced to rain during the night, and continued doing so nearly the whole of the next day, so I thought it advisable to halt, which, indeed, I was not sorry to do, for I had worked hard on the Koonowlie hill, and a day's rest was anything but disagreeable. It cleared up towards evening, and the villager who had been with me came and asked if I would like to take a stroll, saying we should probably find some goral, and that there were lots of kalleege and cheer pheasants close by. He took me over the hill-side behind the village, on which the grass had been burnt some time previously. The fresh green shoots were just springing up, which made the walking very pleasant, and the recent showers had given a freshness and purity to the atmosphere. The clearness and distinctness with which objects, either near or remote, are seen after rainy weather, in comparison with what they are at other times, is nowhere more striking than in the Himalayas. A continuance of fine weather is always attended with an undefinable haze or dimness in the atmosphere, while nothing can be conceived more clear than it is after rain.

We soon espied three goral feeding on the short sweet grass on one of the little slopes, near some very steep rocky ground, where they had probably been hid during the day. I got up within eighty yards without much difficulty, having only to draw back a few paces, and creep up behind the little ridge which ran parallel to where they were. A deliberate pot knocked one over, which rolled some way down the slope, and lay for some moments as if dead; but ere we reached it, it got up and went over the next ridge, untouched by the other barrel I fired. The man ran to the ridge and saw it lie down amongst the rocks, but in such a position that we could not from anywhere get sight of it, and the place appeared to me quite inaccessible. My companion pointed out a spot from whence he thought the goral would be visible; but to reach it a steep face of rock must be crossed, with only a few tufts of grass growing out of the crevices as a support to the hands and feet, and the least slip would be certain destruction. It appeared such a tempting of Providence to venture over it that I at once declined; but the villager, against my express command, walked across, and after peeping from the spot he had pointed out, returned to where I stood without much apparent difficulty. He said he could see the goral, which was still alive, and offered to conduct me safely across the rock, and when I would not assent to this, asked me to let him take the gun himself. I felt rather nervous as I watched him walk again across the difficult place, with my rifle in one hand, and clinging to the tufts of grass with the other; but he soon reached the desired spot, and, resting the rifle on a stone, took aim for full half-a-minute, and fired. A few moments afterwards a dull thud told me that the shot had been successful, as I knew it was the goral falling from the rocks on to the green slope beneath, and presently I saw it rolling over and over down towards the rivulet below. On examination I found my bullet had gone right through a little behind the shoulder, and it would have been hard to make a shot more likely to kill an animal dead. The goral, however, is, though small, one of the animals so tenacious of life, that the sportsman in time ceases to wonder at their going away with more than one of his missiles planted to a nicety. As we walked home I thought to myself I had been very foolish in allowing the man to walk over a place which appeared to me so dangerous, and with a valuable rifle in his hand, risking both it and his life or limbs for the sake of securing a wounded deer, though, being confident, he saw no risk himself and laughed at my fears. A few weeks afterwards, when I had gained more confidence in my own powers, I should myself have walked across the same rock without hesitation. One might imagine from this that climbing up rocks, and walking over steep and difficult places, are arts that any person may acquire from practice; but this, I think, is a fallacy, and my opinion is corroborated by Wilson, who ought to be one of the best of judges. To make a good, or even a tolerable cragsman, a person must have a natural aptitude for it, and whoever is such, though practice may have given him greater confidence, and improved him vastly in all other respects, may recollect his maiden effort was still a comparatively successful one. When this is a failure, it is certain that nothing can ever make the individual into a good climber.

From Bengallee we went down again to our old acquaintance, the Ganges, a portion of the next march being through a narrow gorge, with only just room for the river at the bottom; on one side the east face of the hill I had just shot over, and on the other, along which the road led, a hill far more steep and rugged than any I had yet met with. Divested of the trees and bushes, which grew out of the crevices of the rocks with little or no apparent soil to nourish them, many places would have presented a nearly smooth face of all but perpendicular rock, running from several hundred feet above, sheer down to the river. Various are the contrivances to make a practicable path across these. Flights of wooden and stone steps, of fantastic form and rude construction, serve the purpose in some of the bad places; and in others long planks are laid along the face of the rock, resting on wooden pegs stuck in the crevices.

The path is at times several hundred feet above the river, and a slip from one of these planks would shoot a person into it, without a possibility of recovering himself. After some miles of this, the valley again opens out and forms a little district containing several villages. The inhabitants might have been taken for colliers or charcoal burners, so black and grimy were their clothes and persons. This arises from their burning cedar-wood in their houses, which contain no chimneys, and not even a hole in the roof to let out the smoke, which makes its exit by the low door and small window. The wood of all pine trees gives a much dirtier and blacker smoke than that of any others, and here they burn little or nothing else. How the people contrive to live in some of the houses would puzzle a philosopher of any civilized country. I looked into one in which a fire was burning; the roof was not more than five feet from the floor, and the upper half of the interior a volume of dense smoke, through which the eye could scarcely penetrate; and it must be remembered the smoke from wood of any kind is very painful to that organ. I asked the villagers why they did not make chimneys, or at least leave a hole to let out the smoke. Some said it kept the house warm, others, that as their forefathers had done so long without, they could do so too; and remarked that, as they were more like brutes than human beings, the houses as they were were good enough for them; but all admitted that some contrivance to let the smoke out would make them much more comfortable.

I was now close under the snowy range, or rather in it, for the river taking a turn and coming from the east, we soon got well behind the great range of snowy hills seen from Mussoorie; but even here there was nothing very grand in the scenery, and little or no snow could be seen until one left the valley and walked some distance up one of the hill sides. At Derallee, the last and highest village on the Ganges, I found Wilson's camp, he himself having been out in the forest for several days; but I was told he would probably either come home himself or send a man for provisions the next day, as his supply must be exhausted. Particularly desirous of seeing him, I determined to await his return, so pitched my camp in the little apricot orchard with his. It was one of the nicest camp grounds I had met with; the village with its noise and dirt out of sight in the rear, the apricot trees forming a nice shade, with a carpet of green fresh grass beneath, and the Ganges running close by in several shallow streams dispersed over a sandy channel three hundred yards broad. In the village there was a large square house six stories high, in good repair, but untenanted. It had but one door, a strong and massive one, being a single plank of cedar six feet wide, and more than a foot thick. There were two rooms and a kind of closed balcony in each story, and in one of the upper rooms were two large wooden cisterns for holding a supply of water. On a rock a couple of hundred yards above the village was another similar building, but falling in pieces; and in a village across the river, a third. They had been built, I was told, in former years for the villagers to take refuge in when attacked by plunderers from other districts, a thing in those times of frequent occurrence. A few yards from my camp, half buried in the sand of the river, were three Hindoo temples; two very small, and the other a tower about thirty feet high. They were built of dressed stones, fitting together without mortar, some of the stones very large, so as each to form individually a layer for the whole side of the building. These I was told were the remains of twenty-four which had formerly existed on the spot, the rest having been undermined by the gradual encroachment of the river, and buried in the sand.

Wilson made his appearance the next evening. He had been out six days, and had killed during the time seven musk-deer. This he said was very indifferent sport, but that these animals in this part of the country were now very scarce, a number of men from Kooloo having snared the greater number. In the western world, hundreds of our countrymen follow hunting in some shape or other as a profession, but in the eastern, I believe Wilson is the first and only one who has attempted it. If not a remunerating, it is, he says, an exciting and healthful occupation followed in the cold and bracing climate of the higher Himalayas. This no one will doubt, but many would object to the solitude and deprivation of intercourse with any but the ignorant puharies. Musk is what he chiefly depends on to supply the sinews of war, but he also collects birds, and the skins and horns of various animals, disposing of some at Mussoorie and sending others to England. After hearing my plans he delighted me by proposing to shoot with me for a fortnight. "I can," said he, "follow my musk-deer shooting nearly as well as if I was by myself, and at the same time show you other sport, which a stranger has little chance of finding without assistance. You will, of course, like to see the glacier at the source of the Ganges,—it shall be our first ground,—there are musk-deer all the way up, and we shall probably find a bear or two and some burrell." We made our preparations the next day, and the one following set out, having supplies for nearly a fortnight. The road was along the banks of the river, through a dense cedar forest, the whole of the first march, Wilson pointing out to me various of his musk-deer shooting grounds on each side, and amusing me with anecdotes relating to them. On all sides the hills were clothed with pine and cedar forest for about two miles up from the river; above which birch alone marked the limits of forest vegetation. These and many other trees were still leafless, for, though it was now the end of April, nature had not yet recovered from her winter sleep. The hills facing north and west were still covered deeply with snow, which extended far **down** into the forest, and my companion pointed **out to me** many places, smooth unbroken slopes of dazzling snow, where he would in another month **be shooting** musk-deer, and which were in **reality** the **sites of** rhododendron and scrub birch forest, **now** completely buried. The banks of the river **and** minor **streams** were indeed beginning to put on their summer garments; green grass and flowers under foot, and green leaves and blossom **on** the bushes and trees over head, with a warm glowing sunshine, made **one feel** it was really spring. But walk **a** mile or two up the hill and you are in the depth of winter; the ground covered deeply with **snow**, and every tree and bush, except the evergreen cedar and **pine**, **still** leafless, and not even budding.

At Byrainghattee we crossed the river on a rude bridge suspended a hundred feet above the water, with wild naked rocks on each side. A few miles further on we encamped, and **it** being still early, Wilson proposed we should take half the coolies and drive some patch of forest in which was a musk-deer that had several times escaped from him. **It** was close by the camp. We posted ourselves on one side of a little open ravine, running from the path down to the river, with its other sloping bank before us, and the men were sent round to beat through the forest towards us. "If the deer is at home," said Wilson, "it will be sure to cross this ravine somewhere, and must pass within shot of one of us. If it stands when it first comes out of the forest on to the open bank-side, as it probably will, you will have a pretty rifle shot; but if it does not, and comes bounding on to pass you without stopping, you had better try the smooth gun and shot, for musk-deer, from the manner they bound, are the most difficult of all animals to hit with a ball when running." I was stationed a little below the path, my companion going down near the river. We soon heard the shouts of the beaters, who indeed made noise enough to frighten all the deer within a mile of us. I had never seen a musk-deer, and though Wilson had told me they were very small, I was not prepared for the little thing, not much bigger than a hare, which I saw presently cross the ravine, close by where he had posted himself. To my surprise he did not fire, though I saw he was looking at it, and it disappeared in the forest behind us. The beaters were now drawing near, and all at once they set up a perfect hurricane of yells, and in a few moments afterwards a musk-deer made its appearance at the edge of the sloping bank right opposite where I sat. I took as steady aim as possible, but as it stood lengthwise towards me I had but its breast and neck for a target, and missed. To my surprise it never moved, and gave me an opportunity of firing the second barrel, which likewise missed. Apparently perfectly heedless of the shots or of me, it now came bounding forward, crossed the ravine, and was passing within twenty yards when I knocked it over with the shot gun. It turned out to be a male, and when

Wilson came up we cut out the pod, which was about the size of a pullet's egg, and worth, he said, about twenty-five shillings, being one of the largest. He had several times before attempted to drive it, but the jungle being very thick, and seldom having more than two or three men to drive, it always managed to slip by them, and never came out into the open ravine. The one that came out near him was a young one, which was the reason he did not fire.

Sending the camp on to the temple at Gangootree, we went in the morning up the hill-side to some grassy slopes, where Wilson expected to find burrell. Traces of musk-deer were plentiful, but we only saw one, and it was out of sight before either of us could get a shot. I should never have dreamed of looking for a path across such rocks as we now clambered over, but my companion knew the ground well, and it was an excellent lesson for me in walking, for seeing the ease with which he sprung from rock to rock, and the perfect nonchalance with which he crossed places where I should have hesitated, taught me to place more confidence in myself. After about two hours' walking, we came to the slopes, if such a spot be deserving of the name, it being only a portion of the steep hill-side covered with grass, and looking gentle, if I may use such a word, in contrast with the wild rocks and crags around. It was a favourite feeding-ground of burrell, and we soon found a flock. Stalking them with an experienced hand for a

F

guide was an easy matter, though they are the wildest animals in this part of the hills, and I was soon taking a deliberate shot from behind a rock, within eighty yards of the flock, and in another moment one of them was rolling over and over down the hill, and the rest scampering up the rocks. Wilson brought down another, but I missed with the second barrel. Both were females, as were all the rest, as well as we could judge; at least there were no large males amongst them. There were about fifteen in all, three or four being last year's lambs, about half the size of the adults. We took several long shots at one of these, thinking it would be tender for our own eating, but did not manage to knock it over. The entrails were taken out of those we had killed, and two coolies took them up on their backs to carry them home, though each was heavier than any two loads in my camp. How the puharies manage to carry such heavy loads over ground where many people would be afraid of walking, is truly wonderful. When we went out purposely to shoot, we always took a few spare men to carry home the game, which was sometimes killed several miles from the camp or bivouac, to which they always took it, however difficult the ground they had to walk over. Sometimes, when we had killed late, they did not reach home till long after dark, and if it was not moonlight their comrades went to meet them with pine-wood torches. This sometimes happened to ourselves, for Wilson never let a good chance escape for **fear of** being late, knowing **that** as soon as night set **in** without our arrival in **camp,** men would be **sent** out in different directions to find us and light us home. He often owned it was very foolish, and a tempting of Providence, as the hills are bad enough to walk over **in** the day time; but the chances one gets when out burrell-shooting are so few, it is difficult to resist the temptation of staying out a little too long to **secure a** good shot.

As we went down to **the** road, my companion showed me a place where he had a narrow escape from being mauled by a large brown bear. The slopes we had just been over are separated from the wooded one below, along which the road lies, by a nearly perpendicular descent of rock and crag, and there are only a few places where it is possible to get down. One **of** these was only made so by the trunk of a pine-tree having fallen in a nearly upright position between two **rocks,** affording a means of descent from the ledge above to a platform a couple of yards broad below. The rocks were nearly at right angles to each other, so that it was something like descending from the ceiling of a high room by a pole placed nearly upright in one corner. Wilson and one of his men **were** looking for a way to get down the rocks, when they for the first time came to this place. He descended first, and as it was awkward getting down with the rifle, he went without, but so far only that the man could hand it to him, and then slid down the pole with it in his hand to the platform; which he had no sooner reached than he was greeted by the loud growl of a bear, as it was rushing on him out of a small cave formed by the rock receding inwards a little at the base, within a few feet of the trunk he had come down. He had just time to cock the rifle and fire, and fortunately shot the bear through the head, and killed it on the spot. The trunk of the pine-tree being so long had saved him; for could the man have handed the rifle to him when he reached the platform, he would to a certainty have come down without it, and most probably have been the victim instead of the bear, which in their relative positions could not, even if so inclined, have got away without first knocking him off the platform.

We got down to the road and breakfasted in a large cave, in which Wilson had often resided for months at a time while musk-deer hunting in the forests around. It bore unmistakable marks of the work. Heaps of musk-deer fur, scores of their feet, bones in abundance, and several pairs of burrells' horns still remained bleaching about the spot. Two miles further on we found the camp, at the sacred place of Hindoo pilgrimage, the Gangootree temple. The river is the object of veneration as the Goddess Gungajee, who, however, is supposed also to reside in the temple in the form of a small silver female image. She is the most chaste and temperate of all Hindoo divinities, having no obscene rites or sacrifices attached to her worship.

A few blades of grass, flowers, sweetmeats, and spices, and money and cloth for the officiating brahmins, are the offerings made at her shrine. The temple is a small, unpretending little edifice, not unlike one of the small tombs one sees everywhere in the plains.

There is nothing very remarkable in the scenery. The valley is narrow and confined, with no view of the mass of snowy mountains so near. From the temple down to Byramghattee, about ten miles, the river flows unseen in a deep narrow gorge, the rocks rising everywhere very steep, and in many places quite perpendicular, from the water's edge to a height of from 100 to 300 feet. So narrow is the gorge in some places, that near the cave spoken of, Wilson had thrown a bridge across from rock to rock, two hundred feet or more above the water. From the gorge, on each side is a slope varying from a quarter to three-quarters of a mile in breadth. This on both sides is well wooded with pine and cedar. Above this rise steep craggy rocks, everywhere very abrupt, and in some places quite inaccessible; still, however, clothed partially with pine or birch forest. These rocks are so steep that, except in a few places, where small portions of the snowy background is visible, they close the view on both sides. By the temple the gorge disappears, the wooded slope coming quite down to the river, which from here upwards has an open channel. The pilgrims who visit Gangootree are apparently mostly of the middle or poorer classes; it is but occasionally any person of rank comes either to this or any other place of pilgrimage in the hills. From all I could learn, the number in one year of all classes seldom exceeds a thousand or fifteen hundred, and the number is said to be decreasing every year. The brahmins who officiate at the temple reside at a village called Muckwa, opposite Derallee. They hold half the village lands, the whole yearly rental of which is but sixty rupees, rent free from the rajah; but there are none attached to the shrine, the offerings of the pilgrims being its only wealth. A slight contrast to the sister temples of Keedarnath and Budrenath, in the *British* portion of Gurwhal, where a *Christian* government apportions the rents of a considerable number of flourishing villages for the support of a number of lazy brahmins. These holy men are not very particular about the origin of their places of worship. An enterprising individual of the fraternity, debarred by residing in another village from any benefit from the pilgrims he saw daily passing his village to lay their offerings at Gangootree for the more fortunate brahmins of Muckwa, was making an energetic attempt to found a place of pilgrimage on a small scale for his own sole emolument. A few marches below, on the opposite bank of the river from the road, but within sight of it, is a hot spring, the steam from which attracts the attention of the passers by. This he deemed quite sufficient to make the place an object of veneration; but, alas! a bridge required to be constructed over the Ganges to enable his anticipated worshippers to reach the place. This he could not do himself, and the unbelieving villagers would not be persuaded to assist him. Determined this should not defeat his purpose, he posts off to the rajah, expatiates on the advantage of rescuing the forgotten sacred spot from oblivion, and offering a present of one hundred rupees, begs the rajah will help him by ordering the villagers to make the required bridge. The order was given, and as I was passing it was in rapid progress under the supervision of the persevering brahmin, who will now only have to use his oily tongue in persuading the passing pilgrims to turn aside a few moments to do homage at the now sacred spot.

Having satisfied my curiosity with the little to be seen about the temple, in the morning we started with the camp for the glacier, which is eighteen miles farther up; Wilson walking through the forest under the rocks, and myself along the river bank, to which the rocks came so near in several places that we could often speak to each other. A musk-deer shot by him was the result of the morning's walk. We could have easily reached the glacier in one day, but to allow time to beat some likely patches of forest for these animals, we made two marches of it. At our first camp we had to cross the river on the snow, with which it was arched over in many places, the steep rock rising perpendicularly from the water and stopping our further progress on the right bank. After passing the obstruction, we recrossed on another mass of snow. The forest was gradually altering in appearance; pines becoming scarcer, and birch and rhododendron bushes the prevailing wood. The valley itself kept of the same character, a slope of a few hundred yards to half a mile running up on each side from the river, from which rose naked rocks and crags still more wild in appearance. The left bank of the river was almost everywhere covered deeply with snow; but on the right it lay only in the hollows and ravines. The narrowness of the valley, and the steepness of the hills on each side, still confined the view; but the snowy peaks were becoming visible. One on the left bank formed an imposing object, rising direct from the wooded slope some 10,000 feet in one steep and unbroken incline, the lower part naked rock and the upper dazzling snow. At sunset the second day we found our camp pitched on a flat by the river, near a grove of pine trees, and still four miles below the glacier, but the last comfortable place we should find on the way to it; and as we were to stay a couple of days, it was better to halt here where wood was plentiful, and the pine trees would afford shelter to the men, than on the nearer but much bleaker spots higher up. In the morning, on our way up, we went about a quarter of a mile up the hill side, to a flat which is always a sure find for burrell. For two miles below the glacier the right bank is changed in character. From the slope above the river, instead of the parapet-like rocks, there is a flat about a hundred yards wide the whole distance, and the hill rises from it again much less rugged. The slope, the flat, and much of the hill above, are covered with rich grass, and being so seldom disturbed, are favourite resorts of these animals. We saw three different flocks, and succeeded in stalking two, killing two females and one very fine old male; and had we seen it before firing at the first lot, we should have had a chance at a snow-bear, the first one I had seen. It was feeding within a hundred yards of us, but concealed by a little knoll; and a few moments after the shots we saw it clambering up the hill. At noon we arrived at the glacier, and breakfasted beneath it. It was very different from what I expected, from the descriptions I had read of the Alpine ones. Without it the valley would have been exactly of the same character as below, and the glacier lay in it as if snow had been collected and thrown up in the middle for an immense railroad. It might be about three-quarters of a mile broad, but came rounded off at its termination over the river; its depth appeared to be about 200 feet. The river, where it issued from beneath the glacier, was about twenty feet wide and three deep; nearly as large as at the temple eighteen miles below. In the rains, when the river is full, it must be nearly thrice the size. The arch of snow above was about twelve feet from the water, and had much the appearance of the entrance of a tunnel before being faced with masonry. The water being shallow at the side, and portions of the ground dry, I walked a little way under the snow. A cold damp wind blew in my face, water was trickling from the roof, which was very irregular, and the feeling was a strange kind of chilliness without severe cold. The water of the river itself was so intensely cold, that standing in it more than a few moments was impossible. Ascending on to the glacier, we walked up it for upwards of a mile. The surface is very irregular, broken up into ridges and hollows, and in many places strewed over with earth, stones, and masses of rock. Pools of blue-looking water, which we could not fathom, some several yards round, others only a few feet, appeared in the hollows; and little streams of water, flowing in channels grooved in the ice, ran in all directions. It is strange that the water in these pools never freezes, even when the river itself, torrent as it is, becomes in winter, for miles below the glacier, a mass of ice in appearance. At a little distance the Himalayan glaciers appear to be discoloured snow; but on closer examination you find it is very hard ice, and some detached lumps have a quite blue tint, and the sides, where free from incrustation, often that of the glass of a black bottle. On each side of the glacier the hills are still for some distance covered with grass, and even small willow bushes. Its height above the sea-level is about 13,000 feet.

The hills on each side are the grandest and most sublime the mind can possibly conceive of such scenery. Rising 10,000 or 12,000 feet above the level of the valley, and covered from their base with spotless snow, they have an inconceivably awe-inspiring appearance. In some places the rock is seen where, being quite perpendicular, the snow cannot lie, and it has a strange white, spectral appearance, which adds much to the grandeur of the whole. The glacier extends with the same gradual slope to the apparent head of the valley, about twelve or fourteen miles, where it either turns, or is bounded by the snowy hills which there terminate the view.

After some time spent in admiring the wild scenery, we returned by the river side to the camp, on the sand meeting in several places with the fresh footprints of a white leopard, one of the most difficult animals to be got in the hills. On my remarking that as there was no cover we might possibly meet with it in our next day's ramble, Wilson said it was very unlikely, as he had hunted over the ground many times, and though always meeting with fresh traces, had never seen one of the animals. In some fourteen years' hunting, some portion of every one of which had been spent in the regions it inhabits, he had not met with more than half a dozen, and only killed three.

The next day turned out a very fortunate one. We had decided on going first to the flats, looking over them and the hill above, and on our return, if we had time, to beat some strips of birch forest for musk-deer; the coolies being instructed to come from camp in the afternoon, and wait for us there. The first thing we saw when we reached the flats was a snow bear. "It is the same we saw yesterday," said Wilson, "and if I am not much mistaken he will shortly lose that beautiful skin, for the deuce is in it if he escapes us this time. The wind is fortunately in our favour, and only let him get behind that green knoll, and I think he's safe." The bear was busy digging up the ground and turning over the stones, and gradually approaching the little knoll which would hide us from his sight as we ran along the flat. We remained quiet for ten minutes, and then, as his body disappeared behind the swell, seizing our rifles, and leaving all the men but one who carried my double gun, stole quickly but softly across the intervening ground, a distance of about 200 yards. Wilson cautiously peered over the knoll, drew back instantly, and motioned me to advance, as he had insisted I should take the shot. I cocked the rifle and looked over. There was the bear within forty yards. I was raising the rifle, when my companion put his hand on my arm, whispering "Let him turn." I understood what he meant, for the bear was in an unfavourable position, with his back towards me, but I thought as he stood I could have hit him in the spine. What a moment of excitement! In a few seconds he slowly turned half round, exposing his neck and shoulder. Now! and bang went my rifle; the bear rolling over like a stone, as dead as if he had had his head struck off. The ball had gone through his neck. "That's how I like to see a beast fall," said Wilson, "and though a bear often gives a lot of sport when not killed outright, it hardly equals the gratification of seeing one knocked over in that style." We now examined our prize. He was a very large one, and had a magnificent skin; the fur at least nine inches long, and of a bright yellow colour. It was soon stripped off and despatched to camp, and when pegged out to dry was nearly eight feet long. The body was very poor and thin, as they always are in spring. We went on our way, ascending for a mile the grassy hill above the flat. What a scene was around us! What can be conceived more sublime? On every side the most majestic snow-covered peaks, rearing their unearthly forms against the deep blue sky, so near as to be awful in their distinctness. The main glacier below, stretching out before us up the valley, while lesser ones, of a quite different form, some not unlike immense fleeces of wool transformed into snow, and piled on each other, filled every ravine and chasm of the spectral hills encircling it. Now and then strange noises, sometimes like the rumbling of distant thunder, and at others like the sharp crack of artillery, broke the stillness that reigned over all, often startling from the suddenness and apparent proximity. This is occasioned by the cracking of the glaciers, and the falling of masses of snow. But the scenery is forgotten. A flock of burrell is discovered. There they are in that ravine, a long way off, and scarcely to be discerned with the naked eye. But the movement of one has pointed out the spot, and the glass reveals the whole flock. There must be thirty or forty, and nearly all are laid down at rest. But they are in a bad place, the ground is very open, and the flock are widely scattered; the stalk will be a difficult one. After examining the ground, Wilson's experienced eye detects a means of approach, and after a long circuit, which occupies the best part of two hours, it is over, and three burrell are stretched on the ground, and another has gone off badly wounded. It is followed and added to the bag. On our return we find the rest of the coolies from camp, waiting, according to orders, to beat the strips of birch forest. We take our posts, and the beating commences. A musk-deer is roused and comes bounding along past me, but it will not stand for a moment, and I miss with both barrels, and it is too far for the shot gun. But it must also pass Wilson, and see, he raises his rifle. It halts for a second, but is off again ere he can fire. What a pity, it will get by after all. No! another momentary halt, and its fate is sealed. Wilson's practised rifle is too sure at that distance, not more than sixty yards. It is discharged, and a fine male musk-deer is added to our list of killed.

After crossing the first snow bridge, we kept on the left bank on our way down, and six men being quite sufficient to carry all the traps we had brought up with us, while they went along by the river, and made everything comfortable for us at night in some appointed place, we beat in succession the strips of forest on the slope which has been mentioned as extending all the way up from the river to the rocks. Some we beat upwards from the river, being stationed ourselves on the rocks above, and others across, taking our posts on the edge of a ravine, as **Wilson, who** of course directed all, thought most advisable. In choosing a post the great object was to have it so that when a musk-deer came by it would have to cross a portion of ground within shot, free from thick forest or underwood, when it would probably halt for a moment more than once while crossing, and offer a very good shot; while, if the space was confined, it might pass without halting at all, and if wooded, when it did halt, it might be behind the trunk of a tree or a thick bush. Though the game was so small, the sport was very exciting, and the shots quite numerous enough to keep up the excitement throughout the day, for sometimes, after missing, you had time to load and fire your rifle twice before the little animal was out of range. It was excellent practice, too, and I know nothing better adapted to make a person shoot well in the field than a few weeks' musk-deer shooting. You get all kinds of shots, and at all distances, and learn to shoot quick, though still taking a cool and deliberate aim, for, the mark being so small, you must shoot to a nicety. In this manner it took us three days to get down opposite the temple, in which time we killed three male and five female musk-deer, having beat about a dozen different portions of forest. In some not a single deer was found; in others one or two, and occasionally four or five. Wilson's men being trained to the work, and many of mine having been also well-used to it while with him in former years, everything went on as well as we could wish. There was never any mistake made in the direction the forest was to be driven, and it was seldom an animal was suffered to double back, which musk-deer will often try to do if the spot has been driven before. Sometimes one would do so notwithstanding all the efforts of the men to prevent it, almost jumping over some of them in its retreat.

Our next ground was up a lateral valley called Rhudagira, the stream from which joins the Ganges about two miles below the temple, on the left bank near Wilson's bridge. For about five miles the lower part on both sides was thickly wooded with birch, some of the trees having had the bark stripped off to sell to the pilgrims by the villagers and the hill-men, who are engaged as porters by those who can afford that luxury in their pilgrimage. On some of the young trees the inner layers of bark are so fine as to resemble silk paper in texture, and in the higher hills it is very generally used as a substitute for writing paper. Birch bark is one of the articles of hill produce exported into the plains, where, amongst other purposes, it is used in the manufacture of hookah snakes. On some trees there are upwards of twenty layers of bark, and when the trunk is free from knots it is taken off in one piece, which is sometimes nine or ten feet long and three wide, but in general the pieces do not average more than three feet by one or two. The inner bark of all adheres to the trunk, so that, though the outer is taken off completely round, the tree does not die, but for many years the bark is not renewed so as to be worth again taking off.

The musk-deer in these forests we left to be hunted up on our return, and proceeded at once to the head of the valley to look for burrell, pitching our little camp nearly at the termination of the forest, but far enough from the first grassy hill not to disturb anything which might be there. In the upper part of the valley the hills on both sides of the stream are extensive grassy slopes, with here and there portions of rough craggy ground, and sometimes almost inaccessible rock. By going a little way up either hill-side, the whole of the opposite one, from the river to the crest of the ridge, about three miles, could be seen. There was a good deal of snow on both sides from about half-way up, but the lower part was nearly free. From the commencement of the grassy region to the head of the valley, where a large glacier — flanked on one side by an inaccessible rocky hill, which joined a mass of snowy peaks above, and on the other by the base of an immense snowy mountain — terminated it, was about five miles. On the left bank, a little distance above the river, was a long flat, about 200 yards wide, very similar to the one below the glacier at the head of the Ganges, and always a favourite resort of burrell. When Wilson first visited this little valley, some ten years before, it had not been disturbed for near a quarter of a century. In that period probably not a single human being had set foot within it, and certainly no gun had been fired. The burrell, which were very numerous, were like tame sheep, and a flock of nearly a hundred, which he found on the flat, stood for ten minutes within gunshot without showing the slightest inclination to escape, though he was standing up before them quite exposed. He singled out and killed one of the largest old males, reloaded and knocked over a second, when the whole flock galloped off for a short distance, and then again turned to gaze at the, no doubt to them, strange apparition. There they stood for some time, while he and his man were skinning the slain ones, and then slowly walked off up the hill above the flat in single file, "a sight," says Wilson, "which probably neither I nor any other person shall ever see again in the Himalayas." They are now here just as wild as anywhere else, and the numbers have greatly decreased; much more so than the few which have been killed will account for, from which it must be inferred that many have forsaken the valley, probably having crossed the snowy mountains at its head.

To have as good a day's sport as possible, we had not disturbed any of the ground on the evening of our arrival, and in the morning went out almost certain of having our first shots on the flat. As we walked up by the river, the surface of this could not be seen, and no animal on it, unless standing on the extreme edge, could see us. We had got just under it, and were commencing the little steep ascent of some 200 yards from the river to its edge, when a snow-bear made its appearance, coming leisurely down the river side on the opposite bank. We had several men with us, but all managed to escape observation; those who could do so getting out of sight, as we did ourselves, behind large stones, and those who could not, lying flat on the ground. Bears, though rather quick in smelling, are not at all so in seeing, and if the wind is in your favour, and you keep still, though partially exposed, they often come very near before becoming aware of your presence. This one came down without seeing any of us till nearly opposite, and was about sixty yards off, when, fearing it might see some of the men who were exposed and bolt back, I took deliberate aim at the shoulder and fired the first shot. It gave a loud roar, turning quickly round several times and biting at its shoulder, then starting back at a quick trot up the river. Wilson fired both his barrels, and I my remaining one, before it had got many yards, and it then turned and commenced clambering up the hill-side. I now took the double-gun, and fired both barrels without any apparent effect, while my companion was reloading his rifle, when he sat down and took two more deliberate shots; but, though evidently severely hit, the bear still continued its progress up the hill, and before I had got my rifle reloaded was nearly 200 yards off. I took the two long shots, but I had not practised sufficiently at this distance, and one we saw strike half a yard too high. We sat down to watch what the bear would do, going a little way up the slope on our side to have a fairer view, and as we had now the whole of the opposite one before us, it would have to go a long way ere it got out of our sight. After a little while it commenced to go slower and slower, frequently stopping as if to rest, and at length lay down under some crags about half a mile up the hill. With the glass we could just see a little of its back, and we waited for ten minutes without its again moving. Now came the question what to do. If we followed it we should partly spoil our day's burrell-shooting, and after getting a little way up the hill-side, should be fully exposed to anything on the flat, supposing it had not been disturbed by our firing. Taking these things into consideration, we determined to leave a man on the spot to keep watch over the bear, and proceed on our way, Wilson being of opinion it would die where it had lain down. When we got up to the flat, which was not more than 200 yards above, nothing was to be seen on it, but one of the men gave the peculiar "isht" which they all used to denote their discovery of game, and looking to where he pointed up the hill, there was a large flock of burrell in full retreat. "Confound the bear," said Wilson, "what a chance it has spoiled. Those burrell must have been on the flat, and what a shot we should have had if they had not been disturbed. But we must not be greedy," continued he, laughing, "nor repine at our bread not being this time buttered on both sides." It was useless going after them, for burrell, once disturbed, rarely give a second chance, unless the ground is very favourable; and here it was quite the reverse, as the only practicable way would have been to go down the river for some distance, and up some ravine, making a round so as to come over the burrell. This would have taken half the day, and then its success depended entirely on whether the animals remained somewhere near or not, a chance hardly worth the time and labour required. We preferred going in search of others, and went on along the flat. About a mile further it was cut in two by a little ravine, the bed of a torrent which drained the hill above, and the swell of the ground was such that, until we crossed this, the further portion of the flat was not seen. When we got to the opposite side, after scrambling with some difficulty down and up the steep banks, the whole was before us, a long narrow strip of slightly undulating ground, covered with rich green grass, and flanked by the steep, and in some places rocky, hill-side. From our position nothing was to be seen on it; but on getting a little way up the hill, so as to have more of a bird's-eye view, some burrell could just be distinguished nearly at the further end. I might have looked over the ground long enough myself without seeing anything at such a distance, but the more experienced eyes of Wilson and the men made them out at once, and when the exact spot was pointed out to me I saw them plain enough. Only five or six could be distinctly perceived with the naked eye, and only as mere specks; but the glass showed a great many more, which, without its assistance, could not be seen distinctly enough to tell they were animals. They were in a very easy place to stalk, as it was only necessary to go down the little ravine to the river, and walk up along its bed till directly parallel to where they were; then, ascending to the edge of the flat, they would be within shot. Wilson proposed that I should do this while he went up the ravine, and along the hill-side above, till in a favourable position for the chance of a shot if they went up, which they were almost certain to do, after my firing. At any other time mine would not have been a very pleasant walk, for I found the banks of the river in some places so very steep that I was often obliged to walk in the water, which was intensely cold, and it was not easy making way against the stream. I had marked the place by a peculiar rock on the opposite hill, and, ascending the little slope from the river, with feelings a deer-stalker only can understand, however well they have often been described, I rested a few moments before looking over, to still the tremor which walking up a steep ascent, however slowly, causes in our frame, and which was now doubly increased by the intense excitement. I raised my head cautiously, when within fifty yards was the black breast and massive horns of a large male burrel, looking, as I thought, intently in my face. An indistinct vision of several more close by flashed in the hasty glance; but I was not practised hunter enough to see the whole distinctly at once, and I was too fearful of spoiling my chance to take a more scrutinizing look. It seemed as if there was no room in my mind for more than the one individual object singled out. Resting my elbows on the flat, my breast resting against the bank, and a man supporting my feet, for it was so steep I could not otherwise keep firm footing, in another moment my rifle was pointed at the black breast; and as I pulled the trigger, with the sight bearing on its centre, I felt certain of the shot. Mountains and merry thoughts,—loves and lady-birds! what a mess I had made of it! The barrels of the rifle rested on the smooth surface of a small stone, which had just slope enough to let the bullet graze on it without my seeing the possibility of such a thing while taking aim. For an instant the black breast, head, and horns remained motionless, then slowly turned round and disappeared. As I rose up a little there was a confused mass of animals moving off, but ere I fired the second barrel, as if by magic there was a general halt, and nearly the whole turned round, as if not knowing exactly what was the matter. Dropping down again, I aimed at the shoulder of what I thought one of the largest males, and then the double-gun being handed to me, fired the two barrels as the flock galloped across the flat. There was nothing to denote one was even hit, as they all reached the foot of the hill together, and sprung lightly from rock to rock up the steep ascent. But in a few minutes a large male stood quite still, and was soon left alone, making no attempt to follow the rest, which were now fast nearing the spot where we thought Wilson must have posted himself. I was puzzled what to do, for I could not get nearer the burrell without walking across the flat right in its sight, so sat down to watch it, and to see what Wilson would do above. Every moment I expected to hear the crack of his rifle, for the burrell, of which I had counted twenty-three, were a considerable way up the hill, when we saw him running as fast as he could along the hill-side right away from them. What his object was we could form no idea, but on he went till lost to our sight. We waited some time without seeing anything more of him, and I was fairly at a loss how to proceed. There was my burrell still standing in the same place, out of range, and no way of getting to it unperceived, but by going either all the way back, and round by the hill-side above, as Wilson had come, or going up by the river to the glacier, and from thence up the hill and round in the same manner. The latter way was much the nearest, so I determined to try it, and leaving a man to watch the burrell, went again down to the river-bed, and up it to the glacier, and had got some distance up the hill, when I met Wilson coming down. He had killed a white leopard. Having taken up his position on the rocks, he saw all that took place, my first miss and subsequent shots; but his attention was taken altogether from the burrell by seeing a magnificent white leopard, which had probably been watching them, steal off along the hill-side some distance below. Waiting till it got out of sight, he then ran, as we saw him, in a parallel direction, dogged it till it began to descend a ravine, and then running up, got a shot as it was going up the opposite bank. This rolled it to the bottom, but as it got up again he gave it the other barrel. Having related to him my mishap, and described the position of the wounded burrell, we went first and skinned his leopard, which had one of the most beautiful skins I ever saw, long, close, and very soft fur, a greyish-white ground with dark spots, and an immensely long and thick tail. This done, we went to finish the burrell, which we found still in the same place, and coming down on it from above, easily got within forty yards. It had lain down, and a shot through the neck put it out of misery. The first shot had hit it in the side, a little too far from the shoulder to be immediately fatal.

It was now getting late in the afternoon, and we had not yet had breakfast; so we adjourned to the river to discuss that meal, and then down to where we had left the man watching the bear. It had not moved, so we went up to see how affairs stood. See us approaching the rock, with rifles ready for instant use, to—a dead bear. It must have been so for some time, as it was quite stiff. On examination we found it had received five bullets, one behind the shoulder, two in the side, one in the back, and one in the hind leg. This ended our day's sport, which, if it had not furnished a bag anything remarkable in the number of animals killed, far exceeded in quality, by the death of the leopard, our most sanguine expectations.

Wilson remained at home the next day to dress his leopard skin, and I went over the hill on the right bank, but only found one lot of burrell, all females, out of which I killed one by a lucky shot at nearly 300 yards. I had stalked them as I thought very nicely, when, on looking over the ridge I intended to shoot from, they were all off, having crossed one little ridge, and they were fast getting out of even a long range. The first two barrels, at about 200 yards, missed, but the next, after having reloaded, and when they had got nearly a hundred yards further, rolled one over dead. The day following we moved down a few miles and beat the forest for musk-deer, killing two, and I got another very fine one with a pod which must have weighed nearly an ounce, while walking quietly in search of them on our way down to the bridge over the Ganges. Wilson, who went in another direction, had **a blank** morning. There are very few birds in the Gangootree forests; **two** or three monalls, which flew out while the men were beating, and a couple of birds I had not before seen, snow pheasants, which I found, but did not get a shot at, on the grassy hill where I killed **the** last female burrell, were all we met **with**.

Wilson's bridge I thought worthy of a place **in my** book of daubs, and with some difficulty **got** down to the river by a little ravine to take a sketch of it. Arrived at the bottom, I found I could walk along the edge **of the** water to nearly under the bridge. The channel was about sixty feet **wide**, a portion **of** the right bank being dry. The rocks rose on each side, as well as I could judge, nearly **250** feet, **and are** something more than perpendicular, **the** distance between them where the **bridge** is thrown across above being only **fifty feet**. The face of the rock is not very regular, but scooped out in some places and protruding in others, and full of cracks and fissures, out of some of which small bushes, and even a small cedar-tree, were growing. Altogether a wilder-looking chasm can scarcely be conceived. **The** bridge, **as** may be imagined, **is a very** rude one; a couple **of slight** spars, **thrown** across from rock to rock, about **two feet** apart, **and** pieces **of** stick and plank laid crosswise upon them, serve a hunter's purpose.

We beat several more places in the **cedar** forest on our **way** down, adding two more musk-deer **to** our bag, and arrived **at** Derallee, where I had **left**

my heavy baggage, after having been away seventeen days. We had killed eleven burrell, eighteen musk-deer, two bears, and a white leopard, which Wilson himself considered as excellent sport. Had I been by myself I should probably not have got more than half a dozen head of game in all, and possibly not that, notwithstanding I had with me men who were tolerably well acquainted with the ground. In all wild countries it is natural that a person well acquainted with the ground and the haunts and habits of the game should succeed in the chase of it much better than a stranger, particularly in a mountainous country; and nowhere perhaps is a stranger more at a loss, or does he receive more advantage from the experience of others, than in the Himalayas, where the chase is on the most stupendous scale.

CHAPTER IV.

At the risk of being tedious I cannot help giving a few more details of my shooting while with Wilson. Though meeting with no wonderful adventures, no hair-breadth escapes, no lucky shot to save either of us or a coolie from some infuriated beast at the last moment, there may still be something interesting to a reader in what I derived so much pleasure from as an actor. The mention of a sheep or a goat doubtless sounds tame as an object of chase, and with the exception of a few bears, these and musk-deer were all we had to pursue; but a sheep or a goat rises into something well worthy of the sportsman's greatest ardour, and requiring the highest exertion of his art, when in the shape of the burrell or tahr of the Himalayas. The pursuit of these will not indeed bear recital with the thrilling anecdotes of elephant-hunting in Ceylon, or lion-hunting in Africa; but every real sportsman who has had the good fortune to enjoy it, will bear me out in saying that even these hardly yield greater excitement at the time, and certainly not more lasting feelings of pleasure. The hard work of walking up such steep and high hills may take away a great deal of the pleasure from some, but those whose physical powers can make light of this, find as much real enjoyment in stalking a flock of burrell or tahr as in hunting the monarchs of the forest. Nowhere does the stalking yield more excitement, and when it succeeds, there is almost as much satisfaction in making a good shot at the longer distance at one of these, as in flooring the largest of terrestrial creatures by a scientifically placed bullet at half a dozen paces. True, there is not the personal danger; but if the hunter would analyze his feelings, he would find it is not the sense of this, but the confidence of being more than a match for them, and the desire to put this to the proof, that render the pursuit of savage and powerful beasts more exciting than that of timid and watchful ones.

A few days were spent in the forests above Derallee after musk-deer, sometimes beating with all the coolies, and sometimes walking quietly out to look for them by ourselves. In the latter way there was no stalking, almost every deer being within shot when first seen. You took your rifle and walked quietly through the forest for a few hours, morning or evening, when the deer were feeding, proceeding very cautiously, and looking well about on all sides. There were no particular places on which to expect finding one — all were alike; the grassy bank entirely free from forest, that covered with small bushes, or those where the trees were thinly scattered, the steep ledge of rock, and the dark wood where the immense pine trees were so close together that the branches interwove and effectually shut out every ray of the sun, might each or all give the chance of a shot. On some ground, even when standing quite exposed and within eighty yards, a musk-deer will often fail in striking even a practised eye, and a sharp hiss, or the animals bounding off, is not unfrequently the first intimation you receive of the presence of one which may have been for some time standing like a statue steadfastly watching your approach. It then depends altogether on the nature of the ground whether you get a shot or not. If it is open, and the deer has some distance to go ere getting out of sight, it may possibly halt for a moment and give as good a one as you could wish, though perhaps at rather a long range; but from many causes it is often shut from view after a few bounds, and your chance is lost. It was considered a good morning's work to meet with three or four, now that the forests had been so thinned; but when Wilson first commenced hunting here he sometimes met with more than a dozen.

Here, too, they were wilder and more cunning than in the Gangootree forests. One day we were beating, and I was posted on a ledge of rock overlooking a patch of rhododendron bushes. A musk-deer made its appearance, but concealed itself in a thick bush ere I could get a shot. The line of beaters came gradually up, and I waited in momentary expectation of its coming out and up past my post; but though two or three men were just below, shouting and beating the bushes, it would not move, and did not even do so when one of them gave a loud shout and a crash on the bush with his stick a few yards from where it must have been standing, but the moment he passed its level, it jumped up behind him and went off at full speed down the hill.

We often met with traces of bears, but were not fortunate enough to meet with one while at Derallee. The hill above the forest is a beautiful grassy slope, extending to the foot of an immense snowy mountain, the sugar-loaf peak, in fact, so conspicuous from Mussoorie. It looked first-rate burrell ground, but, strange to say, none are ever seen on it, though all the other hills in the district, if not regular resorts, are occasionally visited. What the reason can be it is impossible to conjecture, as it is not more disturbed than others, in fact, not so much as some good burrell grounds, and in character and natural productions it is exactly the same.

There were two good valleys for burrell within one day's march, the Nela and Dumdar ones. The former I should have to go up on my way to Koonaur, so we determined to spend a few days in the latter. After a pleasant walk of twelve or fourteen miles we arrived at the camp, or rather bivouac, of the Jallah shepherds, about two miles from where we intended to pitch our own. Our first question was whether they had disturbed the ground higher up the valley, to which they replied no, that they had only come up from below the day previous. The poor fellows were in a sad way, having just met with a terrible misfortune. The flock, which comprised the sheep both of their own and some other villages, had in the morning gone out to graze as usual, attended by one of the men. A pack of wild dogs suddenly rushed amongst them, killed several on the spot, and the terrified flock, collected in a dense mass, rushed headlong down the hill, and unfortunately to the edge of a ledge of rock with an almost perpendicular fall of some sixty feet. One half the flock was precipitated over this by the pressure from behind, and lay in a confused heap below. Many were killed, and being nearly all ewes in lamb, very few survived the accident. We went up to the scene of the disaster, only a few hundred yards away, in hopes of seeing the wild dogs, but they, having gorged themselves sufficiently, had retreated. There were seven of them, one of which was killed by a shikaree from the village the same evening when they again returned. Our coolies purchased several of the carcasses for four annas (about sixpence) each, the price of a living sheep being from two to three rupees. This was a great loss to the villagers, upwards of sixty sheep destroyed here, and many more which were taken home dying afterwards, but fortunately the loss was pretty equally divided amongst the community. A few days afterwards the dogs were seen near one of the villages, and had very soon killed several cows and bullocks.

This damped our hopes of finding many burrell in the valley, as the dogs might have been prowling about it for weeks, which would have effectually driven them all out; but we were glad to find there were no traces of their having been further up, and the burrell were apparently undisturbed. The ground was very similar to the hills near the Gangootree glacier and at Rhudagira, the grassy region between the forest and the snow, which is the burrell ground, being everywhere on the south side of the Himalayan range much of the same character. The climate being somewhat damper than at these places, which partake slightly of the dry atmosphere of Thibet, the vegetation was more luxuriant, and the hills generally were less rugged. Our first attempt was a sad failure. A very fine flock of burrell was discovered, and with some difficulty, and after making a long round, we had stalked nearly 200 yards, when three or four, which we had either not seen or which had strayed from the flock, suddenly got up before us and took the whole flock off with them. This was a bad result of half the day's labour, and another small flock, which we met with in the afternoon, did not give us the chance of a stalk, as they had seen us and were already moving off when first discovered. The only shot fired this day was one by Wilson at a musk-deer, just before reaching camp in the evening.

The following day we crossed the river on a snow-bridge, and tried the opposite hills. A long and steep ascent took us to the crest of a ridge which divided two of the lateral ravines. The one we now looked into formed a kind of amphitheatre, having a very narrow entrance where it debouched into the main valley, and suddenly opening out, formed a nearly circular hollow, the hills on all sides sloping gradually down to the stream in the middle. The bottom of the ravine itself was an irregular flat, about half a mile in length and 300 yards wide. The ridge on which we were was about half a mile above this, and another very similar ridge on the opposite side faced us. Both ran up very abruptly to the main range above, a portion of which formed the head of the little valley. From our position on the ridge we could look over the whole, and the most distant parts were within the scope of our glasses. While we were scanning the ground over with these, one of Wilson's men, a perfect telescope himself, from his wonderful powers of vision, espied some burrell near the stream below, and the glass revealed a very large flock scattered over the stony flat, most of them lying down at rest. Had there been only a few we might possibly have stalked them; but being so many, and scattered over such an extent of ground, there was no possible way of approaching without being seen by some. Every side was well examined, and the advantage every irregularity of the ground would give in covering our advance noted down; but, viewed in the most favourable light, we could see no way likely to be attended with success. The only plan was to attempt to drive them, and this did not seem very promising, as they might take any direction, and we could command but a small portion of the ground. We had five men with us, and two of these were sent back to go down to the river, up the main valley, and enter the ravine where it joined; they were then to keep well on the opposite hill-side till the burrell took alarm, and then run along it to prevent them going in that direction. We went ourselves a little further up the ridge we were on, when I took up my post. If they came up on this side, I could remain where I was, or run down behind the ridge to wherever they were approaching to cross. Wilson went a little higher up, and then for several hundred yards along the hill-side which shut in the valley nearly at right angles to my ridge. At equal distances between us he left two men, and when he had posted himself sent another still further to his left, nearly to the opposite ridge. We had to wait for some hours before the two men sent round to disturb the burrell made their appearance. When they did so, they were very soon seen, and the whole flock began to move off the flat. At first they seemed inclined to go to the opposite hill, but turning, went right up in the direction of Wilson. It was now very exciting work, and I watched them with peculiar interest. There must have been nearly sixty in the flock, males and females. They went up very slowly, frequently stopping for ten minutes together, and often playing with and butting at each other. I had marked the place down where Wilson sat, though I could not see him, as he had got behind a rock, and saw them get right under the spot, when suddenly one of them rolled over, and the whole flock made a rush down the hill, and a few seconds after came the report of Wilson's rifle. They then came a little way in my direction, and again turned up hill, first at a gallop, but soon subsiding into a quick walk. They would have passed between Wilson and myself, but the men he had left now stood up and gave a shout, and the bewildered animals again made a rush down hill, then came across towards the ridge, by which, if they did not change their direction, they would come up to a hundred yards below my post. I waited a little while, and as they showed no signs of doing so, I then ran down behind the ridge and got behind a large stone. I was only just in time, for a few moments afterwards the leading files appeared passing not more than fifty yards below. A deliberate pot rolled the largest one of the first few over, but I had no time for a second shot ere the whole were rushing down the slope. They now divided into two lots, one portion rushing on to the bottom, crossing the flat, and ascending the opposite hill, and nearly running over the two men, who by this time had got well up the valley. The other lot swerved again and crossed my ridge about 200 yards lower down, but at such a pace that neither there, nor as they passed below on the slope we had come up, could I get a decent shot for my second barrel.

Nothing could have been better planned or better carried out, and everything had succeeded admirably. It was scarcely to be expected that the burrell would give us many shots after having been disturbed; and in this and the Nela valley they are very wild, being continually hunted by the village shikaries. We considered we had been very fortunate indeed in getting two.

The next day we went up to the glacier at the head of the river and looked over some very likely ground, but saw no burrell. The scenery, though grand enough in its way, will not bear comparison with what we saw at the source of the Ganges. The grand features are the same on a smaller scale, but the wild, unearthly, shroud-like look of unapproachable eternal stillness which the vastness of the details throws over the giant peaks there is entirely wanting. On our return by the river we had the good fortune to espy a she-bear and two little cubs, feeding on the grassy bank a little way up one of the lateral ravines across the river. It was not fordable, being now much swollen by the melting snow, and we were obliged to go back nearly a mile to a snow-bridge we had passed. Bears, though they will always bolt the moment they see a person, are the easiest things possible to stalk, if the hunter only takes care to have the wind in his favour; and after reaching the spot we were soon watching this one from behind a swell within **sixty** yards; we being **right** above it, and a space of about twice that distance intervening between the bear and the little stream at the foot of the hill. The cubs were very small, and while their mamma **was** digging for roots, were **frolicking** with each other, cutting all sorts of capers, and scarcely remaining still a moment. It really seemed a pity to disturb their felicity. We had three men with us, and it was agreed that, instead of shooting **the** old lady from where we stood, we should all make a rush on them **just** to **see** what she would do, and the men were **to** catch the cubs. So **very** busy was she at her work, that we got over nearly half the ground before she saw us, when she looked up for a moment, and then started off right down the hill, followed by the little ones, which immediately commenced a most awful screaming. The poor little things could not run very fast, and we soon overhauled them, the old one being **some** twenty yards ahead. She had several times waited for them, and we might have shot her at any time **we** liked. At last the men got hold of the cubs, **and** their screaming was now something ridiculous. I could not have believed the little wretches **could** make such **a** noise. This was **too** much **for** the old lady: maternal affection overcame her fear, and she made a splendid charge **up the** hill at us. But coming up a steep ascent the **poor** brute had not the ghost of a chance against **two** double rifles; **a** bullet from each, fired almost at the same instant within a few paces, doubled her up, rolling over and over, like a ball, to the bottom. "What a shame," exclaimed Wilson, in the tone of a person who has been forced into committing some cruel but necessary deed, and I certainly felt myself something very like remorse for the share I had taken in the butchery. Maternal love is everywhere so very lovely, that, even when shown in a savage and destructive beast, we cannot help being touched and softened by it.

When we reached the old bear, we had another scene with the cubs. They no sooner saw their dam than they became almost frantic to reach her, and on being let go they ran up, stroking her head with their little paws, and fondling her in the most endearing manner, seeming to ask, as plain as could be done without words, that she would get up and come away from the strange company they had fallen into. We sent them away while we skinned their mamma, and it was nearly dusk when this was finished. Long before we reached camp it got quite dark, and the men who came to meet us brought no lights. There were no pine-trees so high up the valley, and we had unfortunately neglected to bring a supply of the pine-wood up with us from below. It is wonderful how well one does manage to walk in the dark when obliged. There was no path, the ground was very rough, and there were two or three rather dangerous places to cross, but we got home with much less difficulty than I anticipated.

The next two days were devoted to driving the forests for musk-deer lower down the valley, in which they appeared to be quite as numerous as in the Gangootree or Derallee ones. We got two males and four females. Before we parted, Wilson was anxious to let me see a drive on a larger scale, where something besides musk-deer might be found; and to accomplish this we took the camp down to the foot of the hill below Sookee, on the opposite side of the river. To his and my coolies were added a number of the villagers, forming altogether a band of nearly sixty beaters, all well up to the work, and as anxious for the success of the drive as ourselves. The hill chosen was not unlike the one I had shot over at Bengallee, the lower part chiefly forest, and the upper grassy slopes and rocks. The beaters began at the bottom, and we were stationed about two miles above, at the edge of the forest, two of Wilson's shikaries being also posted with rifles, as it was expected a number of musk-deer would be driven out. The four of us commanded the whole side of the hill. I had great expectations from this beat, as the place was known as a favourite resort of tahr, and had not been disturbed for some months, and I took my seat on the jutting rock to which I was posted with the anticipation of seeing some good sport. Mine was the choice post, which Wilson insisted on my taking, as it overlooked nearly the whole hill-side, and would afford me an excellent view of all that took place. Two hundred yards to my left was Wilson, and on my right the two shikaries. With what feverish excitement did I wait for the first shouts of the beaters, examining the ground within range of my own post, trying to fix the distance of particular points in case a beast should pass there, and thinking which would offer the nicest shot. Fully two hours elapsed ere we heard anything of them, as they had been told to allow for the time we should be in reaching our posts, and probably waited longer than needful to make certain of not commencing too soon. The worst of these large drives is the long time one has often to sit doing nothing, and the restless impatience which in a young hand it engenders. At length a faint sound came, mellowed by the distance, and told they were at work. Slowly and gradually it became more distinct, but it was a long time ere it was sufficiently so to disturb anything in our vicinity. At first it was a low continued murmur, more like the sound of distant water than the shouting of a mob, and had a most soothing effect on the ear. Then it became more tangible, broken occasionally by an abrupt yell or whistle, till, as the beaters drew near, shouting, yelling, whistling, and screeching, as suited each one's fancy, the whole made a chaos of sounds perfectly indescribable. I thought it was enough to have driven every living thing off the hill long before the beaters came near us, and I sat for a long while in momentary expectation of seeing something emerge from the bushes beneath the rock where I was posted, or cross some of the few open **spots in the** thick forest below. **There,** that surely was something moving near yon **thick** bush! — no, it must have been the wind. But there certainly is something, and it will soon come out into that open patch. **Ah!** it is only a moonall. How its brilliant plumage flashes in the sunlight, as it moves its lustrous neck to and fro! See, it **is** on the wing, and with **a** shrill whistling it rises above the trees, and soaring a considerable height in the air, circles round the ridge **a mile** below—its white back fully revealed in contrast to the dark metallic hue of the rest of its body, and **its** broad chestnut tail expanded like a fan; does it not now look the king of the pheasant tribe? But, hark! a shot on the left; — the game is on foot. With what thrilling excitement I now wait for something coming out near my own post! There comes something at last, through those scattered bushes half a mile below. No! it is only **one** of the beaters. Again, what was that passing by those dead pine trees? There it is again, an old tahr, and coming right in my direction. Another and another; four — five — a whole flock. Now they are hid **in** the thick underwood, but they must come **out** again, there, just to my left. Here comes a little musk-deer. It stops every ten yards for **a few** moments to listen. Surely it will see me **and** go back. No! on it comes, and will pass close by. For Wilson's sake I must not miss **it**, and I reserve my fire till it is within thirty yards, when my first shot knocks it over. Another shot on **the left.**

Here come a lot of female tahr, several of them with young ones at their heels. From motives of humanity it has been agreed not to fire at these, and they are allowed to go by unmolested. What an escape for them! How easily could I have knocked a couple over! Again, a shot from the shikaries. Wilson seems unlucky to-day! But where are the tahr?—they ought to be up by this time. The shots above have probably bewildered them, and the jungle being very thick they don't like to leave it. Here they come at last. No! only one of them; he is coming right up the little ridge. A few steps further, and what a shot I shall have. Here he is, his long shaggy hair waving in the wind. Bang goes my rifle, and he rushes back into the forest. I cannot surely have missed so large an animal at fifty yards. A shot from Wilson at last, and I see a musk-deer rolling dead down the hill below him. Bang again on the left. The beaters are now within 200 yards, and the shouting is deafening Such a variety of discordant yells and screeches I never heard. Moonalls are getting up every minute.

Nothing can remain long in the forest now, for the line is compact and drawing nearer and nearer. Here come the tahr again; the men see them, and the shouting is tremendous. I have another shot as the foremost of three, which are passing on my right, halts for a moment, and this time with effect, for he rolls over. The other two swerve for a moment, but come on again as fast as they can up the steep hill. My second barrel misses, for they

don't stand still a moment, and I am not more fortunate with the smooth gun. I load in all haste, thinking to have another shot ere they are out of range; but my attendant exclaims "Sahib! Sahib!" and points to a musk-deer which has already come close beneath us, and is passing as I put on the caps. In my hurry I miss it with both barrels, and it goes bounding on up the hill after the tahr. In a little while another lot come out, nearly midway between Wilson and myself. At these we both fire, and the result is one tahr killed dead, and another with a broken leg, which comes across a little above, and gives me time to reload the rifle ere it gets out of range, when another bullet finishes it. Another lot of females; as before, allowed to go by. At these too I might have had several shots. In the meantime two more shots have been fired by the shikaries, and one by Wilson; and now the beaters set up another tremendous shouting, and a huge black bear comes out of the bushes below me, and shuffles off in a slanting direction to my right. I have a tolerably good broadside shot at about seventy yards; but it only serves to accelerate his pace, and the other barrel and the smooth gun are fired, without more apparent effect, ere he gets over the ridge. I don't see that I have hit him, but the first and second shots were both answered by growls. He is now passing below the first shikaree, whom I see level his rifle and fire, and the bear rolls over. Up again he gets, and keeps on his way, and will run right over the other shikaree, and presently I hear the report of his rifle. But the men are now emerging from the forest; the beat is over. On comparing notes we found I had killed a musk-deer and two tahr; for the first one I fired at was found dead by the beaters a little distance in the forest. Wilson had shot two musk-deer, and we had killed two other tahr between us. The shikaries two musk-deer, a goral, and the bear. The latter had four balls through him, so, as I must have hit him with the first two, he counted as mine. The beaters reported having roused a scrow, and were much surprised we had not seen it, as it came right up hill, and they had not met with it again. We concluded it must have crossed to the next hill, some distance below us.

On our way back to camp I came across and killed an argus pheasant, a great addition to my collection, which was now making rapid progress, and already numbered nearly all the game birds. On arriving at Jallah we found the villagers holding a festival, and, expressing a wish to Wilson to see how the people amused themselves on such occasions, we took our seats on a low wall on one side of the village square to watch them. During the whole of my progress through the hills the gentler sex, whenever I met any of them, had hitherto avoided me as if I had been some wild beast; and I have often laughed to see a bevy of damsels, whom I happened to come upon suddenly in the fields or on the path, scour away in all directions as fast as their legs could carry them. While in company with Wilson I lost whatever it was they thought so terrible about me, and they would even venture to converse with us: this was a good opportunity of seeing them in their holiday dress. I certainly cannot say much for the beauty of the Puharee girls. Many were fair enough, and most had good-humoured, pleasant faces ; but it was seldom, indeed, I saw one decidedly pretty. The children, though fearfully dirty, were on the whole much better looking, and some of them remarkably handsome. Hard work, and harder fare, soon destroy all grace and beauty in many to whom nature has been exceedingly kind amongst the rude mountaineers.

On one side of the village square, which had been strewn with flowers, two men were dancing, with the depta on their shoulders, to the music of two drums and a long brass instrument something like a serpent. On the other the women and young men were singing and dancing. Their method of doing these is quite national. The girls on one side, and the men on the other, they form two long rows, as if standing up for a country dance, except that all link themselves together by each clasping his two neighbours round the waist. They then keep advancing and retreating, meeting and separating, and keeping time, with a voluptuous motion of the body, to the song they may be singing. This consists of single couplets chanted by the girls and men alternately, each couplet repeated by both parties several times over. Whenever the row of women approached very near the men, the latter bowed down as low as possible several times in succession, still singing and keeping time with their bows to the air. The women then acknowledged the compliment in the same manner. The songs were often very unmeaning, but almost invariably turned on love, and, I am sorry to say, generally love unlawful; the delight of sweethearting with other people's wives or husbands, or something of the kind. No wonder the Puharies are so very immoral. The song they were singing when we first sat down was—

> " Legga dooka mooka jooan, bena,
> Mun udal a lee booda, bena.
> Nuhou kya kya bat, sallee?
> Gasseeallee ka bat nowla, bena."

which may be translated —

> " The moon shines brightly, bena,
> And makes one wish to elope, bena.
> Which way shall we go, sallee?
> By the way of the grasscutters, bena."

"Bena" means an elder sister's husband, "sallee" a wife's younger sister. Thus the song goes on, the girl supposed to be persuading her lover, who is her sister's husband, to elope, and suggesting different roads to go, while he points out the difficulties and dangers attendant on them and the probabilities of capture. Another song, which seemed

A FAVOURITE SONG.

to be a great favourite, as it was sung several times, was:—

"Geun legga goona,
Syze legaw chooee, routella ney soonna.
Mara gaalla bairee,
Soonna routella, kaa kerra ameeree.
Bassa jallee mendka,
Soonna routella, keea gardee gendka."

"The wheat is in flower,
Speak only in whispers, that the routella may not hear.
Go and kill a sheep,
If the routella should hear, what can he do to me?
The frogs are loudly croaking,
If the routella should hear, he will put you in the stocks."

The reader may think this translation a joke, but it is very literal. The first line in each couplet has no meaning in connection with the song, being only to rhyme to. This is the general system of the rude Puharie poetry; the idea they wish to express is made to rhyme to a sentence having no connection at all with it. The latter song went on in a number of similar couplets to the above.

The lady is talking with her lover, and tells him to speak in whispers lest the routella, her husband, should hear them; he trying to calm her fears, and saying the routella has no power to hurt him, and what he would do if unfortunately they were discovered. "Routella" means a descendant of a rajah by a slave girl. The young people seemed to enjoy this way of singing and dancing amazingly, and often indulge in it for hours on moonlight nights. In large villages it is a regular amusement while the moon rises early, and is sometimes even carried on by torchlight. One may readily conceive what the consequences must be of this free intercourse of the sexes in a country where chastity is scarcely considered a virtue, and its violation entails no public disgrace, and where parties are married when mere children, leaving it to chance whether any liking or affection may spring up between them as they attain adolescence. These early marriages are the bane of Puharie society, and the origin of half their domestic cares and afflictions. A girl is married when a child; as she grows up she takes a dislike to her husband, and is continually running away from his to her parents' house. Then, as may be expected, she places her affections on another man, probably with a wife he dislikes, and ends by eloping with him. Then comes a divorce, with its attendant expenses, and she begins life anew with her second husband, perhaps plunged into debt which it will take him years to discharge. The attachment between lovers is often fervent in the extreme, and so strong as to battle with and overcome all that can be arrayed against it; the authority of parents and husband, the decision of magisterial authority, fines and imprisonment, and sometimes severe bodily punishment. The loves of many a Puharie couple would form the ground-work of a romance.

It was now high time I should be proceeding

on my travels. I had **been more than a month** with Wilson, and a very pleasant time it **had been**. Always something exciting **going** on in the **day**, while our evening chat over **the** fire was **to me** particularly interesting, and **often** prolonged far into the night. Anecdotes of his singular and solitary life amongst the rude mountaineers, hunting adventures, and village legends whiled away many an hour; and European and Indian politics, **of** which he was fond of talking, showed **the** interest he still took in the world he had almost forsaken. One of his anecdotes I will venture to repeat, as **it** tends to show **what** deference is **paid** to a European in some native states.

One winter while busily engaged collecting birds, the rajah's phoundar came into the district to collect the revenue and decide criminal and litigious cases. Wilson had always been careful not to interfere with these officers in the discharge of their duty, and from having given way to them in several cases in which his men were concerned, sooner than have any misunderstanding, they **were** beginning to fail in the respect hitherto shown him and imputed his forbearance to fear. When this officer came to the village near which Wilson had taken his quarters, he was told that if he wanted any of the villagers Wilson had in his employ they should immediately **be** sent to him on his mentioning their names, but was requested particularly not to seize them without such intimation having been given, as they might at the time be engaged on important work. Accordingly several men were mentioned as having misdemeanours to answer for, and were given up by Wilson and duly fined. The phoundar went away to a village a day's march lower down, and some days afterwards Wilson started a man off to Mussooric with letters. He had to pass through this village, and was there seized by the phoundar and detained two days, being obliged to borrow a few rupees to pay the fine directed to be levied by him on some frivolous pretence ere he could obtain his release. On doing so he came at once back to Wilson, and related the circumstance. This was too much, and if allowed to go unpunished would probably be used as a precedent by other phoundars, and it was high time to give them a lesson. An appeal to the rajah would, in all probability, have been attended with the punishment of the offender, but this would not give half the prestige that a speedy personal chastisement inflicted on him on the spot would certainly do. It was an example that was required, *pour encourager les autres*. Getting together half a dozen of his men, Wilson proceeded to the village, at which he arrived a little before sunset, and found the phoundar holding his court in the village square, surrounded by the usual satellites of an eastern official. In a few words he explained to the astonished assembly how matters stood, cautioned them and the chuprassies and sepoys not to interfere with what he was about to do, and giving a signal, the phoundar was seized by four men previously instructed how to act, thrown down, and stretched spread-eagle-fashion on the ground; Wilson then, tearing off his inexpressibles, administered, with a few well-twisted hazel rods, such a flagellation on the seat of honour as a phoundar probably never received before. "He roared," said Wilson, "in a glorious manner, and I thrashed him till every rod was in shivers, and my arm fairly ached, while not one of his attendants mustered up courage to interfere." To this day the phoundars are influenced in their conduct to Wilson by the remembrance of this summary proceeding. The phoundar went at once to complain to the rajah, and, anticipating this, Wilson sent a letter detailing all the circumstances of the case at the same time. The result was, that the rajah, much to his honour, declared the official had been served exactly as he deserved, and hoped it would be a caution to others to pay due respect to every European they met with in his country; and to show he did not in the least blame Wilson, he sent him, with the answer to his letter, a very handsome present.

Of the travellers who, like myself, had made Wilson's acquaintance, and joined him in little shooting excursions, he had some entertaining stories, and criticized their proficiency in his loved art of woodcraft, in some cases so sarcastically, that I was glad I had acquitted myself tolerably while with him. Of all whom he had met with, General

Markham was decidedly his favourite. "He is," said he, "the beau-ideal of a sportsman; never tired, never disgusted with bad luck, and while at it throwing his whole heart and soul into whatever may be going forward. Quick in deciding what course to pursue, and generally displaying great judgment, he is withal, a trait in his character I much admire, not at all self-opinionated, and always ready to give due consideration to the suggestions of others, when knowledge or experience are likely to give them some value. The tact and judgment displayed in woodcraft are the same that will, if opportunity offers, shed lustre round his professional career, and I expect to see him amongst the first of our generals. It may seem a strange idea, but I cannot fancy that any man possesses within him the ability requisite for the leader of a body of soldiers, who, calling himself a sportsman, would blunder seriously when engaged in the pursuit of wild animals. If a good general be a sportsman at all, I cannot imagine him being anything but a good one."

Wilson has been mentioned in terms of some disparagement in the letters of Dr. Hoffmeister, describing his travels in the Himalayas, while in the suite of Prince Waldemar of Prussia. Our conversation turning one evening on this subject, Wilson gave me an account of the progress of the party through this part of the country, and laid all the blame of the failure of their attempt to get into Thibet, which the Dr. seems to think was Wilson's fault, upon

Count O., the real leader of the party, who would not be persuaded the Puharies were anything but what he imagined them to be; and, acting according to his idea of their character, he treated them as if they were a race of sturdy, independent freemen, men who would scorn to tell a lie, and take it as an insult if you doubted their word. "In fact, the truth I believe was," said Wilson, "he thought, or wished to think, them worthy of their majestic mountain land. A pardonable error, if it had not been persevered in against daily examples to the contrary."

Our manner of life was half in what is generally called the comfortable or luxurious way of travelling, and half in that termed roughing it. We took with us one small tent, our bedding, and a change of clothes. My servants were left at Derallee, and one of Wilson's men cooked for us. If his culinary productions were not particularly artistic, they were always substantial; and appetites sharpened by the cool mountain breeze and violent exercise did them ample justice. The men who carried our beds saw that everything was made comfortable about the camp, washed our clothes, and acted as valets. The tent was used only to sleep in, and might almost as well have been dispensed with. Wherever we encamped, if only for a night, a little hut open in front was hastily constructed of a few stones and long sticks, and covered with a large piece of wax cloth. Before this a large fire was made, and after the day's shooting we reclined in this hut, which was well bedded down with grass or green leaves, ate our supper, and then smoked and chatted till bed-time. So comfortable was it that I often felt inclined to roll myself in a blanket and sleep where I was. It was called by the men "the messcut," a word which rather puzzled me at first, till I learned it was their corruption of the English term mess-court. Were I to make another hunting excursion in the Himalayas, I should certainly dispense with many things I had brought with me on this one, as a chair and table, cot, &c. After a hard day's shooting I found it much more comfortable to loll before the fire in the mess-court, after Wilson's fashion, than to sit on a chair in the tent.

I left Derallee for Koonawur on the 28th of May, having stored up a lot of information from Wilson about the countries I was going through. As an addition to my journal, he afterwards wrote and sent to me a description of the hill country of Gurwhal we have hitherto been travelling through, which, coming from a person who knows it so well, may perhaps be interesting, and I will give it now, before proceeding to other scenes.

CHAPTER V.

THE hills north of the Deyrah Dhoon form the little protected hill state of Gurwhal. I am not acquainted with its early history, but it appears to have been an independent state until conquered by the Goorkhas at the beginning of the present century. It was ceded by them to the Company, together with Keemaon, after the Nepaul war of 1815. The rajah had been killed, but his son who had taken refuge in the British territories, was sought for and placed on the throne of his ancestors, to rule over a portion of the ceded country, which was given to him and his heirs in perpetuity. This portion has since been known as Independent Gurwhal. It extends from the foot of the hills to the borders of Thibet, and from the Alucknunda branch of the Ganges to the western branches of the Tonse, being about eighty miles in length and breadth, and forming a complete section of the Himalayan range from the plains to the snow. Its general features may be thus described. The hills rise abruptly from the Dhoon to nearly 8000 feet in some places, and 6000 in all; and for about forty miles keep nearly the same elevation, the valley between being from 3000 to 5000. The hills then rapidly increase in height till they reach an elevation of from 15,000 to upwards of 20,000 feet. In detail these hills are long, narrow, and extremely tortuous ranges, leading up from the plains to the snow, to which they all lead, though with an infinite variety of twistings and turnings. Take for instance the first, on which stands Mussoorie. You trace the course of the ridge first south-east for about twenty miles; then turn round the head of the Oglia valley, and go north-west till again opposite the station; and so it goes on to the snow, this ridge running up to the great snowy peaks between the sources of the Ganges and Jumna, which form so conspicuous an object from the Sanatarium, until nearing which, the ridge has never been less than 6400, or more than 8500 feet high. There are no isolated hills or ranges, nor is there a river or stream which divides into two branches. Until we cross the great backbone and get on the Thibetian side, the outline is sharp and angular, the ranges nowhere having the rounded forms of our English hills. The slopes vary to every degree of incline, the south and east being generally the most abrupt. Some are little removed from the perpendicular, others at an angle of not more than 20°. What is rather strange is that though the ridges are so irregular, depressed in one place and rising abruptly in another, the valleys everywhere keep a tolerably gradual slope. This may vary a little in different places, so that a river may flow through one in a gentle current, and a few miles further be a foaming torrent; but there nowhere occurs any sudden sinking, so that a waterfall in the larger streams is nowhere to be found.

"To about 11,000 or 12,000 feet, which is near the extreme limits of forest trees, the hills are everywhere well wooded, particularly on the northern and western slopes, which are almost everywhere clothed with forest of some kind. The opposite, the south and east, are more partially so, these sides of a hill being sometimes on the lower ranges nearly destitute of trees altogether. Commencing at the foot of the lower hills, we first find trees similar to those in the plains, and the forest here is only remarkable for the gigantic creepers. The common pine then makes its appearance, and is the principal tree, many hills in the lower ranges being clothed solely with it. The common oak begins at about 4000 feet, and the rhododendron the same. Between 7000 and 8000 feet the common oak gives place to the khursoo, and at this elevation the trees of the colder European climates also appear: chestnut, sycamore, box, yew, filbert, and others; besides the rye and morenda pines, the pride of the Himalayan forests. The cedar grows at almost all elevations; you find occasional groves as low as 3000 feet, but the great cedar forests are not common at a lower elevation than 6000. At 9000 feet birch becomes prevalent, and a little higher, with the exception of dwarf rhododendron, monopolizes the forest Above these come juniper and a kind of willow, with some other shrub-like bushes, till at 13,000 feet arboreous vegetation entirely ceases, and grasses, herbs, and mosses only are met with from thence to the snow.

"In the lower ranges the forest is in detached portions, and nowhere covers uninterruptedly any great extent of country, so that, seen from a distance, the hills form a light ground with dark patches, large or small, and more or less numerous as forest predominates. The ravines and hollows are almost everywhere thickly wooded. Nearer the snow the forests become dense and continuous; on the northern and western slopes the eye sometimes rests on miles and miles of country where not a glimpse of the ground can be discerned through the dark foliage. Some of these forests have a very imposing appearance; a rich green forming the ground—of different tints, according to the kind of tree that predominates, oak being everywhere the principal—while sometimes singly, sometimes in groups, the long tapering summits of the pines appear piercing through the dense mass, their very dark foliage setting them in clear relief against the rest. Here and there occurs a little glade or open spot, entirely free from tree or bush, and not unfrequently with a little miniature lake in the centre. In winter the scene is little changed until covered with snow, the forest being composed mostly of evergreens. A brown patch here and there marks a cluster of chestnuts or sycamore, and, if the hill is high enough, a brown border the region of birch.

"This is the prevailing character of forest throughout the middle ranges, but in some places, particularly near the snow, it is composed almost exclusively of pine trees, as in the higher part of the Ganges valley from Sookee upwards, where there is not a single oak tree. In such places cedar and cheel predominate on dry rocky ground; morenda and rye in others; but in many forests all four are so intermingled that each and all may be found on almost every dozen square yards of ground. Many other trees are found scattered singly or in groups, as poplar, willow, filbert, cypress, and many others, but their numbers are so few in comparison with the pines that they are scarcely observable.

"The underwood is exceedingly varied, but nowhere particularly dense. In the middle ranges red and black currant and raspberry bushes form a portion of it. The fruit of the two latter is almost equal to that of our English gardens. In the rainy season the herbaceous vegetation springs up to a great height throughout the forests of the middle and higher regions, so as to render walking, except on the beaten pathways, extremely unpleasant. In many places the tangled grasses are higher than a person's head, and a peculiar herb, with a single long reed-like stem, often eight or ten feet high, shoots up in a few weeks throughout almost all the great forests. At the close of the rains as rapidly decays, and is soon laid prostrate; but lower down the hill the tangled grass and ferns remain a great hindrance to comfortable travelling till withered by the autumnal sun. In the lower ranges this perennial vegetation is not nearly so luxuriant; but after the rains the spear grass which covers many of the hills is equally unpleasant to walk through, unless the pedestrian is clothed in some material its barbed seeds cannot penetrate.

"Being no botanist I cannot give a technical description of the individual trees composing the Himalayan forests, but I may venture to say a few words about the most remarkable, some of them having been introduced into England, and many others which would be useful or ornamental being well adapted to our climate.

"The cedar grows at almost any elevation and on any kind of ground; small groves or single trees being met with in the most widely different localities; in the low warm valleys and near the everlasting snow. Its favourite habitat is between 6000 and 9000 feet, and here only extensive forests of it are found. It seems to thrive best in a dry rocky soil, and it is wonderful to see the places where some trees take root. In the perpendicular face of a smooth granite rock is a little crevice; into this a seed in some manner finds its way, vegetates, and becomes a large tree, flourishing perhaps for centuries where to appearance there is not a particle of soil, deriving sustenance probably from the rock itself.

The cedar grows to a great size, some having been measured with trunks upwards of thirty feet in circumference a yard from the ground. When in forest most shoot upwards in long, tapering, straight trunks, with rather short branches, and having the cone-like form of most pines; but when scattered singly they often stretch out long massive arms, the ramifications of which being all horizontal, each with its foliage forms a surface almost as level as a table. The highest cedars attain to a height of 100 feet. The wood is everywhere in the greatest esteem for building purposes, as it is easily worked, almost imperishable, and splits easily into planks, an indispensable requisite in a country where saws are unknown.* The bridges over the Jhelum in Cashmere, which are constructed of this wood, are a fair criterion of its lasting qualities. Some portions are always under water, some only so half the year, and the rest always exposed to the atmosphere. These bridges have been standing for nearly a century, and are standing still, though so constructed that a few rotten timbers must of necessity cause the downfall of the whole. When subjected to the process by which tar is extracted from other pines, cedar-wood yields a much thinner liquid, of a dark red colour, and very strong smell, known as cedar oil. It is used

* Since writing the above, I have found that the wood of the cedar (*Pinus deodora*) growing in the lower hills is much inferior to that near the snow, the latter being far more durable, and of much finer grain.

by the Puharies as a remedy for the itch and other diseases of the skin, and all scrofulous diseases in cattle. The length of time this tree requires to arrive at even a tolerable size unfits it for introduction into other countries except as an ornament.

"The cheel pine is, I think, identical with the Scotch fir, or *Pinus excelsa*. It grows only in the higher regions, being seldom seen at a lower elevation than 6000 feet. Some hills near the snow are covered almost exclusively with it, and it is generally found intermingled with cedars, wherever the latter are numerous enough to give a character to the forests. The wood, being very full of turpentine, is used for torches, and serves the purpose of a lamp or candle in the dwellings of all classes. It is seldom used for any other purpose. The turpentine, as it oozes out of the living tree, is used as a dressing for sores, and as a poultice, and is a certain and speedy cure for chapped hands.

"The morenda pine is, I believe, peculiar to the Himalayas, and grows in the middle and higher regions, from an elevation of 6000 feet to near the limits of forest. In the great oak forests of the middle ranges it occurs at intervals, sometimes singly, sometimes in clusters, and its very dark foliage, and spire-like top towering above the other forest trees, render it a conspicuous object. On some of the hills nearer the snow, where pine is the prevailing wood, it almost monopolizes the forest. The morenda is a large and very handsome tree, the trunk perfectly straight, often upwards of twenty feet in circumference at the base, and sometimes reaching a height of between 150 to 200 feet. The branches, which in a large tree commence about twenty feet from the ground, are very short, in some cases not extending more than a few feet from the trunk, and very regular all the way up, which adds to the apparent height of the tree. The wood is of little use except for indoor work, as when exposed to the atmosphere it soon decays.

"The rye is generally found growing with the morenda, but is not nearly so plentiful, and never forms a forest of itself. Seldom, indeed, are a dozen trees seen together without some of the latter or the cheel amongst them. It is in all respects a more tender tree, and entirely ceases upwards of a thousand feet lower down. In size it is nearly equal, and is perhaps still more ornamental. The branches are slender and drooping, and the foliage partakes of the same character. The wood is of much the same quality as that of the morenda.

"The kolin, or common pine, grows only on the lower hills, ceasing altogether at a little above 6000 feet. Forests of it extend over a great portion of the lower ranges, where it and common oak are the principal trees. The kolin forests are always very open, the trees some distance apart, and it is rarely or never any underwood grows beneath them. In many places spear-grass alone covers the ground for miles where these trees form the forest. The kolin has little ornamental about it. It is often a large irregular tree for a pine, with wide-spreading and crooked branches growing far apart. The wood is a common coarse deal, only fit for indoor purposes, and probably would not repay the cost of cutting and transporting to the plains, even where the rivers are available; but as it yields excellent tar, these forests may yet be turned to some advantage in a commercial point of view.

"These are all the cone-bearing pines in this part of the Himalayas. The leure is a kind of cypress, the berries and leaves of which are similar to the long slender species in our English gardens and pleasure-grounds, but here it grows into a tree nearly as large as the morenda or rye. It is very rare, and found only in a few places in the middle regions. The wood is hard and extremely heavy, but does not appear to be very durable. A peculiar quality, the very reverse of all pine, is, that it is very difficult to burn; so much so that it is impossible to make a good fire of it alone. Another cypress, a much smaller tree, is found when we approach the dry atmosphere of Thibet, the wood of which has a fragrant smell and is often used to burn as incense. The yew is scattered through all the forests between 7000 and 9000 feet; though itself often a tolerable sized tree, it is so overtopped by the gigantic oaks and pines as to have almost the character of underwood. Its wood is valued as much as cedar, and supposed to be still more durable.

"The first oak met with is the banj, which I have named common, to distinguish it from the two others. It begins at about 3500 feet, and almost ceases at 8000. The oak forests of the lower ranges are composed almost exclusively of this species, as well as the lower part of those further in the interior. There is nothing remarkable about the tree; it is in appearance something like the English oak, but seldom attains to any extraordinary size. The wood is coarse, and rarely used except for firewood. Burning well while green, it is the principal wood consumed in the houses at the different sanatariums. The three Himalayan oaks are all evergreens.

"The next in order is the moura, a large and handsome tree. The branches are rather slender and very numerous, and the leaves small and of a particularly bright hue. It grows sparingly, near the summits of the lower ranges, amongst the common oaks, becoming more common in the great forests of the interior, but is nowhere so numerous as to give a decided character to any part. It seems to prefer sheltered nooks and hollows, and a rich damp soil. Its range is from 5000 feet to nearly 9000. It attains to a great size, the trunks of some being twenty feet in circumference. The wood is excellent, uniting in itself the best qualities of English oak and ash, the hardness and durability of the former with the toughness and flexibility of the latter. The leaves of both this and the common oak are eaten with avidity by sheep and goats. In winter, when the grass is so dried up as to afford little nourishment, the shepherds ascend the trees, lopping off all the small branches, which as they fall are soon stripped of their leaves by the hungry flock underneath. Large bundles are also taken home regularly every evening for them to eat during the night. Of the two trees the moura is considered the most nourishing, and in some districts each family has one or more trees planted near the village, which furnish a ready supply for a few days after severe snow, when it could not be otherwise obtained without a great deal more exposure to the inclement weather. These, being stripped of their small branches almost every year, grow as compact as a clipped box tree, and, being often of enormous size, are the most magnificent trees of the kind one can conceive.

"The khurso is an oak confined to the higher hills. It is first met with at an elevation of about 7000 feet, and extends to nearly 11,000. In the great oak forests of the interior the lower portions consist of the two former, which gradually get mixed with khurso, till this becomes the sole occupant of the higher. In appearance it somewhat resembles the common oak, but has some peculiar characteristics. The leaves, particularly in young trees, are very prickly, as much so as holly, and the acorns are about three times the size of those of the other oaks. The trunk is generally very straight, and for forty or fifty feet scarcely decreases at all in thickness. The branches are short, so that the trees grow very close together. An acre of ground in any khurso forest would yield more than treble the quantity of timber the same area in any other oak one would. The wood, though inferior to the moura, is of a very fair quality. Though found on all faces, the khurso prefers the southern and eastern slopes, as the morenda and ryc pines do the northern and western. It is not unusual to find the forest on one side of a ridge all khurso, while on the other it is composed chiefly of the two pines.

"The horse-chestnut grows to an immense size. It is generally found in groves of from fifty to a hundred trees, in the oak and morenda-pine forests of the interior, where the ground is rather damp and not very steep. These chestnut groves, surrounded closely by the other forest trees, have rarely any growing amongst them, appropriating the entire space to their own species; and it is but seldom a chestnut tree is found growing alone amongst other kinds. The sycamore and filbert grow scattered at random in similar localities in the higher forests. The former attains to a great size, and several majestic individuals are sometimes found growing by themselves in an open glade, or some grassy flat bordering a large stream, and giving quite a park-like appearance to the spot. The round knobby excrescences on the trunk of the sycamore are cut out, and form a considerable article of export with Thibet, where they are made into drinking cups something the shape of a tea saucer with a turned rim. They take a beautiful polish, and the wood is very pretty, being mottled something like bird's-eye maple. Roughly turned into something of the required shape, they sell in Thibet at from four to eight for a rupee, but one is occasionally found which itself fetches from ten to twenty rupees. These are called jat ones, but to a stranger they do not appear to differ in the slightest degree from the others. Even the men who collect them in the forest can see no difference; and when they are so fortunate as to find one, which they know by the bark all falling off on giving it a slight tap, they keep it apart from the rest, or mark it in some particular manner, as the only means of knowing it again. The Tartars, they say, can distinguish them at once. The alleged reason of their great value is, on this side the hills, that any poisonous liquid poured into the cup is at once detected; what the real one may be it is impossible even to conjecture, and, their ideas being so much at variance with our own, perhaps no one but an inhabitant of the celestial empire could appreciate it. These jat cups are but rarely met with. A man may cut a thousand from the trees, and not find one; but he always gives every knob the gentle tap by which they are discovered before commencing to cut it out. In Huc's 'Travels through Tartary' he mentions going into a cup shop at Lhassa, and, on asking for a cup, being shown one of these jat ones, which was carefully taken out of several wrappers of silk paper, and being astounded at the price asked for it. I cannot remember whether he was told what there was peculiar in it or not, but it seems to show that the Tartars, at least, do see something.

"The birch, it has been before mentioned, is not met with till we are approaching the limits of arboreous vegetation. Besides the oak and pine, it is the only tree which ever forms a forest entirely of itself. So well-known, it requires no description. The tree rhododendron is first met with about the same elevation as the common oak, 3500 feet, but extends higher up, being sometimes seen as high as 9000 feet. It is very common throughout all the lower ranges, being scattered over the hill-sides amongst oak, pine, and other trees, rarely forming a forest of itself, and the trees generally a little distance apart. Further in the interior, groves exclusively formed of this tree are occasionally met with. On the lower hills the flowers are invariably a deep crimson, and few flowering trees equal in beauty a rhododendron in full blossom, its dark green leaves almost hidden by the mass of flowers. When found higher up the flowers are of all shades between pure white and the same dark crimson, and a grove of these trees in such situations is one of the fairest of nature's gardens. The effect produced by hundreds of trees covered with large and handsome flowers of all shades of crimson and pink to pure white, collected in one spot amongst the wildest scenery, may be easily conceived. I am not aware whether the tree rhododendron has been introduced into England or not. It is many years since I left the country, and, to the best of my recollection, all I ever saw belonged to an altogether different species — the bush rhododendron. The wood is of very coarse grain, very brittle, and of no use except as firewood. A full-grown tree has a trunk from six to nine feet in girth, and is from thirty to forty feet high.

"The bush rhododendron is found only on the higher hills, beginning to grow nearly at the same elevation as birch, and arboreous vegetation ceases with it. It has never any trunk, but springs up in a lot of crooked zigzag branches, about the thickness of one's arm, many of these lying on the surface of the ground. In some places under the birch-trees this rhododendron covers the ground for miles, and is often so dense that it is impossible to make way through it but by climbing along from branch to branch; a slow and very laborious method of progressing. The bushes are seldom more than eight or nine feet high, and generally not more than four or five, but the arms are sometimes twelve or fifteen feet in horizontal length. They are very tough, it being almost impossible to break one of moderate thickness. The flowers are of different shades, from white to a kind of lilac, rather smaller and not so numerous as on the tree rhododendron. The leaves are slightly poisonous. The dead and dry branches burn the clearest and brightest of any wood whatever, with scarcely any smoke at all. In many situations the bush rhododendron is completely buried under the snow nearly half the year. It is much more common on the northern and western slopes than on the opposite; and in the little narrow ravines on a hill facing the south or east, one side is densely clothed with birch and rhododendron, while the other is quite open.

"Walnut trees are often found in the forest; but, both there and in the village orchards, nearly all in these hills produce fruit with such a hard thick shell, that the kernel is only extracted with difficulty in small pieces by means of a needle. It is gathered chiefly for the sake of the oil which it yields, the women amusing themselves on winter days, when nothing better is to be done, by extracting the kernel. The wood is of much coarser grain, and in all respects is much inferior to that of the English walnut.

"Apricots grow only in the orchards, and most abundantly in the higher regions. The fruit is small, and often very sour, the effect probably of the trees never being pruned; but some are of really tolerable flavour. Being cultivated merely for the oil, quantity, not quality, is what the Puharie looks for. When ripe, the fruit is collected in large heaps, and covered with green grass and bushes till completely rotten, when the mass is taken in baskets to a spout or fall of water, which soon carries away the pulpy portion, and leaves only the stones. These are put by to have the kernels extracted at convenience. So fond of spirituous liquor as they are in the higher hills, and regularly distilling it from grain, it is wonderful the Puharies have not discovered that a spirit might be obtained from the fruit, and thus the pulpy portion, now entirely wasted, made of use as well as the stones. When they take it to wash, it appears to be in a state of fermentation just ready for the still. The pounded cake, after the oil has been extracted, is kept for various purposes. It is considered a good thing to eat when crossing high passes where the air is very rarefied, and, when old, is an excellent remedy for certain urinary diseases. Though perfectly innoxious to the human system, it is a deadly poison to the canine race. A small quantity of the best and ripest fruit is dried in the sun, and some, when partially dry, is pounded and made into small cakes seasoned with salt and pepper. These cakes are also considered a good remedy or preventive for the sickness and headache invariably expected when crossing very high passes. The other fruit-trees of these hills are mangoes, peaches, nectarines, pomegranates, limes, wild cherries, figs, mulberries, medlars, and a few others peculiar to the Himalayas. These, and many other forest trees not described, being in no way remarkable, it would be uninteresting to notice them in detail.

"Of the underwood, the only thing worthy of particular notice is the ringall, a kind of hollow bamboo cane, which grows throughout the middle regions. There are several varieties, differing but slightly in appearance, each having particular localities determined by elevation. All are used for basket-making, and the best, which grows in the great oak and morenda-pine forests of the interior, forms an article of export to the plains, where it is used to make hookah pipes. The cane is cut into pieces about four feet long, and carried in bundles to the marts at the foot of the hills. A man will carry 500 pieces, for which he gets from two to three shillings — no very handsome remuneration for the trouble of cutting, drying, and carrying them five or six long days' marches on his back. The ringall, when most luxuriant, grows in clusters, the largest canes being from three to six inches in circumference, and from twenty to thirty feet long. When dead and perfectly dry they burn well, and are used for torches where pine-wood is not procurable. The ringall is well worth introducing into our English woods, where, the climate being very similar to that of its native region, it would doubtless be easily naturalized. It would not interfere with the forest trees, and would be of great value. Nothing can be better adapted to basket-making in all its branches; it makes handsome walking-canes, and can be used in the same manner as molacca-cane, for making mats, &c.

"Above the forest, where the hills are high enough, comes a region of herbaceous vegetation, extending from about 12,000 to 14,500 feet, from whence the hills on the Indian side are clothed with perpetual snow. This region, from the first general fall of snow, which sometimes occurs as early as October, is covered with it till May, and is not entirely free till near the end of June. In its short summer it is clothed with rich and luxuriant herbage, which springs up as soon as the snow disappears. The grass in a few weeks is in many places two or three feet high, and a great variety of flowering plants deck every slope with a thousand colours. The cowslips particularly are very rich, of all colours, from the brightest yellow to a dark purple, and are much larger and finer flowers than any of the kind in an English garden. This region forms the summer pasture-ground of the flocks possessed by the mountaineers; the shepherds being careful to avoid those places where the poisonous aconite grows in profusion. On the Indian side of the great Himalayan chain there is little or no space between the limit of vegetation and that of perpetual snow; they join together without any appearance of that entirely barren strip of bare ground which on the Thibetian side divides the two. A great deal of controversy has arisen in trying to decide at what elevation to fix the limit of perpetual snow; but in truth no limit can be fixed, as it varies, and is entirely determined by the climate. Where the hills are fully exposed to the influence of the rainy season, as is the case in the greater portion of Gurwhal, it is lowest, and may be fixed generally at 14,500 feet. Where the hills are less exposed to the rains, the climate becomes drier, and the limit of perpetual snow higher, till, as in Thibet, entirely beyond their influence, and with a cold, but remarkably dry climate, it is not less than 20,000 feet; corn growing at 14,000, and the pasture-grounds for cattle being often between 16,000 and 17,000 feet. If we search for immediate causes, the principal one may be that on the Indian side the sun throughout the summer is generally obscured by clouds, and has little influence; while on the Thibetian, a sky rarely obscured by even a passing cloud leaves the hills exposed to its full power. When speaking of the limit of snow, it must be borne in mind that this is always calculated on exposed hill-sides, as in ravines and sheltered places it remains all the year round much lower. In such situations, beds of snow are often seen at the close of summer at 12,000 feet, and many of the large glaciers are not more than 11,000.

"Nothing can exceed the beauty of the scenes presented from the high pasture grounds in summer. They are too generally shrouded in clouds or mist to make them comfortable spots to encamp in for any length of time, and the rain often continues for days together; but when the weather is fine the first few hours of daylight are delightful. If you get on a ridge from whence you have an extensive view, you see the valleys filled with a dense white mist or cloud, out of which the ridges and hill tops appear like islands out of a sea. The atmosphere above this is so clear and transparent that small objects on distant hills, which at other times would be merged in the general mass, can be distinctly made out; and the snowy hills, some of which are always in the scene, appear to great advantage, so wonderfully distinct that you fancy the smallest speck on their smooth white slopes would be visible. Then long before it reaches you the sun rises on some of the highest peaks, and throws a flood of golden light on the glistening snow, which makes them perfectly resplendent. The scene remains unchanged for an hour or two, till the sunshine reaches the hitherto motionless clouds in the valleys, when a commotion may be observed on their surface; soon large masses begin to roll about, gradually creeping up all the lateral valleys and ravines; higher and higher they come, still keeping their dense opaque appearance, conveying no idea of dampness or of mist, as it appears to us when enveloped in it, but more like white smoke, or the round white fleecy clouds of a summer's evening. As they approach nearer, the commotion becomes more violent; portions are whirled round and round, and drawn upwards from the rest; the compact appearance gradually dissolves, till, as they reach your elevation, you find yourself and all around you fairly enveloped in the clouds; and you now see and feel what they really are, a thin, sleet-like vapour, making your clothes quite damp. The clouds generally remain enveloping all the higher regions till sunset, driven about from place to place, first freeing one spot, then another, but never for any length of time; and then sink again to the bottom of the valleys, giving promise of another fine day, for in rainy weather the clouds remain at night **on the upper** hills, while the valleys are free.

"The valleys in this portion of the Himalayas are very narrow, the hills generally rising in a slope of greater or **less** incline, either direct from the rivers or from within a few hundred yards. **In** many places the hills on each side are so **near each** other that, while walking along one a quarter **of** a mile above the stream, animals may be seen and killed with a good rifle on the opposite. In the lower hills, where the valleys are widest, the level ground at the bottom is rarely more than half a mile or a mile in breadth; **but** in some, **the** hills for a mile or two on one or both sides are **on** a very gentle **slope, so** as to form in a manner the bottom of the valley. They are very irregular; a few miles may be open, with a broad strip of level ground at **the bottom, and** the hills receding in gentle slopes; and **the** next few very narrow, with but just room for the river to pass through. In some places one side is very steep and the other a gentle slope, and in others both are alike. The ridges are **the** same, **by** far the greater number, or rather **in** most places, having very narrow summits, but being sometimes rounded, and at rare intervals with a small portion of table-land. There are no large lakes, as in British Gurwhal and Keemaoon, except one in the Kelso valley, said to be upwards of three miles in circumference; but small ones, if sheets of water **a few** hundred yards round can be called so, are frequently met **with.**

These are all on the hill sides, the rivers or large streams never forming one in a valley.

"The principal river of Gurwhal is the Bhaggerette branch of the Ganges, considered by the Hindoos as by far the most sacred of the streams whose united waters form their sacred river, and bearing to its source the name, *par excellence*, of the Ganges. It rises in the great glacier above Gangootree, and is a considerable stream when it first sees the light. Joined by several smaller ones from the snowy hills on each side, after a course of thirty miles it receives its first great tributary, the Jad Gunga. This is in reality the parent stream. It rises in the Thibetian hills beyond the snowy range, and flows in a clear current, generally fordable to near Nelang, a village owning allegiance to both the Tartar and Gurwhal authorities as well as those of Koonawur, where it is joined by a stream much larger than itself from the snowy hills which form the north-west boundary of British Gurwhal. At the junction it is curious to mark the very gradual amalgamation of the two waters, one beautifully clear, the other turbid and dirty. For a long distance they keep quite separate, one half of the river being blue, the other almost yellow. Twelve miles lower down it receives the Choor-gade, from the hills bordering on Koonawur, and becomes a rapid, turbulent river. For sixteen miles it flows through a narrow gorge with high rocky hills on each side, and joins the Ganges at Byramghattee. At the confluence each stream is, when full, about fifty feet wide and ten or fifteen deep. All the **Himalayan rivers that rise** from **the glaciers are in** summer more or **less** discoloured, many being perfect torrents of mud. **At the** end of **August** they begin to clear, but throughout **the winter** remain only half pellucid **and of a** bluish tint. Those that have their rise in the lower ranges, or where there are no large glaciers, are clear as crystal, and quite colourless in winter, and in summer **only** discoloured after heavy rain. It is always easy **to** tell what kind of a country there is at the head **of** any river, from **its** appearance below. **From** Byramghattee the Ganges **for** twenty miles runs through **a** tolerably open country, the little district of Tangnore, and receives several large streams from the high snowy hills on each side; it then enters a narrow gorge, in which it is confined **for** nearly twenty miles, when the country again opens out, and so it flows **on** through alternate defiles and open valleys, receiving **a** multitude of tributaries, and enters the plains near Hurdwar, after a course of nearly **200** miles through the mountains. **It is a** very tortuous river, first flowing north-west, then west, then south, and in some parts of its course nearly east. The rivers that are fed from the snowy ranges vary so much in size and appearance at different seasons of the year, that it is impossible to give a correct idea either of this or any other. The Ganges **in July** is a very different affair from the Ganges in December; at the former period it is a large river, rolling on an

L

immense volume of muddy water, and rushing over the rapids with such impetuosity as to be for miles like a great cataract; at the latter a moderate-sized, clear, and by no means rapid mountain stream, sleeping in large glassy pools, and gently rippling over the shallows and rapids. When full it discharges more than twenty times the quantity of water it does in the cold weather, and is from 50 to 100 yards wide. In the upper part of its course its bed is full of immense masses of rock, which entirely preclude the possibility of turning it to account in floating down timber, so that, unless some convulsion of nature entirely alters its present aspect, the splendid cedar forests close to its banks in Upper Tangnore and about Gangootree, worth lakhs and lakhs could the trees be transported to the plains, must ever remain to flourish and decay where they are growing, of no benefit whatever to the human race.

" The Jumna rises from the foot of the first range of snowy mountains, but not like the Ganges from a large glacier, and one consequence is that it is always pretty clear, and in the cold weather remarkably so. It is not nearly so large a river as the former, and none of its feeders coming from valleys within the snowy ranges, it is not subject to nearly so great a change in size and appearance. After a very straight course of about ninety miles it debouches into the Deyrah Dhoon. The Tonse rises in several branches from the range of snowy mountains between Gurwhal and Koonawur, but there being no very large glaciers, its waters, though partially discoloured with snow water, are not nearly so turbid as the Ganges. It is much larger than the Jumna, which river it joins where it enters the Dhoon, after a course of 120 miles through the hills. It is the comparative freedom from snow-water which renders the Jumna in the plains such a beautifully clear stream compared with the Ganges and other large Indian rivers which rise in the Himalayas. Another large river which drains the north-eastern part of Gurwhal, joins the Ganges at Teree. The number of smaller streams which drain the ranges on each side the large rivers is almost countless. Every little ravine has one running through it, and many from the lateral valleys are themselves tolerable-sized rivers. All in the lower hills are well stocked with fish, but those that rise from the snow are entirely without them till joined by others from the lower ranges.

"Of the snowy mountains which form the northern boundary of Gurwhal, the highest are above the Gangootree glacier. These majestic peaks are upwards of 23,000 feet above the level of the sea. The range stretching south-east has peaks 21,000 feet high. That to the westward is much lower; with the exception of the double-topped peak so conspicuous from Mussoorie, and a few others further in, few are more than 19,000 feet.

"The passes over the higher ranges require a brief notice. At present there is but one open leading into Thibet, and this goes rather through than over the snowy mountains. It is up the Tartar branch of the Ganges, past the village of Nelang, from which it derives its name, to the head of one main stream, where a low range of hills almost free from snow forms the water shed line, the streams on the north side running to the Sutledge. This range is crossed in several places, but the main road leading to the large Tartar towns of Chapung and Toling may be considered the actual pass, and is called the Jeela Kanta. From the last encamping ground on the stream it is a gradual ascent of three miles, up a shingly hill-side, covered with small prickly bushes and scattered tufts of grass nearly to the summit, and the only difficulty experienced in crossing arises from the rarefied atmosphere. The descent on the Thibetian side is gradual for two miles, and then very steep for two more to the bed of the first Tartar stream. The height of the pass is between 16,000 and 17,000 feet. From the crest there is a grand panoramic view of a great portion of the Sutledge valley and the hills between it and the Indus. After the green hills of Gurwhal everything wears a frightfully barren and sterile character. The first impression is that of a country entirely desolate, one wide waste of sandy hills and valleys where vegetation had never been, and could never be, and it is some time before this feeling wears away. The hills are of various colours, some yellow, some brown, some red, and some of a bluish tint, but all wearing the same look of utter sterility.

"Of all the passes between Hindoostan and **Thibet** there is not one possessing greater natural advantages than this; yet **the** traffic is confined to a little salt and grain exchanged through the hands of the **Tartars** of Nelang. Grain, which must always be the staple article **of** import into Thibet, is much cheaper and more plentiful in the hills on our side of this pass than in any other. The pass **itself** is perhaps the easiest of all, with abundance of excellent pasture-ground for cattle nearly **to its** very crest; there are several large Thibetian **marts** near, as accessible as from any other pass, and **it** remains **open** perhaps the longest of any, being regularly crossed from April to November. **The** principal reason, **no** doubt, **is the want of** roads, these being throughout Independent Gurwhal the **merest** tracks imaginable, unfit for any beast **of** burthen except sheep or goats, **and** in many places difficult even **to** them. In all other hill countries very fair roads, on which ponies and mules, or asses, can safely travel, extend from the plains of India to the very confines of **the** Chinese territories. On these roads a couple **of** men will drive a flock **of** upwards of **a hundred** loaded sheep, while on the miserable **paths in** Gurwhal the same number would **require** six **or** eight, and even then the chances of some being lost over the precipices are **double.**

"The little trade carried on over the Nelang pass is entirely in the hands of the inhabitants of that village, about thirty families of Tartars, who reside there during summer, and come down into Gurwhal in winter. The Gurwhalees themselves rarely or never go into Thibet, and not one of them can speak the Tartar language. They take their grain to Nelang, and exchange it for salt with the Nelang people, and even should other Tartars be there, are not allowed to exchange or trade with them. The Nelang people take the grain on into Thibet, exchanging it for salt or wool, or the Thibetians come down to Nelang. Scarcely any other article of merchandise crosses this pass.

"The Puharies of the eastern part of Gurwhal, who now get their salt either from Nelang or from the traders of British Gurwhal, say that formerly there was another pass open by which they brought it from Thibet themselves. This pass they say was over the hills at the head of the Billing river; but as these hills are marked down in our latest maps, and the country has now been accurately surveyed, it seems altogether impossible such a pass should exist.

"There are several passes which were known to the Puharies some fifty years ago, when the people of one valley were constantly stealing the flocks belonging to those of another, which probably no one now living has crossed. Of these may be mentioned one from Nelang to Manna in British Gurwhal; another from Gangootree to the same place; and one from Gangootree to Gungee in the Billing valley, and to Keedarnath. The highest and most difficult pass now crossed is the Changso Khaga, between Nelang and Chitkool in Koonawur.

It must be nearly 18,000 feet above the sea, and no European has yet crossed it. It is considered so dangerous that the Chitkool people, who go to Nelang every year to receive a portion of tribute paid by the inhabitants of that village to the rajah of Koonawur, generally prefer coming over the Nela pass to Muckwa and up the Ganges, a route nearly twice the distance, to crossing it.

"The Nela pass is up the Goomtee, a little tributary of the Ganges in Upper Tangnore, to the head of the Buspa in Koonawur, being five long marches from Muckwa to Chitkool, the villages first reached on each side. It is nearly 17,000 feet high, and one march, when the dividing ridge itself is crossed, is for twelve or fourteen miles entirely on the snow. A more detailed description of this pass is given in another chapter, which will give some idea of what nearly all the high passes on the southern side of the Himalayas are like. The Dumdar pass crosses the same range of snowy mountains in another place, from another tributary of the Ganges to the head of the Tonse in Burrassoo, and is only a few hundred feet lower than the Nela. The Chya and Bamasoor passes, the latter being a shorter but higher route over the same hill, lead from the Ganges to the head of the Jumna. They are respectively 13,500 and 15,000 feet high. From the different sources of the Tonse river, passes lead into the Baspa valley in Koonawur, all crossing at different points the one long range of snowy mountains which divide that valley from Gurwhal.

Of these the most frequented is the Ropin, 15,000 feet high, which is one highway between the two countries. The others, which are higher and more difficult, are rarely, if ever, crossed except by the inhabitants of the villages near. The spurs jutting from the snowy ranges are crossed by different paths from almost every village, at elevations of from 9000 to 12,000 or 13,000 feet; but though some are as bad or even worse to cross than the higher ones, the roads over them are not dignified with the name of passes. In the native dialect they are called "dandas," while those over the snowy ranges are called "khagas." The higher passes are open from April to the first heavy fall of snow in autumn, which may happen in September, or not till November; but peculiar circumstances in the character of each pass render all easier to cross at one time than another in this interval. Some are easy to cross in April and May, and scarcely passable the two following months; and others are exactly the reverse. The chief governing cause may be stated in a few words. Where the road lies on the snow in the *bottom* of a valley or ravine, the pass will be easiest to cross early in spring, before the winter snow has all melted, and when it is of such a consistency that the traveller only sinks in it a few inches. At this time the lyes or cracks in the ice, which are so troublesome and dangerous when the snow has altogether disappeared, or become too soft to bear the weight of a man on the surface, are securely covered, and there is less chance of being ingulphed in one of them. Where much of the road lies along the *face* of a steep hill-side, the pass will be best to cross later in the season, when the winter snow has melted, for while hard, if the incline was great, steps would have to be cut in it the whole way, and there would be great danger of slipping down the smooth surface. The difficulty and danger of crossing the higher passes of the Himalayas have often been greatly exaggerated, though no doubt it is to many a severe trial. To say the danger is quite imaginary would be wrong, for there is danger in crossing any hill when a fall or slip would peril life or limb, and it must naturally be considerably increased when the hill is covered with ice and snow; and as it is everywhere hard work to walk six or seven miles up-hill, it is easy to conceive this may become a real difficulty where the rarefied atmosphere so seriously prostrates our physical powers.

"The rivers having been mentioned, the means of crossing them require a slight notice. In the cold weather most will admit of temporary bridges, but except in some favoured spots these are washed away soon after the waters rise in spring. The force of the torrent is far too great to admit of any artificial support for a bridge in the current; and where very wide, the rivers are crossed by a rude suspension bridge made of grass ropes. These are so narrow as only to admit of one person passing at a time, who takes hold of the supporting ropes, and steps on small pieces of stick half a yard apart, the ends of which are tied to the lower ropes forming the road-way. They enable people to cross from side to side, which is all that can be said, for only experienced hands venture to carry loads across, and even a goat is unable to cross itself, and must be carried. Another way of crossing a river that is too wide to bridge, is by a single rope stretched across, called a "tune." A crooked piece of stick in the form of a small triangle, generally cut from the bush rhododendron, as the toughest wood, is put over the rope, and a string attached to one end is passed under the waist and fastened to the other. The traveller then hangs suspended horizontally from the rope, supported by the stick and string, and pulls himself across, hand over hand. Loads of every description, sheep and goats, women and children, are taken across by suspending them from the triangular stick, or a small ring of twisted shreds of ringall cane, put on the rope for the purpose, and pulled along by a cord from the opposite side. Accidents often occur where the rivers are crossed in this manner. Sometimes the rope breaks, and the passenger is precipitated into the river. He has of course hold of the rope, and if he keeps his presence of mind and can retain it, is immediately washed to the shore and saved; but the torrent is often so impetuous that it breaks his hold in a few seconds, and sweeps him away without a chance of rescue. Few of the Puharies of the middle or higher hills learn to swim at all, and the strongest swimmer would have little chance in some of the torrents over which these tunes are made. Sometimes the string or triangular stick that supports the body gives way, and few have strength to complete the remainder of the passage without, but, utterly exhausted, drop off into the river. A singular accident occurred to one unfortunate passenger on a tune over the Ganges. It was rather low, and the river having risen, or the rope itself having become slacker since the last person crossed, when he got over the centre of the river the waves and spray dashed over him so continuously that he was drowned on the rope ere he could get across.

"The regular Puharie bridge is on the lever principle. Two or more long trunks of trees are laid parallel, a few feet apart, with their small ends projecting a little over the river, and the counterbalance is increased by large stones laid on the thicker ends. A cross piece is laid over the projecting ends, and serves as the fulcrum of another pair or set of sleepers, as they may be called, which project still further out over the river. The same process is carried on on the opposite shore, till the space between is reduced to forty or fifty feet, when two long poles are laid across, a few feet apart, and planks or sticks laid crosswise over them for a road way. The sleepers vary in number according to the width of the river, from a single pair to half a dozen layers, and where a substantial bridge is made are generally imbedded in solid masonry.

"The cereal productions of the hills are very similar to those of the plains, but some in the higher regions are peculiar to the country. Wheat, rye, and barley are the spring crops, sown in September, October, and November; and reaped in April, May, and June, according to the elevation of the place, that which is high up being sown earliest and reaped latest. At Nelang, and in hill countries out of the influence of the rains, and where the winter is very severe, these crops are not sown till spring, in April or May, and are reaped in September or October. In the lower and middle hills, where reaped early, a second crop of some autumnal grain is always obtained from the same ground. Rice of several qualities is cultivated on the irrigated lands of the lower hills; and a kind peculiar to the hills, which grows without irrigation, is cultivated to a great extent up to an elevation of 6000 feet. The grains of this kind of rice are larger and rounder than of any which grows on irrigated lands, and it is one of the most useful crops for home consumption the Puharies have. Cheena is what is called and used in England as bird or canary-seed. Here, in the middle and higher regions, it is one of the chief autumnal crops, sown in April and reaped in September. Kownee grows in the same regions and in the same manner; but the plant is higher, and the seeds, which are smaller and rounder, are contained in a long ear which bends downwards from the slender stalk; while the flatter ones of cheena are in a loose bunch, like what is familiarly called trembling grass. Bettoo is a gigantic kind of kownee, confined to the higher hills. Jungeroo is similar to the budjera of the plains, and grows only in the lower valleys. All these are used for food in the same manner as rice. Marcha is, I believe, the plant which in English gardens, is cultivated as a flower, and called 'Prince of Wales' feather,' or one nearly similar. It is one of the principal autumnal crops of the middle and higher regions, sown in April and reaped in October, and makes a coarse brown bread. Koda or mudwa is an autumnal crop of the lower hills and of the Dhoon, and makes a still darker coloured and coarser bread. Popra, ogle, and chabra are three kinds of buckwheat; the first is confined to the higher hills, where it is the principal autumnal crop, sown in April and reaped in September and October. It makes a light, palatable, and wholesome bread. The second kind grows in the middle regions, but is more sparingly cultivated. The third, chabra, is a peculiar kind confined to the higher hills. It is very quick in coming to maturity, and is sown as late as July, in the fields from which the spring crop of wheat has been reaped, and is ripe even sooner than the others. This kind is ground into flour for bread, and also used in the same manner as rice. Bears are very fond of buckwheat, and when the grain is ripening, the fields have to be carefully guarded at night, or it would be totally consumed. Koda in the lower hills, has to be carefully watched from the same cause. Indian corn, extensively cultivated in other hill countries, is in Gurwhal only seen in the gardens or small plots of ground near the houses, appropriated to the production of kitchen vegetables, pumpkins, cucumbers, French beans, spinnage, &c. The oil-seeds are, teel, mustard, rape, and poppy. The pulse, several kinds of dal and vetches. In the lower valleys a little cotton is cultivated, and manufactured into a coarse strong cloth for home consumption, generally long, narrow pieces adapted for waist-belts. Potatoes and onions have lately been introduced, but as yet are but sparingly cultivated."

CHAPTER VI.

" THE hill country of Gurwhal is but thinly populated, and, as has been before remarked, must at some former period, if we may judge from the vestiges of old cultivation, have contained nearly double the number of its present inhabitants. I have no means of correctly ascertaining what this may be, but some idea may be formed. The land revenue is said to amount in round numbers to 100,000 rupees. A village paying 100 will be found to contain something like 150 inhabitants, which would make the present population 150,000, probably somewhat near the mark. This appears very scant for something near 10,000 square miles of surface; but it must be remembered a great portion is too high to be habitable, and of the other not a twentieth part under cultivation. There are no towns, not one even where the rajah resides, and the largest villages seldom contain more than 100 families ; from ten to thirty being the usual number. The villages are built in the most favourable spots in the valleys, and up the hill-sides to an elevation of 6000 feet. The houses are substantial cottages, generally of two stories, the lower being occupied by the cattle, while the family reside in the upper. In the higher hills, where timber is plentiful and near, many are three and four stories high, and some even five or six. These are all old ones, the Puharies of the present day, when they build a new house, being contented with two, or at most three stories. In the lower hills they are thatched with a long rank grass called halim, or slated where the material is procurable. In the higher hills they are roofed with thick planks, cedar, wherever it can be got, being used in preference to any other wood, as it is easily worked and very durable. Many of the finest trees are useless to the Puharies, as they have no saws, and few, except the pines, split easily. Even of these, those only which are free from knots or twists can be used for planks, and then only the portion of the trunk without branches. To get a couple of dozen decent planks, a Puharie carpenter uses up a tree, from which with a saw more than a hundred of the same size could easily be procured. The rooms are very low, the lower and middle stories being rarely more than five feet, and the upper four at the sides, and eight in the centre. They have no chimneys, or any contrivance to let out the smoke. The windows are small openings a foot square, and the doors are so low that a grown-up person must stoop considerably to enter. Wooden balconies are generally attached to the better sort of houses, and a few planks, over which the roof is extended, form an entrance to others. The Puharies seem to have an utter contempt for comfort or convenience in their **dwellings**. Houses **of three** or four stories high, **really** imposing-looking **buildings** of the **sort**, have **an** entrance only through the dark and **dirty** ground-floor occupied by the cattle. Furniture is almost unknown; a few cooking utensils, brass vessels **to eat** and drink from, a covered basket or two **to contain** clothes, **a** few larger ones or wooden boxes **for** storing grain, and in the lower hills sometimes a **small cot** or bedstead, form the whole of it to be found **in a** Puharie's house. In the higher hills, in this, **as in** everything else, there **is a** little improvement; a wooden granary is constructed outside, in which is stored the grain and everything not daily required in the house, **so** that its occupants have **at** least a little room to move about. The whole family use but one apartment, in which they **cook**, eat, and sleep, unless in fine warm weather, when some prefer sleeping outside; **visitors taking** their chance with the rest. **It** is not unusual for a man, his **wife,** his son, and son's wife, other grown-up children, and perhaps two **or** three visitors of either sex, his **own,** or his wife's relations, to sleep in a small room not more than **18** feet by 12. The young Puharie girls must **find** it difficult sometimes to complete their toilet, for until **they** become mothers they are very **particular in not** for a moment exposing their **bosoms** to any **of the** other sex. Bedding is a luxury possessed only by the wealthy, except sometimes a sheep or deerskin; **the** clothes worn in **the** day serve for covering at night. When the houses are of several stories, each is generally occupied by a branch of the parent family, or the spare apartments are used as store-rooms.

"The Puharies of Gurwhal are all Hindoos, divided, as in the plains, into several castes. To describe the inhabitants of one large village, or a cluster of small ones, gives a good idea of the entire population. There is generally one or more families of Brahmins, who officiate at the religious ceremonies, fix the days for marriages and betrothments, for commencing any particular work, setting out on a particular journey, casting nativities, horoscopes, &c., but they have not nearly the influence possessed by their brethren in the plains. A blacksmith is indispensable; he makes and repairs the agricultural instruments, and for this receives from each family, yearly, a certain fixed quantity of grain, about 16 lbs. of each kind harvested, but no pecuniary compensation. The shoemaker is supposed to supply every male in his village with a pair of shoes yearly, and to receive also a certain quantity of grain from each family. Formerly this custom was universal, but now that money is more plentiful it has fallen into disuse, and he gets paid in cash or grain as he sells his wares. One or two families of carpenters or masons, the two trades being always united, are located in almost every village, but only a few of them work regularly at their trade. When employed by any person, they are supplied by him with food, and receive a certain amount in cash, and sometimes a pair of silver bracelets or gold ear-rings when the job is finished. The jumaries are musicians attached to the village temple. In large villages there are two or three families; in smaller ones generally but one, and some are without. Their women are natch girls, and twice a year, in spring and autumn, they go about dancing and begging from door to door, both in their own village and the neighbouring ones, every family giving them either a small present in money or grain, and sometimes wearing apparel. At times they make excursions to distant districts, remaining away from home for months together. This is not from want, but from custom, and in their own village and the neighbouring ones, they seem to consider they have as much right to the *douceur* they receive for dancing before a person's house as the artisan who built it had to the remuneration he received for his labour. When at home the men are tailors and barbers, and in their character as musicians perform at all the festivals, religious or otherwise, and night and morning beat on their small drums the 'nomtee,' a kind of watch-setting and *réveillé*, performed in every village where a family of these people reside at day-break and bed-time. If they fail in this, or are too late in the morning or too early in the evening, they may be fined by the villagers for the benefit of the temple. In large villages, where there are several performers, the nomtee puts one in mind of the watch-setting and *réveillé* of a military cantonment. It is considered as daily honour paid to the Deity by the inhabitants collectively. The jumaries receive from each family in their village a fixed quantity of grain yearly, and, on all occasions of public or private feasting, cooked victuals. For their tailoring they are paid in grain or cash by whoever employs them. Cultivating only the small portion of land they generally receive rent-free, attached to their office as musicians to the temple, they lead an easy, idle life; having so much spare time, many learn to shoot, and it is amongst this class the greatest number of shikaries are found. Their women, from not being subject from infancy to hard out-door labour, like the generality of Puharie girls, are, as a class, the best-looking, free in some measure from the masculine appearance common to the rest, and with some share of the grace and softness of the gentler sex. They must not be confounded with the natch women of the plains, and of some other hill countries, who are mostly unmarried and lead a life of prostitution. Here they are as respectable as any other class of the community, and though it would be difficult perhaps to find one of unsullied virtue, they are in every respect as moral as the rest of their countrywomen.

"With the shoemakers, the lowest caste in the hills, are classed the domes or slaves, the serfs of the wealthier inhabitants, several families being found in every tolerable-sized village. The rest, forming the bulk of the population, are chutree rajpoots, occupied exclusively in the cultivation of the land. No one, however, of the other classes lives solely by his profession, every family cultivating some portion of ground, enough to yield, with what they receive for their office or for work, sufficient for their own consumption, if not a surplus for sale. Besides those enumerated, common to almost every village, there are scattered throughout the hills a few workers in brass, called 'tamotas' and 'komars,' or manufacturers of earthen vessels, and in the lower hills, where cotton is grown, a few families of koolees or weavers.

"A person's caste is hereditary, and though he may please himself whether or not he works at the trade supposed to be attached to it, it cannot be changed. A carpenter, blacksmith, or shoemaker, if he entirely forsakes his trade and occupies himself exclusively with farming, still retains his family caste, which descends unalterable to his posterity. A person may forsake his own and enter a lower caste, but by no possibility can a person become of higher caste than that in which he was born. In order, the different castes stand thus:—1. Brahmins; 2. Rajpoots; 3. Carpenters, masons, blacksmiths, and jumaries; 4. Weavers; 5. Shoemakers and slaves. Each caste is again divided into different grades, though the distinction is seldom observed. The different castes never intermarry, except occasionally Brahmins and rajpoots; but a member of one sometimes elopes with a partner of another, the higher in this case losing his or her caste. Working at any particular trade does not injure a man in caste; a rajpoot may leave his farming and work altogether as a carpenter or mason, and still remain a rajpoot, and the workers in gold and silver are of no particular caste, Brahmins, rajpoots, and blacksmiths learning and working at that trade without reference to it. The Brahmins eat bread cooked by rajpoots, but it must be with butter or ghee, however small the quantity may be. The rajpoots may not eat with the lower castes, nor these again with each other. This has relation only to food cooked with water; if that element does not enter into its composition, no distinction is made. Thus, flesh, or any other thing roasted at the fire, parched grain, fruit, and everything that does not require cooking, may be eaten by all classes together. Neither can a member of one caste enter the house of a person of superior, except rajpoots those of Brahmins. It would be considered as defiled, and a goat have to be killed in it, and the blood sprinkled about, ere fit for its former occupant. The prejudices of caste are not nearly so rigidly observed in the higher hills as in the lower ranges bordering the plains, the rough and hardy inhabitants of these regions setting at defiance many of its minor trammels. A rajpoot will often, when in the forest or on a journey, eat with men of inferior caste, and in some places they allow them to enter their houses. Of the entire population, the rajpoots form about three-fourths, the rest are in nearly equal proportions. The generality of villages are peopled with a mixture of classes as above described, though a few are exceptions, some being inhabited entirely by Brahmins, with a family of jumaries, and a few of slaves; others by a preponderance of the lower castes, and many small ones by rajpoots only.

"One of the most influential of the rajpoot inhabitants is selected by the rajah or his official, in each large village, or for several small ones, and appointed as a kind of headman, called siana, mukeea, or pudan, to keep the village in some kind of order. If obeyed as he ought to be, his authority is great, but it is often set at open defiance, and he not unfrequently suffers for the faults of his villagers. Travellers passing through apply to him for Coolies, provisions, or whatever they may be in want of, and he gives orders for the supply; the villagers do not bring all that is wanted, and the indignant traveller or his servants give the unfortunate siana an undeserved thrashing. All the affairs of the village community are settled through him, and he is supposed to watch over their individual interests in any quarrel with other villagers. The emoluments attached to his post are, a large field rent-free, a *douceur* on the marriage or divorce of any of his villagers, and on deciding quarrels, and if he chooses, when travelling to another village, a person to attend him without compensation. If he can enforce it, he is also entitled to a leg of every sheep or goat killed in the village, and of any wild animal brought from the forest by the shikaries. The office is often held for life when the villagers are satisfied with the siana, and he likes to retain it; the rajah enforces a change at his pleasure, but the wishes of the villagers are generally attended to, if they express a desire to have any particular person retained in the office.

"Another official is the pauree, a kind of constable selected by the villagers themselves from the lower castes. His duty is to enforce on each family or individual their share of any general work; to see that each person takes his turn in performing duties common to the village, as transporting the baggage of travellers, carrying letters, or accompanying any person entitled to a guide to the next village; collecting from each family whatever is required from the village collectively; and carrying to each any general order of the siana, to whom he is a kind of subordinate. He receives also for his services some ground, rent-free, attached to his office, a certain quantity of grain from each family, and a trifling *douceur* at marriages and births of first male children. If ordered to arrest any one by order of the siana, he is entitled to a tumassee (the fifth of a rupee) from the person on executing the order. The affairs of a village are settled in punchayet, every grown-up male having a voice and being invited to attend. The siana, if he is an intelligent individual, has great influence at these meetings, and can generally have the decision agreeably to his own views.

"The country is divided into districts, each containing from twenty to sixty villages. The rajah appoints yearly to each an officer called a phoundar or petwarree, who collects the revenue, decides all disputes, inflicts punishment for all but capital offences, and is in fact the magistrate and collector. For these purposes he makes one and sometimes two tours through the district; visiting every village, and deciding all cases on the spot; while thus employed being supplied with food and carriage for himself and attendants, free of cost, by the villagers. This is an office much sought after, both from its emoluments and the consequence attached to it. A man will often make the rajah a present of 200 or 300 rupees to get the phoundarship of a district for a single year, the whole revenue of which may not amount to more than 1500. They receive no salary, but are thus remunerated. While the land revenue goes to the rajah without deduction, fines, the duty on divorces, and other fluctuating income, which goes under the general name of fida (literally profit), is shared in by the phoundar. It sometimes amounts to as much as the land revenue, and a third is what the rajah generally allows them to retain as compensation for their services. An excellent plan for obtaining as much as possible from the country, but the worst that could be devised for the administration of justice, for, as might be expected, the phoundar thinks of nothing but getting as much fida as he possibly can; indeed, if this was not something considerable, he would be disgraced, and probably have to make it up out of his own pocket; while the larger the amount, if unaccompanied by any very serious complaints of flagrant injustice from the district, the better is he considered to have performed his duty.

"More than fifty per-cent of the fida is collected by fines for adultery. The Puharies are so careless in their intrigues that they are soon known to the whole village, and some one is sure to inform the phoundar when he arrives; and, where immorality is carried to such a frightful extent, it may be imagined how numerous they must be. It is not unusual for a phoundar to make a present to any good-looking girl, reported to have a number of admirers, to tell him who they are that have enjoyed her favours. No other proof is required, and each is fined from five to fifteen rupees, according to his means or the pleasure of the official. Even if a man is innocent, and determined to establish the falsehood of the charge, if once preferred against him, no matter by whom, he has to pay nearly as much as the fine would be for having his innocence made patent to the world. The women receive no punishment whatever, unless their husbands think fit to give them a thrashing; and a Puharie belle rather prides herself on the number of young men who have been fined for her sake, considering it, no doubt, a proof of her charms. Lamentable as such a state of morality may be, no one of those concerned is much shocked by it; the husband himself, as long as his frail wife shows no particular aversion to him, or wastes any of his substance on her admirers, treats the matter very coolly, rarely himself being the informant; and the phoundar, instead of viewing the matter in a serious light, often makes a joke of it, and will tell the culprit that the favours of such a woman are worth twice the amount of the fine he is about to inflict. There is little doubt that if the authorities really wished to decrease this fearful amount of immorality, it might easily be done; but it is to be feared the phoundars are rather desirous it should increase, to swell the amount of fida collected in the district. If the accused parties were punished more severely when guilty, and not at all when innocent, and some mark of disapprobation at least, if not of punishment, inflicted on the frail fair ones, the whole community would soon look on the crime of adultery as something really disgraceful, and it would not be half so frequent. The favour, again, shown to a person who runs away with another man's wife into the Company's territories, tends greatly to encourage the evildoers, particularly of the poorer classes, who have little to lose by forsaking their homes. If the husband follows, and complains he can get no redress, and the adulteress is told she may please herself, whether she shall go back to her home with her husband, or remain with her paramour. A woman will sometimes tell her husband, if he expresses great anger at her loose conduct, that if he does not take care she will elope with some one to the Company's territories, the Deyrah Dhoon being the principal place of refuge; and the knowledge that a husband's authority ceases there often deters him from taking measures to reclaim her. Non-interference in these matters may answer very well in the plains; but in the hills, where society is quite differently constituted, morality on a much lower scale, and unlimited freedom of intercourse amongst all classes unavoidable, it would be productive of the most disastrous results.

"Elopements are, as might be expected, of common occurrence. In these cases the parties have generally agreed to join their fortunes together, and the man is prepared, or trusts to his relations, to pay the husband double the amount of the original purchase-money, which, with a fine to the rajah, is what it costs him, and the general end of such adventures. The couple generally hide in the forest for a few days, and then reside together, either in their own or another village, till the phoundar decides the case. Sometimes the husband will not agree to give up his wife on any consideration, while she as resolutely declares her determination to remain with her lover; a good thing for the phoundar, as both parties try to bribe him with small presents to grant or withhold a divorce.

The lovers, however, generally gain the **day, the** law, or rather custom, being that if **a woman can** from any quarter offer double the **amount of** her purchase-money, with the expenses of a divorce, she is entitled to it. The duty paid to the rajah is about six per-cent from each party **on** the gross amount of purchase-money, with **a** rupee to the phoundar **as** his due, and whatever else he can cajole out of the parties as a favour; and two **or** three to be divided amongst influential villagers and sianas, who, with the phoundar, hear the case, though having **no** voice in the decision.

" If **a** girl of the Brahmin **or** rajpoot **caste** intrigues with a man of a lower, it is a regular windfall to the phoundar. The man is fined from fifty to **a** hundred rupees, and the girl being considered to have lost caste, her husband, her relations, every family of her own caste whose house she may have entered, and every person who may have partaken of **food** from her hands, or cooked in her house, are considered to have profaned theirs, and have to pay a rupee as a fine for **the** unwitting violation. This is called chundraee; and as companionship **in** misfortune makes it more endurable, the **first** denounced, true to the adage, tell on others, **till,** though the amount from each is but a rupee, the sum realized from all amounts sometimes to more than a hundred. Intrigues of this kind, from the heavy penalty entailed, are far less frequent than others; the men fearing **that,** and the women the disgrace and probable loss of caste. The husband sometimes insists on a separation and divorce, receiving from her parents some portion of the purchase-money; and sometimes, seeing no chance of receiving back anything like what she has cost him, unwilling to part with her, or knowing himself too poor to buy another, he puts up with the calamity, performing the necessary ceremonies to reinstate her in caste. Some prefer losing both money and wife to keeping one who has thus demeaned herself. The adulterer, if he cannot pay the fine, is sent to prison; but this does not often happen, as if he cannot borrow, he may sell himself, or his own wife or children, to raise it. Until it is forthcoming he often receives some other punishment, as being kept in the stocks, beaten with sticks, or made to stand for hours with a large stone on his head. When these cases are sent for the decision of the rajah, he generally puts both parties in prison. To reinstate the woman in caste, she must make a pilgrimage to Gangootree, bathe in the sacred stream there, and at home sacrifice a goat and make some pecuniary offering to the village deity. On some occasions the pilprimage to Gangootree is dispensed with, a simple ablution in the Ganges at any spot being deemed sufficient.

" Personal quarrels, of whatever nature, are also productive, and add something to the fida account; the individual declared to be in fault pays a fine, and the other gives a *douceur* for the honour of gaining the day. Whoever makes a complaint against another, of whatever nature it may be, must at the same time make a present, generally of a rupee, to the Phoundar; the accused has to pay four annas, or a quarter of a rupee, to the peons sent to apprehend him, and a rupee to the phoundar ere allowed to enter on his defence. With all these drawbacks, the Puharies are so litigious, they will seldom settle their disputes amicably, though well aware an appeal to the rajah or the phoundar can only end in loss to both parties. If complaints were heard without loss to the complainant, and cases decided with what we should call but justice, there would be no end to litigation; every Puharie would find some hole in his neighbour's coat, and false or exaggerated charges be of every day occurrence. The phoundars are easily bribed, and sometimes decide cases with the greatest contempt for right and wrong; but the rajah not unfrequently wrests from them a portion of their ill-gotten gains, by fining them at the close of their official career a few hundred rupees for some flagrant act of injustice; though next day, perhaps, on receiving another present, he will appoint them in the same capacity to another district. Any person fined by the phoundar may appeal to the rajah, but this is attended with so much inconvenience that it is seldom resorted to, except where the fine is heavy and the injustice flagrant. For the sake of five or ten rupees, it is not worth a man's while to make a journey to Teree, the residence of the rajah, and remain there till his case is heard and decided on in the durbar, besides having to disburse a few more rupees in presents to the rajah's officials there. The knowledge of this makes the phoundars unsparing in levying small fines on all on whom they can fix any trifling cause for doing so.

"The judicial administration of the country may seem to us most oppressive and corrupt, yet there are few independent native states of which the inhabitants are treated more leniently; and with all the expensive paraphernalia of the Company's courts, and the boasted justice and freedom from oppression they are so fondly thought to confer on all beneath their sway, it is very doubtful whether the poor cultivators of the soil in the British territories are at all better off, and not just as much oppressed by a lot of venal official subordinates as the Puharies of Gurwhal are by their phoundars. Indeed, in one respect the latter have the advantage, for they have but one huge oppressor, and that but for a day or two once or twice in the year, while the former are subject to a host of lesser myrmidons all the year round.

"The revenue is paid principally in cash; a small portion in produce from each village serving for the consumption of the rajah, his family, and adherents; the nearest furnishing grain, and the more distant, butter, oil, and salt. Musk and falcons are taken in lieu of rent, the former in pod at about three rupees per ounce, and the latter at from seven to thirty-five rupees each, a young female bird being valued at the last-named sum. Heavy fines are inflicted if either are sold to strangers; but musk, being easily concealed, and saleable at more than double the price given for it by the rajah, is very generally disposed of without detection. The land revenue, considering the low price of produce, and the want of a market, except at Mussoorie or Rajpore, seems excessive. It is calculated on the amount of seed necessary for cultivation, and amounts to, in some cases one third, and in others one half, the value of the gross produce. This makes the Puharies, except in particular spots near the markets, careless about cultivating more ground than will suffice to raise grain for their own consumption, and they depend on other sources for the means of raising their quota of rent and what other money they may require, as taking service for a few months at Mussoorie, or with some traveller or pilgrim, or gathering such of the spontaneous productions of the hills as are saleable.

"The other sources of revenue are a few trifling taxes; one on sheep, another on milch buffaloes, a small duty on mills, on the holy water carried from Gangootree to the plains for sale, and an occasional levy of from one to three rupees each on all the artisans, goldsmiths, blacksmiths, masons, and carpenters who work at their trade; this being made every three or four years. Formerly a duty was levied on all merchandise, on everything brought from the plains or carried out of the country for sale, and was rather productive, being six per cent on the value; but within the last few years it has been abolished in this and all the protected and tributary states, a portion of territory on the frontiers of each having been given as compensation to the rulers for the decrease of revenue thus caused.

"Considering the trifling amount realized by the sale of natural products, with the fact that of the 150,000 rupees or thereabouts drawn from it yearly by the rajah, not twenty per cent is again disbursed in the country, it appears at first sight a puzzle where it, and half as much more expended in the purchase of foreign articles, cloth, domestic utensils, &c., comes from. It would be difficult to form a correct estimate of the amount of each particular item by which the Puharies yearly realize this sum, but a guess at their probability, calculated from what data we possess, may be interesting.

"The value of goods, the natural product of the hills, sold out of the country, may be 50,000 rupees. These consist of grain, clarified butter or ghee, ringalls or reeds used in the plains for making hookah pipes, a few medicinal roots and herbs, draught bullocks, sheep and goats, and a few other trifling items, musk, skins, birch bark, &c. The men in service at Mussoorie, and employed in transporting goods up the hill from Rajpore, send or take to their homes at least 60,000 rupees. The pilgrims and other travellers expend in purchasing food, and for the transport of their baggage, 10,000.

Three or four thousand of the **Puharies go every** winter to Gwalior, **where** they receive from **the** rajah of that state from five to seven rupees each as a charitable gift on some religious ceremony; which, with what else they bring back by begging, the sale of Ganges water, and other things, produces perhaps 20,000 rupees. A great number go **further into** the plains with the Ganges water, **some** even into the Dekkan, a journey occupying several months, and these may bring back 10,000. These sums amount together to 150,000 **rupees,** leaving half that amount, or whatever other **sum** the entire population may expend in their foreign purchases, to find its way **back** through various channels from the coffers **of the** rajah and other miscellaneous sources. **These** estimates may perhaps be far from the truth, but they will serve to demonstrate the means by which **the outlay** of the **country** is realized.

"The Puharies may be divided into two classes, the inhabitants of the higher and those of the lower hills; and though the same in race, religion, and customs, the difference is very striking. **The** hardy, rough dwellers in the upper and **colder** regions look down with something of contempt **on** their lowland neighbours, engendered, **no doubt, by** their **habit** in former times of robbing them with impunity. In local parlance, the latter **are** called Gungarees, from gungar, the lower hills and valleys, and the former style themselves Perbuttees, from perbutt, the higher regions near the snow. The

Perbuttees are in most respects a better race of men than the Gungarees; the few good points in the general character are brought out more prominently, and a few of the many bad ones in some degree softened. They are less envious of each other, have something of generosity in their disposition, have more regard for truth, sometimes show that gratitude is not utterly unknown amongst them, have stronger affections, and are far more hardy, enduring, and courageous. The men wear thick woollen loosely-fitting coats, giving full play to the limbs, but confined tightly round the waist by a long cotton belt or woollen rope; wide woollen trousers, tight at the ankles, a round or peaked woollen cap, and shoes of net-work, half leather, half woollen thread. They have no under garments, but in very cold weather wear two coats. To complete their costume, when travelling, if even but to the next village, they generally stick in their belts the national weapon, a dangra, or light broad-bladed hatchet. The women ordinarily dress in a coat a little longer, but of the same form and material, as that of the men, a long cotton cloth wound round the waist, and a large cotton turban. At festivals the men often change their woollen trousers for cotton ones, and all wind round their caps a long, narrow, white cotton turban. Some of the women keep the same dress, merely putting on a cleaner or better suit if they have one; but others change it entirely, putting on a jacket or spencer of printed cotton cloth, a very full white cotton petticoat, and over it another made of masoor, a striped cloth of silk and cotton. A gold **nose-ring**, large silver ear-rings, necklace, and collar, weighing altogether half a pound, a few strings of beads, and bracelets of silver, pewter, or brass, complete the *toilette*. The costume is picturesque, and the turban, as they wear it, wound twice **or** thrice round the head, and the ends thrown backwards over the shoulders, has a very graceful appearance. They wear their hair long, gathered to the **back of** the head, where, with the addition of some **very** finely twisted woollen thread, it is made into a large knot. In the lower districts many of the men wear only a blanket wound round the body, so as to leave the legs and arms bare, and fastened round the waist by a rope or cotton belt, and a small cotton skull cap. The holiday dress, and that worn by the better classes, is a long, closely fitting white or coloured cotton tunic, trousers, and turban. The women wear the spencer and petticoat, or a blanket or cotton sheet fastened tightly round the waist, and enveloping in not ungraceful folds the whole body, except the arms and one shoulder, which remain exposed, and a little party-coloured under-dress, just sufficient to confine the bosom. The men go unarmed, except a few who substitute for the dangra of the Perbuttees, a Goorkha **knife**, wearing it in front, while the latter wear theirs behind; both, if they can afford it, wear silver bracelets, and often gold ear-rings; these often serving to pay the fines inflicted by the phoundar.

"To a casual observer, the Puharies appear a harmless, unimpassioned, simple race; and, if not possessing many of the amiable qualities, at least free from some of the worst vices of the human family; but a closer and more intimate acquaintance reveals much that lies hidden beneath the smooth exterior. They are envious, vindictive, uncharitable, and extremely selfish; servile and abject to superiors, and arrogant and overbearing to inferiors. If not cruel, their humanity is confined to pity, and seldom goes so far as to make any personal sacrifice to relieve the distresses of a fellow-creature. Gratitude is almost unknown, or confined to heartless expressions. Falsehood, in the lower hills particularly, is a besetting sin. The Puharies will lie with unblushing effrontery, and seldom appear to feel the least shame when found out and exposed in doing so. Their immorality has been before alluded to. It is something almost incredible, chastity being little appreciated even where it does exist. Industrious through necessity, sober and frugal from inability to procure the means of debauchery, their very virtues are forced upon them. Their honesty has been frequently extolled, and is undeniable; but even it will scarcely bear scrutiny, and is more the effect of local causes, than an inherent quality. In their small communities it is almost impossible to become dishonest; every man's actions being patent to the rest, detection and disgrace, or punishment would be certain; while away from home a Puharie has not cunning enough to be a rogue. In his own country he is seldom tempted, undergoes no severe ordeal, **and unless** influenced by connection and intercourse with some other loose characters, he probably grows up without thinking at all on the subject, seeing no beauty in his own honesty, and more of daring than of any detestable vice in the roguery and deception he sees or hears of. In comparison with the inhabitants of the plains, the Puharie certainly shows to advantage in this respect, for the robbery of a stranger in the hills, or theft amongst themselves, is unknown, or of very rare occurrence; but he is not difficult to corrupt, and some of those who remain long in service at Mussoorie become as untrustworthy as their compeers in the plains.

"Love of home is universal, and in the higher hills a perfect passion. A Perbuttee rarely or ever leaves for good his own native hills and valleys, and can scarcely bear even a temporary absence. When tempted on a long journey or sojourn in another country, he soon wearies of the new scenes, and is for ever thinking and talking of his own loved home, calculating the time that must elapse ere he may return to it, and noticing, with childlike glee, each day that shortens the time of his probation. The passion is much less strong amongst the Gungarees; but even there almost sufficient to make it a national characteristic. Love of kindred is another amiable quality, but linked with strange contraries. Relations will quarrel furiously with each other, inflicting injuries without compunction, but fly with alacrity to each other's succour against strangers. They are passionately affectionate and loving parents, but often undutiful and unkind children; solicitous for the welfare and comfort of their own offspring, for whom they will suffer uncomplainingly almost any deprivation, but seldom showing much regard for the authors of their being, and neglecting many of the kind offices that should smooth and cheer their declining years. So strong is parental affection, that it overcomes all selfish considerations, and parents, however neglected, rarely complain or repine at the unkindness of those for whom they have done so much, showing for them to the last the same unchangeable passionate regard.

"The Puharies are rather short in stature, but generally of well-knit, robust frame, and many are seen with limbs that might serve as a model for a miniature Hercules. They are strong and hardy, and capable of undergoing a great amount of privation and fatigue. Brought up from infancy on frugal diet, they perform the most arduous service on the most simple fare; a few cakes of the coarsest flour and a little salt are their daily food for weeks or months together, when travelling or employed away from home, and on this simple fare they keep up their strength as well as if supplied with the most nourishing food. A small flat-iron plate, on which to bake their cakes, is often the only cooking utensil of a large party; and even this is sometimes dispensed with, a thin flat stone serving the purpose. In this manner they **transport** the baggage of travellers across their mountains, carrying no additional or superfluous weight of their own, the single suit of clothes worn in the day serving for bedding at night. Except in warm weather, in the lower hills, they sleep round fires, every five or six men making one for themselves. They form excellent material for irregular troops, as testified by the behaviour of the hill-regiments, composed now of men from this and the neighbouring states. Wherever they have been tried, they have shown themselves almost equal to Europeans in bravery, and in every other quality of a soldier may certainly challenge any portion of the native army. The best of their natural qualifications, however, their rough and ready way **of** life, and power of endurance, are entirely neglected, and probably eradicated. What are real luxuries to the race, they have been taught to consider as simple necessaries; and never being required to do without them for a few days, they would feel it some hardship if obliged by circumstances to do so. In cantonments it is all very well to make **them as** comfortable as other native troops, **but if advantage is** taken of what nature has made them, on the march, on detached duty, and occasionally **at** other times, they ought to revert **to** their own primitive way of living and travelling, so that, when in the field, they might be moved about without the usual attendant train of baggage. A Puharie, however comfortable he may make himself at home, never dreams of taking with him, when he leaves it for any time, more than a coarse blanket or cotton sheet; and how he must open his eyes when he sees the bed alone of his brother, whom he meets going up the hill to Mussoorie to mount guard, make a good Cooly load! A regiment of Puharies ought to be a body of men who would think it no hardship whatever to start on a journey of twenty days, provisioned for the whole time, so as to be independent of any extraneous aid, and without, except perhaps their field-hospital, a single baggage-cart or animal, or a single camp-follower.

"The Puharie women, as has been noticed, have nothing particular to boast of in regard to beauty, though many would in any country be considered pretty. They have, however, naturally very fine forms, and in youth many in this respect could hardly be surpassed. It is not for long, for hard labour, and their practice of keeping their infants at the breast for two or three years, soon spoil the graceful contour of the finest figure."

CHAPTER VII.

" THE religion of the Puharies is a simple form of Hindooism, free from some of its worst features as followed in the plains. They rarely or ever set up idols themselves, even in their temples, though they will own and make the usual offerings to one set up by others in their own or any other country they happen to pass through. The village temples are dedicated to no particular divinity of the regular Hindoo mythology, but to the supreme ruling power of the universe, an individual essence, as it were, being supposed to reside in each temple. They speak of the divinity of each as distinct and separate, not as such and such a god, but as the god of such and such a place. Almost every remarkable hill has also an individual protector, and the small lakes and ponds are considered as particularly favourite places of the deity's abode. The principal sylvan deity is the Nag Rajah, a god supposed to clothe himself in the form of a serpent. Fairies and demons are supposed to inhabit every spot not daily subject to the intrusion of mankind, and to exercise great influence both for good and evil over all. The spirits of the departed are also believed to revisit the scenes of their mortal career, and to possess the power of afflicting individuals of the family of which they were once members.

"In the higher hills they keep in the temples, or rather as attached to them, a kind of ark, as a dwelling-place for the deity. This consists of a small framework of wood, in which is placed a basket containing a little silver image. It is fixed on two long poles, and covered and dressed with pieces of cloth, of more or less value according to the wealth of the village. Several chowries or yaks' tails are generally added, and it is encircled by a broad silver belt, and has a small golden bird perched on the top. At festivals and religious ceremonies it is dressed and brought out into the village square, and two of the villagers take it on their shoulders, resting the end of a pole on each, and dance with it to their rude music, being relieved by others when tired. At this time the deity is supposed to have entered it, and supplication is made by those who have anything to ask or to thank for.

"The great characteristic of Puharie worship is the number of sacrifices made and the manner of making them. Sacrifice indeed is the universal and almost sole method of manifesting thanksgiving for benefits received, or making supplication to avert calamity. This would almost lead one to believe Hindooism in the hills had been grafted on some other religion, the rites of which were still blended with it. To see a Puharie family sacrificing in the forest, the sheep or goat for a victim, the pastoral appearance of the people, the fire, and the rude altar of rough stones, carry one back at once to the early ages of the world. Sacrifices are made to the depta of the village, to the divinities of particular places, to the fairies, demons, and spirits of the departed. They consist of a sheep or goat, or of bread, sweetmeats, or flowers; some divinities being propitiated with any, and others with a particular sacrifice. The supreme Deity is satisfied with incense and adoration alone, and requires no sacrifice. When a person is taken ill, or suffers any grievous calamity, it is considered as owing to the displeasure of the depta, or some particular divinity, or to the malevolence of fairies, demons, or the spirit of some departed relative; an oracle is consulted as to which, and a sacrifice made as directed. On emergent occasions, as a very sudden alarming attack of illness, a severe fall, or other accident, a sheep or goat is often brought at once, led round the sufferer, and sacrificed on the spot, without any reference to any particular power or divinity. A person in tolerable circumstances, when dangerously ill, has often more than half a dozen sheep or goats sacrificed over him in a few days. They are led once or twice round the individual, and then, while standing erect, have their heads struck off, almost invariably at a single blow, with a dangra or Goorkha knife. Oracles are consulted by inquiry of the depta, of individuals into whom some divinity is conjured for the purpose, or while dancing the pundap natch, and by counting strings of beads. In sickness the Puharies trust almost entirely to these sacrifices, for medicine is almost unknown, and the few articles in their possession supposed to have medicinal properties are often so misapplied, as to check rather than assist Nature in her operations. Not one of their own native plants or herbs has been discovered by them to possess any medicinal virtue, and black pepper, ginger, cloves, and other spices brought from the plains, are almost the only things used as internal remedies. When a person is ill, first one thing is tried, then another, so that if he remain so any length of time, almost every procurable remedy has its turn. At the same time an oracle is consulted, and probably declares some particular divinity, fairy, or demon is angry, and requires to be propitiated with a sacrifice ere the patient can recover. If, when this has been made, no amendment takes place, another oracle is consulted, which points to some other offended power as the cause, requiring another sacrifice, and so on till the patient dies or recovers. If the former, it is supposed to have been the will of the great Almighty power to whom all other divinities are subject; and if the latter, to the acceptance of the last sacrifice made by the power sacrificed to.

"The depta is also supposed to watch over each family in a sort of individuality as its household god, and a corner of the dwelling is often considered as consecrated to its abode, where nothing unclean should be put. Some keep a round pebble, a piece of crystal, a small iron trident, or other such thing, as the visible incarnation of their household god. The belief of the Puharies may be summed up as a belief in one great ruling power, to whom all things human and divine are subject, but requiring from mortals no particular worship; in a number of inferior divinities and spirits ordained by him to watch over the human race, and to be constantly feared and worshipped; in a future state of purgatory for the wicked, and happiness for the good; and in the devil, whom they call Jewra or Jim Rajah. Uninstructed even in their own professed creed, their religious ideas are vague and indefinite, particularly with regard to a future state, and were it not for the division of caste the missionaries would find no difficulty in converting the Puharies to Christianity. This will always be, here and wherever it prevails, the great obstacle to the spread of Gospel truth. It is not difficult to satisfy a Hindoo of the absurdity of his belief, but very difficult to prevail on him to eat with those of lower caste than himself. In the hills the feeling is not of a religious nature; it is more like what would be felt by the nobility of our own land if obliged to eat at the same table and on an equality with scavengers. In almost every case where I have heard the Puharies converse about a convert to Christianity, the subject has been, not his changing his religious faith, not a word about forsaking the worship of the Hindoo divinities, but by eating with people without caste, debarring himself from social intercourse with his family relations.

"Amongst the religious ceremonies the most remarkable is the pundap natch or dance. It is performed at no particular period, but at the pleasure of the villagers, or any individual who likes to bear the expense, and is often resorted to on a continuance of unfavourable weather, or any public calamity, and as an oracle to consult on any important occasion. The entire neglect of it would be expected to bring some misfortune on the village. When it is about to take place, the village square is swept, and a fire lighted in some part of it to burn incense. The jumaries, or musicians, call the people to assemble by beating their drums. Two or three individuals of either sex sit down at a time; the jumaries, standing immediately in front of them, beat their drums in a peculiar manner, increasing their strokes in violence and rapidity to the highest pitch possible, while their listeners gradually work themselves up into a state of intense excitement, whether real or pretended it is difficult to say, but so violent that they no longer seem the same beings. At first they begin to shake and tremble, and breathe very quickly; the jumaries, seeing this, increase their exertions, standing as close to them as possible, so as almost to deafen them with the noise; then their whole body partakes of the excitement, and at last they jump up, sometimes uttering loud shrieks, and leaping and dancing about as if perfectly frantic. One of the five pundaps, or some being amongst their followers, **is** supposed to have entered their bodies, and they continue in the character till the ceremony ends, or till tired; after the **first wild** burst becoming less furious, walking mooningly about at one time, and at another **dancing** wildly to the music, or breaking out into a state of pretended inspiration. When the spirit is about to quit them, they get a person to stand ready, and running backwards and forwards very quickly several times, they spring into his arms and fall apparently devoid of sensation for several moments. Others, in the meantime, have become **similar** recipients, so that several are always up at a time while the ceremony lasts, and sometimes half the people in the village. It is generally continued two **or** three days, and the last, all night long. While dancing the men strip to the waist, and daub their faces and bodies with pitace, a yellow powder from the pine-tree flowers, which gives them a wild and savage appearance, particularly **at** night, when a stranger might fancy he had got amongst a lot of demons. A club, dangra, **a bow** and quiver, or some other weapon, is flourished about by the male performers, who in their lively moods realize exactly one's idea of an untutored warlike savage dancing after performing some great feat. **Some** heat a crowbar red-hot in the fire, and while flourishing it about in one hand draw the hot end quickly through the other, **or** lick it with the

o

tongue. Others walk barefoot on the sharp edges of a long line of dangras, hatchets, and other weapons, held with their backs to the ground for the purpose. Some are faqueers, going about covered with ashes, and begging flour in the village, which they bake into cakes at the fire; some are monkeys climbing and swinging about on ropes; and others bears, eating an incredible quantity of raw pumpkins, cucumbers, or anything of which bears are fond, and drinking large bowls of buttermilk. These antics are performed in accordance with the character of the spirit supposed to have entered them, and they will point to the handling of red-hot iron without being burnt, and the walking on the blades of sharp weapons without being cut, as proof of the reality of the inspiration. In one village near Gangootree they were rather discomfited by seeing a young officer of a Queen's regiment, who happened to be a spectator of a pundap natch, and to whom they were insisting on supernatural influence to enable them to do these tricks, coolly go through both ordeals in his natural state. Some of the Puharies fail in the attempt, and get burnt or cut, in which case they are thought to have been only pretending to inspiration, and are laughed at for their pains. While in their assumed characters they drop their own entirely, and are inquired of as oracles, their answers, which are given in a kind of chant, being considered as inspirations from the divinity. The ceremony generally concludes by all who have joined in the dance being feasted while still in their assumed characters, either at the expense of some individual or the village collectively.

"A few of the Puharie festivals, as the Dewalee, are general in common with all Hindoos, while others are peculiar to particular villages or districts; and these are far more thought of than the regular Hindoo holidays, many of which are entirely neglected. The first of Bysakh (April) is in some districts attended with a peculiar ceremony. The men of each side the valley assemble by the river in opposite bodies, each on their own bank, armed with slings and blunt arrows, while the women and children seat themselves on some eminence near as spectators. Each party with their deptas, and the ark before mentioned, approach the river, and a mimic battle commences between the two, stones being slung and arrows discharged with all the skill and strength of the combatants, who encourage each other by shrill whistles and loud shouts, while the collected jumaries, with their drums and discordant music, increase the din and tumult as much as possible. The deptas must be brought down to the river and sprinkled with water; and when either party attempts to do this, the opposite direct their united fire on the spot, and raining on it a shower of stones and arrows, often succeed in driving back their opponents several times ere they can accomplish their object. The fight lasts about an hour, the distance preventing much harm being done; but many get struck with the stones they are not quick enough to avoid, and receive severe bruises, each successful shot being hailed with loud shouts of applause by the side from whence discharged. Instances have occurred of a leg or arm being broken; but these are very rare, and a broken head is the worst to be expected. The day ends with singing and dancing at the different villages.

"The first of Assooj (September) is in some of the higher villages another great holiday, a kind of feast of flowers. Some days previous, every one sows a little wheat and barley in a small box or basket filled with earth, and kept in a warm part of the house. It shoots up rapidly, and by the festival is nearly a foot long, and, from the forced growth, of a rich yellow colour. Tufts of this are stuck in the cap or turban as bouquets, and in the windows and doors of the houses. Several large baskets of flowers are brought, some always from the kylass or grassy region above the forest, and scattered thickly over the village square; a fine to the depta being a penalty incurred by any one who treads on them till all is ready. The villagers stand round headed by the siana, all dressed in their holiday clothes; and when he gives the signal, the whole rush forward, jumping and dancing, shouting, screeching, and whistling, and in a few seconds the variegated carpet of flowers is no more. The day, as usual, ends in singing and dancing.

"Another festival peculiar to some villages is on the 20th of Saween (July). For three days previous all the milk given by the cows in the village is kept as consecrated to the depta, no one using the least quantity. On the festival a member of each family brings into the village square a large vessel full. The siana dips a bunch of flowers into each vessel, and sprinkles a few drops of milk on the depta, dressed and brought out for the occasion. The contents of all the vessels are then mixed together in one large one, and a portion distributed to every one in the village who likes to partake of it, or any stranger who may happen to be a spectator. At this festival, too, the village square is strewn with flowers, of which the Puharies of the higher hills are very fond, the men rarely passing any without sticking a few in their caps, and the girls in their turbans, or fastening bunches to their ear-rings. Drinking is very common at all festivals, particularly in the higher hills, and many of the men get inebriated. Their liquor is a spirit distilled from grain, fermented with the aid of sprigs of green juniper; it has a very disagreeable taste, but is often nearly as strong as whisky.

"When sheep and goats constitute the chief wealth of the villages, they have a singular custom of once every three or four years uniting all in one flock and racing them round the village. The shepherds first lead the flock round slowly, and gradually increase the pace till they run as fast as they are able, the sheep following them at full speed several times round the village, without one attempting to leave the flock or lag behind.

"Another characteristic national ceremony is chasing and killing a young buffalo bull. Bulls of the milch buffalo, except the few required for breeding purposes, are of no use whatever in the hills; many are destroyed as soon as calved, but others are kept till nearly full grown, and sold to the villagers for this rather cruel purpose. He is first led round the village, then teased and goaded into as mad a state as possible, and let go. After a start of forty or fifty yards, he is pursued by the young men and boys of the village, each armed with his favourite weapon, dangra, Goorkha knife, tomahawk, or tolwar, and striving for the honour of drawing first blood. When the bull is savage and powerful, the chase is very exciting, for he often turns on his pursuers; and if but slightly wounded at first, proves a difficult customer, rushing madly from place to place, first charging one, then another, till, disabled by some well-directed blow, all rush in, and the poor brute sinks literally cut to pieces.

"The marriage ceremonies are simple, and attended with little expense. The relations and friends of the bridegroom go to the house of the bride's parents, remain there feasting for a day or two, and bring her to his or his parent's house, attended by her friends and relations, who, in like manner, are feasted for a few days. A Puharie's constant thought on becoming the father of a boy is where to find a wife for him, and the parties are often betrothed while mere infants. No ceremony is performed at this time, but the Brahmins are asked to examine each child's horoscope, and see that no misfortune is likely to attend the union.

If their **answer is** favourable, a few **rupees** are given by the parents **of the boy to** those **of the girl** as earnest-money. From time to time **other small** payments are made **in money,** cattle, **clothes,** or other valuables, till **the** united **value** amounts to from **twenty to** sixty rupees. **If the** match is broken **off** during this time, **the** money **or its equivalent is** returned without any further expense on either side. When the girl reaches **ten** or **twelve,** and sometimes even at six **or** eight years of **age,** the purchase-money is made up to something **near** the amount agreed upon, and the marriage ceremony takes place, the parents **of the** bride returning a dowry of perhaps one-fourth **of** what they have received, the greater **portion in gold** or silver ornaments for her person. Whatever either party gives is carefully noted down on paper **in** case of any misunderstanding, and some of these papers **are** amusing documents, **in** which much of the selfish, litigious character of the individual Puharie **may** be traced. **The** bridegroom's parents' account will be something like this, copied from **one** handed to **a** phoundar on the occasion of a divorce, and which I had the curiosity to read over:—

Money and Goods (tuka) *paid to Durmoo, of Ritul,* **by Man** *Sing, of Bujoolee, for his Daughter Minah.*

	ru.	a.	p.
Paid in cash, **on** making the proposal and its being accepted	1	0	0
Paid in cash as earnest-money . , .	10	0	0
Paid in cash on his visiting my house . .	1	0	0
A goat	2	0	0
Three sheep	6	0	0

	ru.	a.	p.
Sixteen measures of barley	0	4	0
Ten measures of wheat	0	4	0
Two measures of ghee	0	4	0
A woollen coat	1	0	0
Raw wool	1	0	0
Two measures of salt	0	4	0
A cow and calf	4	0	0
A silver bracelet	8	0	0
Sixteen measures of rice	0	8	0
A turban	1	0	0
Paid to his son on his visiting my house	1	0	0
Paid in cash on the marriage	25	0	0
A pair of gold ear-rings on ditto	16	0	0
Paid in cash on bringing the bride to my house a second time	10	0	0
Paid in cash on his visiting my house afterwards	1	0	0
A new woollen coat	1	8	0
Raw wool	1	0	0
Four measures of salt	0	8	0
Total	92	8	0

"Against which the parents of the bride presented their account as follows:—

Cash and Goods (deige) *returned to Man* Sing *on Account of my Daughter Minah.*

	ru.	a.	p.
Paid in cash to him on visiting my house	1	0	0
Paid in cash to his son on the same	1	0	0
A turban given to his son	1	0	0
Paid in cash to him on a similar occasion	1	0	0
A gold nose-ring given to my daughter on her marriage	12	0	0
A pair of silver ear-rings on ditto	6	0	0
A silver coin for ditto	3	0	0
A pair of pewter bracelets	0	8	0
Fifty measures of wheat	1	0	0
Thirty measures of ghee	3	0	0

		ru.	a.	p.
Two measures of ghee	. . . .	0	4	0
Two ditto, ditto	. . . .	0	4	0
Two ditto, ditto	. . . .	0	4	0
Paid in cash to his son on visiting my house after the marriage	. . . . .	1	0	0
Total	. . . . .	31	4	0

"The marriage had only been celebrated about nine months, or the latter account would probably have been considerably longer, as many, if they have not many daughters, give back in course of time nearly as much as they have received.

"The amount paid for a wife varies greatly, according to the wealth of the parties. From 50 to 150 rupees may be considered as the average extremes, but some go as far as 200 or 300. After the marriage, if the girl is very young, she goes back to her parents' house and resides with them some years longer; and in riper years, until she becomes a mother, often visits and remains with them for months at a time. If, when she goes to her husband for good, she does not like her new home, and cannot be induced to remain, she is taken back to her parents and remains with them some time longer, when, if still unwilling, they either force her to go, or agree to her entreaties for a divorce. If a man wishes himself to divorce his wife, he receives back but two-thirds of the amount he or his parents may have paid, and that not till she gets another husband. If the woman or her friends insist on a divorce, he receives double, or half as much more, as the phoundar may decide;

one half the amount at the time of the divorce, and the remainder when she gets another husband. If young, and there has been nothing unusual in the circumstances of the divorce, a girl seldom remains many months before she is again married, as the grown-up young men whose wives have died or been divorced, or whose parents, from abject poverty or other circumstances, have been unable to purchase them one, consider her by far a more eligible match than a girl of more tender years still with her parents, their only alternative, as there are no grown-up girls that are not, or have not been, married. To have been divorced more than once is rather prejudicial to a woman's character, though some might be found who have been so several times, and their discarded husbands all living. The Puharies in general have but one wife, though some marry two, and even three; but unless in default of male issue, these must be considered as exceptions to the rule. Those who do, lead but a sorry life, continual quarrels being the result, and their partners generally insist on having separate establishments.

"It has been thought that in the hills several brothers sometimes marry but one wife amongst them, who is common to all. This odious practice does exist to some extent in Koonawur and some other states, but is certainly not the case in Gurwhal. The belief has doubtless arisen from the fact that in this, and most other hill countries, a brother's wife is not looked upon at all in the light of a sister, and intimacy with an elder brother's is not considered **at all criminal**. A younger brother's **wife, on** the contrary, **is treated** by most as a daughter-in-law, though some form **an** improper intimacy **with her** also. These amours, however, **except** amongst the lower orders, are not more common than other intrigues. A wife's sisters, again, are treated with **almost as** much familiarity as herself, and intrigues with them, though fined as severely as others by the **authorities,** are not looked upon as so deserving **of** censure by the people themselves; indeed a man would be thought ungallant if he did not **pay some** little attention **to** his wife's sisters. The relationships caused **by** these customs are rather curious. A sister's children only are a man's nephews and nieces, **a** brother's being called sons and daughters. By the same rule a woman's nephews and nieces **are her** brother's children only, her sister's being sons and daughters. A child **calls** its father's elder brothers big fathers; and his younger, little fathers; their wives being its big and little mothers. Its mother's sisters it **also** calls mothers. Its only uncles are its mother's own brothers, and its aunts its father's sisters. Cousins are all brothers **and** sisters, that relationship being unknown, and **there** being no word for it in the language.

"A man never calls his wife by her name, but by that of the village she came from, **or one** derived from it. Thus, a man's wife from **a** village called Ritul would be called by him Ritullee; others Derallee, Deraitee, and so **on**. He will not even pronounce her name, **and** when speaking of any other woman with the same, he intimates the person he is alluding to in some other manner. A woman has the same objection to utter her husband's name.

"The funeral ceremonies are the same as amongst other Hindoos; the body is burnt, and the ashes thrown into the nearest large stream, every village selecting a particular spot for the purpose. The male relations of the departed shave the head and beard as a token of mourning, and for ten or twelve days the family partake of no flesh, oil, or ghee, and no member goes out hunting or shooting. At the expiration of that time an offering is made to the manes of the deceased, and all resume their usual habits. An exception is made in cases of people who die of any epidemic disease, as small-pox, and also of infants, these being buried in the ground, and no public mourning made for them. If a woman, on her husband's death, determines to remain a widow for life, she retains her nose-ring; but if she takes it off, it is a token she intends to marry again. If she has a son, the choice rests entirely with herself, and she generally marries some one who will leave his own home and live with her; but if she has no son, she is obliged to marry again, her purchase-money going to the revenue of the country. A man's property at his death is divided equally amongst his sons. Should he have no male issue, it reverts to the rajah, together with his wife and any unmarried daughters. These are given in marriage as soon as possible, and the sums paid for them added to the district revenue. This is complained of as the greatest hardship of all the rajah's exactions, and no evil is so much dreaded as having no son to avert the possibility of such a calamity.

"Slavery is carried on to a great extent, almost every person in affluent circumstances having a family of slaves, who are bought and sold like any other commodity. Free people become slaves in many different ways; sometimes a man has borrowed money and cannot repay it. The sum, though insignificant at first, amounts in a few years to one which there is little chance of his ever being able to liquidate by ordinary means, interest being never less than twenty-five, and sometimes fifty per cent. When his creditor proceeds to extremities, and he cannot by any other means meet the demand, he himself, or some member of his family, is sold as a slave. Some have become slaves from their parents dying in debt, and in former times many poor people of the lower castes were forcibly taken by any powerful family on some trivial pretence, and kept as slaves. In general the slaves are of the lower castes, but some are rajpoots, and while living in slavery still retain all the privileges of their caste. If inquiry was made, the right of many slaveholders to their human property would be found to be based on the most frivolous grounds; a few rupees' worth of grain furnished by the forefathers of the stronger to those of the weaker party, or something of that kind. As an instance, I found one large family, a man, his wife, and several children, who had become slaves merely by the circumstance of the man having broken the leg of a goat. He was made to pay for it, and had to borrow two rupees for the purpose. This was allowed, most probably for the very purpose, to remain accumulating interest till it amounted to twelve rupees, when he was seized and sold as a slave by the man who had lent the money. The individual who bought him had, besides the work of the family, realized sixty rupees by selling one of the daughters, and it was a quarrel arising from the father's endeavouring to prevent him disposing of another in the same manner that brought the history to my notice. Since the country has been under British protection, the slaves are much better off than formerly, and hundreds of families have run away and settled in the Company's territories, where of course they are at once free.

"Like the inhabitants of most cold, mountainous, and half civilized countries, the Puharies are extremely dirty; dirty in their persons, in their clothes, their cooking, their dwellings, and, in fact, in everything. They will wear their clothes for months without washing, and may often be seen hunting for those little animals whose presence is the natural consequence. Their religion obliges them to wash their hands and face before eating the morning meal, but it is generally what we should call a rub and a promise, and the rest of the body is seldom treated to the same indulgence. Their villages are built without any regularity, and the excrement of cattle accumulated in heaps in front of the houses, while there are no drains to carry off the moisture. In the rains, in bad weather, the mud, filth, and pools of stagnant fetid water in every quarter of the village are perfectly inconceivable, and would, but for the salubrity of the climate, certainly cause some fatal disease.

"Farming occupies the greatest portion of a Puharie's time, the women joining in all its details except actually ploughing the ground, and a great deal falls entirely to their share. Though each family cultivates so small a portion of ground, the labour is far from light; some fields, too rough for the plough, are turned over entirely by hand, and the autumnal crops require weeding several times. The grain must be all carried to the village to be thrashed, except rice, which is trodden and beaten out on the rice grounds; and manure must be carried in baskets from the village to the fields ere seed can be sown, the nature of the ground forbidding the use of even a wheelbarrow. In their leisure hours the lowland Puharies loll listlessly about, and occasionally go out to catch fish, if there is a fishing stream near. They have few games of any kind. In the higher hills, and wherever woollen clothing of home manufacture is worn, they are seldom, except when at actual labour, seen without their spinning machine, the inseparable companion of their spare time. It is used only by the men, and consists merely of a piece of stick a foot long, with a small wire hook at one end, and a round flat piece of wood at the other. The wool, in a long loose coil, is contained in a small basket suspended over the left wrist. A twirl being given to the stick, it is left to spin as long as it will, while the fingers rapidly draw out the wool and keep the thread at a regulated thickness. It is slow work; what a man spins in a day might be performed with a wheel in half an hour. The weaving is performed by two people in just as rude a manner, nothing being used but a few sticks. It takes them several days to weave a piece ten yards long by eighteen inches or two feet wide. In the higher hills almost every one spins and weaves his own and family's clothing; if he has no sheep, purchasing raw wool. The wool of the country is very coarse and short, the sheep being shorn three times during the year, but it makes a strong and durable kind of cloth, almost impervious to the rain.

"Hunting, either singly with the matchlock, or in a body with dogs, is much followed in the higher hills, but more for the sake of the flesh of the animals killed than as a pastime. All Puharies are passionately fond of flesh, which is considered a great luxury, for they cannot afford, except at rare intervals, to kill a sheep or goat, and depend mostly on wild animals for it. In the lower hills, where these are not plentiful, there are many people who do not taste flesh more than once in a twelvemonth. Their cookery is very simple; leaven is never used in the bread, which is in the form of thin cakes baked for every meal, unless rice, or some of the other grains used in a like manner, take its place. Whatever they eat with the rice or bread is called sâg, and with the poorer classes is for nearly the whole year round a small portion of some boiled vegetable from the garden or jungle. Those in tolerable circumstances can add occasionally butter, honey, milk and flesh, but the wealthiest seldom kill a sheep or goat purposely to eat, except one fatted in the house for some months and killed in November, the flesh of which is often made to last throughout the winter. Poultry, which every one might keep without a farthing of expense, they are forbidden by their religion to eat, though eager enough to get hold of forest birds of almost any kind. Half a dozen men and boys in the lower hills will hunt an unfortunate partridge, flushing it from place to place till it allows itself to be taken or knocked down, and divide the flesh with as much apparent satisfaction as more orthodox hunters would share a deer. The other out-door amusements, or labours which partake of woodcraft, besides hunting, shooting, and fishing, are setting snares for muskdeer or pheasants, traps for bears or leopards, or watching a net for falcons.

"The want of games, even amongst children, is a peculiar trait, the Puharies rarely amusing themselves in this manner. In the evening, the older men will collect in the village square to canvass the news of the day, and the younger and women to sing and dance; and this, except at festivals, seems to be their only out-door amusement. Story-telling, as a fire-side pastime, and to while away the long evenings in the forest or when on a journey, is universal. Some of their stories are very like those of the Arabian Nights, and others still more improbable, though scarcely less amusing. The legends of their own hills and romances, woven from the adventures of real characters, sometimes take the place of these. They are told partly in prose and partly in verse, the latter being chanted in a not unpleasant manner. These tales are learnt orally, there being no books in the hills except a few versions of portions of the Shastras or religious works written by the more learned Brahmins, and but few of the Puharies can read. There are no schools, and if a man wishes his children to learn he employs a private tutor, or two or three families engage one amongst them. The course of instruction never extends beyond simple reading and writing, and an attempt at the first rules of arithmetic. The written characters are somewhat different from the Hindoo ones of the plains, and many words in the language being also different, the Puharies cannot read so as properly to understand the works printed in the plains in the Hindoo character.

"The almost total ignorance of medicine has

been alluded to. Scarcely a single natural product in their extensive vegetable world is known by the Puharies to possess any medicinal quality; and, strange as it may appear, they have never learnt what properties are ascribed to the few drugs they collect and take to the plains for sale. They bring from thence spices, and any other thing which the venders can persuade them are medicines, and doubtless often use them in diseases where they prove very injurious. In surgery they are a little more advanced, as they manage to set broken limbs, to cup, and perform other operations, but have no ointments, and do not even know how to make a common poultice, all they use being made from green herbs bruised on a stone, or the simple raw turpentine of the pine tree. The latter is certainly one of the best of poultices and healing salves, but unfortunately they rarely decide correctly when the application of it would be of service, and sores and wounds often get into a frightful state from injudicious treatment. The actual cautery is their best and most universal remedy for pains of almost every description, and they apply it for rheumatism, pains in the side or stomach, liver complaints, and many internal diseases, without the least scruple. Infants but a few days old, if they appear to be uneasy, are at once severely cauterized on the stomach, and certainly no bad effects ever appear to follow such an off-hand proceeding. The general way of applying it is to rub the part with a handful of cold wood-ashes, and then strike it repeatedly with a pin of red-hot iron, something with a rounded point being selected. Another, but more painful, method is to put a piece of lighted tinder on the affected part and allow it to consume entirely away. No one follows the healing art as a profession, but occasionally people come from some other country and travel through the hills as hakeems. As physicians they are seldom much better than the Puharies themselves, and the only surgical operation they perform well is extracting the stone, in which they are very successful. One or two individuals in each large district inoculate for the small-pox, but only when the disease has made its appearance in a village, when an inoculator is sent for, and all who have not been so previously are inoculated with virus from the person attacked with the disease. The operation is a rather painful one, being performed on the wrist with a bundle of needles, as in tattooing. If the disease is in a virulent form, the result, as may be anticipated, is often disastrous, many of those inoculated falling victims to it.

"In the lower hills buffaloes and cows constitute the chief wealth of the Puharies; in the higher, sheep and goats. A man is considered well to do if he has fifteen or twenty of the former, or a hundred of the latter; but the generality have not more than one-fourth of the number. The value of a milch buffalo in the hills is from fifteen to twenty rupees, of a cow about three, and of a sheep or goat from two to four. In some of the lower hills a great number of draught bullocks are reared, which are sold in the plains at from fifteen to forty rupees a pair. The price of grain and other natural products varies in different districts, but the average may be cited as follows:—Rice, 30 seers per rupee; wheat, 50; barley, rye, marcha, kooda, and other coarser grains, from 60 to 80; ghee, 5; honey, 8; oil, 6; and wool, 3. Salt in ordinary seasons sells at Nelang at 20, in Upper Tangnore at 15, and in the other districts at 8 and 10 seers per rupee. Every article, except wool, is bought and sold by measure, a patta, which contains about two seers weight of grain, being the standard, and the largest measure used.

"Bees are pretty generally domesticated in the middle and higher hills, but are rarely seen in the lower valleys. If a little care and management was bestowed on them they would be very plentiful, and might be a source of considerable profit. The domesticated bee in the villages of Gurwhal, and the wild one in the forests, is one and the same insect, and swarms often come from the forest into the houses, and leave the houses for the forest. Those that may be called domesticated are kept in the walls of the houses or outbuildings; but no trouble is taken with them, the young swarms even being left to go where they like, and the only time a Puharie ever troubles himself about his bees or their hives is when he takes the honey. In building a house, or any substantial outbuilding, small oblong apertures are left at intervals in the walls, generally of the lower story, about twelve inches by nine. An oblong piece of board, with a small triangular hole in the centre, secured in the wall while building, closes the aperture outwardly; and a similar board, without any hole, and made so as to be removed at pleasure, serves a similar purpose inside. Six or eight of such hives is the usual number made in a moderate-sized house. Sometimes a portion of the hollow trunk of a small tree, if a piece can be found adapted to the purpose, is made into a hive by closing each end with circular pieces of board, and building it into the wall. All is now left to chance for swarms of bees to take up their abode in the hives. They may all get occupied, or only two or three, or perhaps none. To take the honey, the board which closes the hive inside is taken off, and a piece of ignited dry cow-dung is held inside, and soon fills it with smoke. The bees hurry out, and the combs are separated from the roof of the hive with a knife, and drop into a dish held beneath to receive them, scarcely a single bee being killed. The board is then put in its place, and, as soon as the hive is free from smoke, the bees, which have been during the time clustering to the wall outside, re-enter it. The hives are taken twice a year, in May or June, and September or October, but are sometimes opened to take out a small quantity in the interval. The honey taken in spring is very dark-coloured, rank, and of a disagreeable flavour, while that taken in autumn is white and of excellent quality. In the forest the bees make their hives in hollow trees, and sometimes in the cleft of a rock, and a great many of these wild hives are found and taken by the villagers.

"The only beasts of burthen in Gurwhal are sheep and goats, which are used in most of the hill countries, and throughout the table-lands of Thibet, for the purpose. In Independent Gurwhal the miserable roads forbid the employment of any other animal; but in others ponies, asses, yaks, and bullocks are also used. A good goat, when full-grown, will carry from forty to fifty pounds, and a sheep thirty, and travel ten or twelve miles daily. In these hills a man is required for every fifteen or twenty sheep, as, owing to the extreme roughness of the miserable apology for roads, they often throw their loads, or get them on their necks, and many get pitched over precipices by coming in contact with some jutting rock. They travel from daylight till near noon, when, after a rest, they are allowed to graze the remainder of the day. Where the roads are tolerable one man is sufficient for fifty or sixty, and in the table-lands of Thibet three or four men will take charge of a thousand. There they travel often for two days and nights without any regular halt, the loads not being taken off their backs the whole time. They are then given a rest for a day or two, when another couple of days and nights are devoted to travel, and so on till the journey is ended. The length of time occupied in loading is the reason they are kept at work so long at a time. A thousand sheep, catching and loading, will employ half a dozen men nearly the whole day.

"In the lower hills the dogs are sorry curs, much like the village dogs in the plains; but in the higher, a more powerful breed, originally from Thibet, or dogs brought from thence, are employed to guard the flocks. Two of these are at any time more than a match for a leopard, and a single good one not unfrequently fights with and kills one of these animals; yet the end of almost every dog is being killed and carried off by a leopard. When sprung upon unawares, they have little chance with their powerful antagonist, and are probably rendered powerless at once; but if a dog can once turn and defend himself, the leopard is generally beaten off. The cattle — kine, and sheep, and goats — have to be at all times closely watched, even when near the villages, and notwithstanding every precaution the destruction committed by wild beasts is terrible. Leopards are the chief depredators, but bears occasionally join, and when once one of these animals commences killing cattle, they never cease till destroyed. Wild dogs are seen but now and then, but their visits are generally attended with still more disastrous consequences. A pack will rush suddenly on a flock of sheep, and besides killing a score or two in a few minutes, so terrify the rest that they rush over some precipice, and are nearly all killed or maimed. They attack anything they come across, **and** though **not larger** than a moderate-sized setter, two of them will **kill** a large milch **buffalo in a few seconds.**

"The wild animals of this and other parts of the Himalayas have been so fully described in the *India Sporting Review*, in a series of articles entitled 'Game of the Himalayas by Mountaineer,' and some others, and are now so generally known, that it is almost needless to mention them. However, as these pages may be read by those who have **not** seen these descriptions, and are totally ignorant **of** the animals, a brief notice may be taken of those which come under the denomination of game.

"The largest of the deer is the gerow or burra singha. It is found in the lower and middle hills, and in the Terai, and appears to be the same animal known in the Neilgherries and other parts of India, under the name of samber, and in Ceylon as the elk. A full grown stag stands fourteen or fifteen hands high. The antlers vary considerably both in size and shape, scarcely two being alike. The largest are twelve or thirteen inches round at the burr, and from three feet to three feet six inches in length, but the average is much less. The usual number of tines is three on each antler, but many of the large ones have four on one and three on the other, and some four on each. **The** colour of the animal is dark brown, the hair or fur very coarse, from one to two inches long on the body, and five or six on the neck, forming a coarse bristly mane. In the hills it inhabits **the** forests of every description, but is nowhere numerous. The great oak forests of the interior, and the secluded nooks of the pine-clad hills of the lower ranges, are its favourite haunts. The old stags are generally found singly, and the young ones and hinds in small parties of from three to six, but exceptions to this rule are of everyday occurrence. Keeping in the undisturbed recesses of the forest, and avoiding the thickly-populated districts, they are not so commonly met with as their numbers might lead one to suppose, and but few are killed by sportsmen visiting the interior. At night they sometimes visit the grain fields, the young wheat and barley when a few inches high tempting them most. In winter, after severe snow-storms, they are hunted by the villagers with dogs, and then fall an easy prey, and at any time are easily run down by two or three that hunt well by scent. Fortunately for them, such are rare in the hills, the Puharies not knowing how, or never taking the trouble to train any.

"The serow is a stout-built, clumsy looking animal of the chamois family, about two-thirds the size of the gerow. The large coarse head, long ears, and thick legs, give it something of a jackass-like appearance. The horns are from nine to twelve inches long, slightly curved, and slanting backwards very close to the neck; round, black, and ringed at the base, where they are five or six inches in circumference, and tapering to a fine point. The female, as well as the male, has these appendages. The neck is adorned with a strong bristly mane of long coarse black hair; the rest of the body is a reddish brown, inclining to black on the upper, and white on the under parts. Its favourite habitat is in the dry rocky forests of the middle regions, and a few are found in the wooded ravines and oak forests of the lower ranges. It is a very solitary and recluse animal, moving little about, and two being rarely seen together. It is a stupid beast for a deer, and, when come upon in the forest, not unfrequently stands for some time watching a person's approach before it attempts to move away.

"The goral is the Himalayan chamois, and is numerous from the foot of the hills on all the lower ranges, and on the middle and higher, to an elevation of 7000 or 8000 feet. Though gregarious and several being generally found near each other, and often in company, the movements of each are very independent, and a single one shows no disinclination to be left alone. Where most numerous they are scattered over the hill, one here, two there, another behind the next swell or ridge, and so on, several often getting together. They are found on grassy and rocky hills, and in dry forest where there is not much underwood, the favourite haunts being rocky hills clothed with the kolin pine. The goral is about the size of a domestic goat, both sexes having short, black, slightly curved horns, very similar to those of the serow. The general colour, except the throat, which is white, is brownish grey, the fur about two inches long, and tolerably fine. It is not particularly shy, and being found in such favourable ground, and giving so many chances during the day, it is just the thing for a beginner in the art of deer-stalking.

"The kakur, or barking deer, the muntjack of naturalists, is found in the Dhoon, along the foot of the hills, and like the goral, generally up to an elevation of 7000 or 8000 feet, but is not found so near the snowy ranges. It is a forest animal, but more partial to the wooded ravines and coppices than the great forests. It is rather solitary in its habits, and generally found alone. This deer and the goral, though not perhaps the most numerous, may be called the most common of the Himalayan ruminants, as they are frequently found close to the villages, while the rest prefer the more undisturbed regions. The kakur is of a light-reddish colour, white on the under parts, and the head slightly tinged with dusky grey, the hair throughout short and very smooth and glossy. In size it is rather less than the goral, and very slightly made. The horns are curious, being miniature antlers six inches long, rising from continuations of the skull, which, covered with skin and hair, protrude from the forehead several inches. The male has two short tusks in the upper jaw.

"The musk-deer is occasionally found on the first range, where above 7000 feet high, and on the summits of all the high wooded hills of the interior, but is common only on the spurs jutting from the snowy ranges, where it is general from an elevation of 7000 feet to the extreme limits of forest. It is a solitary animal, and though several may inhabit one patch of forest, each selects a place for itself, like hares in our own country; and a pretty correct idea may be given of the general habits of the musk-deer by saying they resemble hares as much as a deer can possibly do. They are about three times the size, without horns, but the male has two tusks about three inches long depending from the upper jaw. Their colour is a dark grey, inclining to black on the hinder parts, the hair very thick and brittle, each something like a miniature porcupine quill. The musk, found only in the male, is contained in a small pod, between the skin and the flesh, attached to the navel. For two years it is a yellowish milky substance, with a disagreeable smell. When first changed to musk, there is not more than a quarter of an ounce; it increases as the animal grows, till in old males it varies from an ounce to two ounces. The way the Puharies take them is by snaring. A slight fence, a few feet high, and often upwards of a mile in length, is made on some ridge or across the hill in the forests where they are numerous. Openings are left every ten or twelve yards, in each of which a strong hempen snare is set, fastened to the end of a long stick fixed firmly in the ground, and bent down to the opening in such a manner that, when anything tries to pass through, the stick springs back and tightens the snare round its leg.

"The tahr is a species of wild goat found in the middle and higher regions, and is perhaps the most numerous of the wild animals in Gurwhal. It is gregarious, and, with the exception of an occasional old male, is rarely or ever found single, and when one is left so it always appears uneasy till it meets with others. The flocks vary in number from five or six to fifty or sixty, and are larger or smaller as the country is more or less disturbed. It inhabits the grassy and rocky hills, and forest where the ground is dry and rocky. In summer the males keep entirely separate from the females, resorting to a quite different part of the hill, and remain very quiet and secluded, moving about only at night, or morning and evening, and lying concealed during the day in the forest, or in caves and thick bushes. An old male tahr is a noble-looking animal, very stoutly built, and three times the size of the largest domesticated goat. His hair is long and shaggy, particularly about the neck and shoulders, of an ashy colour, inclining to black on the hinder parts. The horns are about fourteen inches long, curved backwards, with flat sides, and ten inches in circumference at the base. The female is not more than a third the size of the male; she is of a reddish-dun colour, and the hair is much shorter.

"The burrell is a species of wild sheep found in this and other parts of the Himalayas on the grassy hills between the forest and the snow, and is common in many parts of Thibet. Like all of its tribe, it is gregarious, and is seldom or never found single, and generally in pretty large flocks. The male is rather less than the tahr, and a clean, well-made animal, rather stoutly built, but beautifully proportioned. The colour is light ashy grey on the upper, and white on the lower parts, with a black breast, and a black line down each side, dividing the grey of the back from the white of the belly. The horns curve outwards, and in the largest are thirteen inches in circumference, and about twenty-four long. The females are half the size of the males, the same colour, but with much less black about the body, and scarce any at all on the breast, and have short flat horns. The hair in both is short, very thick and compact, and brittle like that of the musk-deer.

"These are all the wild animals of the ruminating class found in Gurwhal. Of the feline race, the tiger is sometimes seen nearly up to the snow, but is very rare; it is the same in every respect as the one found in the plains. The leopards are of several varieties. The white one, or ounce, is confined to the snowy ranges, and is very rare. Of the red there appear to be three well-marked varieties — a large dark-coloured one in the middle and higher ranges, preying on wild animals, and generally keeping aloof from the inhabited districts; the common species, which commits such havoc amongst the cattle; and a smaller one, distinguished by the spots being much smaller, more numerous, and less defined, which preys on monkeys, sheep and goats, and the smaller deer. Though so very numerous, leopards are but seldom seen, prowling about chiefly at night, and when out in the day so circumspect and stealthy in their movements that they generally manage to escape detection, crouching behind stones and bushes to let people pass. One will often hang about a village the whole day, and though the cattle by their anxiety and uneasiness denote its being in the vicinity and put the people on their guard, it is rarely seen till it seizes some unfortunate cow, or a sheep or goat.

"The black bear is common on all the lower and middle ranges, and grows to an immense size, being often upwards of eight feet in length, and the fat alone will sometimes load four or five men. In spring they keep in the forests, feeding on roots, grasses, and scorpions, beetles, and other insects, which they find under stones, and occasionally at night trespassing in the fields, and greedily devouring the young green shoots of barley. As soon as the grains and fruits commence to ripen they turn their attention to these, and in autumn feed in the forest on various berries, and at night commit great havoc in the grain fields, which have to be regularly watched. From October acorns form their principal food, and they all resort to the oak forests. This is the proper time for bear-shooting, when it may be followed as an acknowledged sport, as they may then be seen in the trees nearly all day long, while at others finding them is very uncertain. Though generally **fleeing from mankind whenever met with,** the black bear sometimes attacks people from sheer ferocity, **and** many of the inhabitants get fearfully mangled by them. **The face is** almost invariably the part selected by the savage brute, **and** in a twinkling the flesh is completely torn off, leaving the unfortunate victim a frightful spectacle. This seems **to** satisfy the bear, as they never kill a person **outright,** but decamp after thus venting their fury. **I will** venture to relate two well authenticated incidents, serving to illustrate the ferocity of the bear, and the difference **in** character **of** the Puharies of the lower and higher hills. A man residing in one of the villages near Mussoorie had turned shikaree, and bought a single barrel gun to shoot pheasants and partridges for sale in the station. While on a visit to his wife's parents, who resided further in the interior, he went out one **day** to shoot pheasants in a jungle near the village. Hearing something move in the bushes, he crept towards the place, but instead of a bird, as he expected, it was a large bear, and it **no** sooner saw than it rushed at him. Instead **of** saluting it with **the** charge of shot, which at such close quarters would **probably** have killed, or at least turned it, he **threw** himself down with his face to the ground, **and** suffered the bear to bite him severely in several places. It then left him, and when it had got a little distance he got up and started to run. The bear immediately turned and **gave** chase, and the man, perfectly paralyzed with fear, again threw himself down with his face to the ground; but this time the bear turned him over and took his face completely away, cheeks, nose, lips, and one eye, leaving him a frightful and sickening object. The man is still alive, and with his skeleton features concealed in a large cotton wrapper, he follows his usual avocations. Fearing his young wife would decline to live with such an ogre as he now was, he gave some hints of an intention to cut off her nose, and by thus spoiling her beauty prevent any one else from taking her, which so frightened the poor girl that she would never go near him afterwards, though declaring she would otherwise have remained with and done all in her power to console him in his affliction.

"The other rencontre had a happier result, though more of foolish daring than prudent courage was displayed by the actor. Two men, inhabitants of one of the higher villages near the snowy range, went out tahr-shooting with a matchlock. They found a lot of females and killed one, which they covered over with leaves and stones, and went on in pursuit of others, and were fortunate enough to kill a second. This one of them took on his back to carry home, going the nearest way; and his companion went for the other, both agreeing to meet at a certain place where their respective routes to the village would join. The first retained the matchlock, while the other had in his belt a dangra, a kind of light broad-bladed tomahawk, the national weapon of the Perbut Puharies. When he got to the place where they had left the tahr he found it gone, carried away as he thought by a leopard; but, on following the traces a little distance, he found a large black bear quietly making a meal of it. His first thought was to run back to his companion for the matchlock; but reflecting that in the meantime nearly the whole of the tahr would be consumed, he thought it better to frighten the animal way, which he did by shouting and throwing a stone at it. The bear immediately bolted, and thinking all was now right, the man went up to his tahr and began making it up into a load; but, while he was doing so, the bear returned and showed an evident inclination to dispute possession of the prize. Nothing daunted, the man, who prided himself on his strength and daring, again tried to frighten the animal away by shouting and throwing stones, the result of which was a rush by the bear to close quarters; when the intrepid fellow, by a well directed stroke with his dangra, clove the bear's skull down the middle, and laid it dead at his feet.

"Bears devour flesh, either fresh or putrid, whenever they meet with it; but fortunately they seldom attack the flocks or cattle, though, when once one has made a commencement, it never leaves off the practice, and is a great pest till destroyed. Every now and then it comes into the jungle near a village, generally the one where it made its first carnivorous meal, and kills one or more sheep or goats, or a cow or bullock; and, if unsuccessful in the jungle, will often at night come into the village and break into some outbuilding where the cattle are confined. They are seldom suffered to continue their depredations long, as, if not shot, a trap baited with flesh generally seals their fate. The trap is a large triangular framework, constructed of trunks of young trees, and weighted with large stones, which falls on the bear when it attempts to pull the bait from underneath, and crushes it to death.

"The brown bear is common in the higher hills near the snow. It is not quite so large as the black, though some are full seven feet in length; nor is it so savage or ferocious, rarely or never wantonly attacking mankind. In spring and summer it resorts to the grassy regions above the forest, and the green banks and open glades near its limit, feeding on grass and roots; and in autumn remains chiefly in the forest, feeding on fruit and berries. Like the black it trespasses on the grain-fields, and one occasionally turns carnivorous and takes to killing cattle. These last, both black and brown, are almost invariably old he-bears. In winter the brown bear always conceals itself, and probably remains asleep, or in a torpid state, till spring. The retreat chosen is most probably a cave, as no remains of any kind of nest is ever found in the forest. The black bear has the same habit, but it is not universal, many being found roaming about throughout the winter.

"The wild dog is not common, which is a gracious

dispensation of Providence, for if it was, all other animals, both wild and domesticated, would soon be exterminated. The few there are roam in small packs from one part of the hills to another, and except when the bitches have pups, seldom remain in one neighbourhood any length of time. They are the most voracious of all animals; three or four will devour a sheep or a deer in a few minutes, leaving nothing but the skin and a few bones; and so quick are they at the work, that when seen to kill one, it is often completely eaten before the bystanders can get to the spot. Once upon the track of any animal, its fate is almost certain; the only possibility of escape is by its taking refuge on some ledge of rock on the face of a precipice, where the dogs cannot follow, and many animals are incapable of doing this. They hunt wild animals of every kind, as proved by the remains found near their breeding places, but gerows seem to be their favourite chase. There are said to be several varieties of the wild dog in India. The one common to the hills is rather larger than a jackal, of a reddish-brown colour, with shorter and rather coarser fur, short erect ears, and more of a wolf-like appearance. When we reflect on the fecundity of the canine race, and the fact that wild dogs are seldom killed, either by mankind or other wild animals, it seems surprising their numbers do not increase, and there must be some cause unknown to us constantly operating to prevent it. It may be they are subject to some fatal disease; or the young ones, when first hunting with the pack, may get lost, and, unable to hunt for themselves, die of starvation. It is easy to account for the non-increase, or even the gradual extinction of most other animals, for we know of many causes tending to effect it; but with the wild dog all is conjecture, for we know of none except natural decay, which in no case is of itself sufficient to keep the numbers of any animal from rapidly increasing.

"The wild boar is found in the forests of the middle and lower ranges, but is nowhere very numerous. Though the domestic swine is held in such utter abhorrence by all but the very lowest caste, the flesh of the wild is much esteemed by all classes; even the Brahmins officiating at the Gangootree temple, who in strict observance of their creed ought not to eat flesh of any kind, consider it a great treat. Amongst the smaller animals there are jackals, foxes, polecats of several kinds, weasels, wild cats, leopard cats, otters, flying squirrels, and porcupines.

"The game birds are the horned pheasant, commonly called the argus, the moonall, cocklass, cheer, snow, and kallidge pheasants; the snow, wood, black, and chuckore partridges; the woodcock and solitary snipe, and a few quail. All except the last are numerous. The other orders are very numerous, but none have any remarkable peculiarity. The lammergeyer, or bearded vulture, the largest bird of the tribe, most being nine feet across the extended wings, is very common; and of the eagles and falcons there are many large and beautiful varieties.

"Reptiles are not numerous. The boa is occasionally met with, and snakes are common, though most would appear to be harmless, as death from a snake bite is of rare occurrence. Scorpions are very common, and of two varieties, the black and red. The former is found chiefly in the higher hills, where in some places there is one under almost every stone; the sting is not more painful than that of a wasp. The red is not so common, and confined more to the lower valleys; it is very venomous, the sting being attended with excruciating pain. In the insect-world there is nothing remarkable, if we except a few gaudy-coloured butterflies and moths.

"The brief account I have given of the country, if not interesting, will I hope give some idea of what it is like; and if it does not, I can only beg indulgence for any obscurity of style, or omission of detail necessary to have done so. To describe the features of a strange country, and the manners of a strange people, in such a concise form as to give the reader a correct idea of every peculiarity, requires ability of a much higher order than a hunter can be supposed to possess, and I frankly acknowledge myself unequal to the task. Then you should not attempt it, some may say; but if none but those properly qualified to do so gave their recollections to the world, we should know little or nothing of many places which persons of inferior capacity alone are tempted to visit, and the acknowledged axiom, that every little helps, induces me to hope mine may not be considered a mere waste of time and paper. There are many things relating to the country not touched upon, for it was never my intention to attempt giving a full and complete account, but merely to delineate its leading features, so that some idea might be formed, knowing that in a narrative of sporting incidents, the interest felt by the reader is heightened by having something as a guide in picturing to himself the locality of each adventure."

So ends Wilson's description of Gurwhal, and I will now proceed with my own narrative.

CHAPTER VIII.

BEFORE I had parted with Wilson I had received letters from Mussoorie, and a few supplies to replenish the commissariat, and so far my trip had been all that could be desired. In pursuance of my original plan I now turned towards Cashmere, with the pleasant anticipation of having a most interesting journey, for Wilson had given me such a minute description of the route, that I knew where to expect sport, and where there was anything natural or artificial worth going out of the way to look at.

The route led first over the Nela pass into Koonawur. Many years ago I read, in one of the Mofussil papers, a most interesting account of a trip over this pass, by Mr. E. C. Bayley, of the B. C. S. He crossed with some difficulty, as he missed the real pass, and after a night and two days spent in the regions of everlasting snow, reached the other side in safety, but without his tent, which he had been obliged to abandon. None of his party knew the road, and he crossed the ridge at a place several miles above, and nearly a thousand feet higher than the proper pass. I set out under more favourable auspices, and without much likelihood of meeting any such mishaps. The time of year was more favourable, and many of my men knew the route well, having crossed several times. Leaving Derallee, the first march was half way up the Nela valley, and nearly to the verge of forest vegetation, birch and bush rhododendron being the only trees where the camp was pitched. The length of the march entirely precluded the possibility of leaving the road in search of game, but I went on ahead in hopes of seeing something near the camp-ground, it being a very likely place for burrell. One spot passed on the way had a very inviting appearance, and I almost regretted not having made arrangements to encamp on it for a few days, and shoot over the hills around, which are all good for bears, burrell, and musk-deer. It was a large green flat near the river, quite level, with a clear little brook winding through, and adorned with several majestic sycamore trees, just like a park in England. The hill above the camp was a very fair specimen of the grassy region of the Himayalas in summer. It was a gentle undulating slope of considerable extent, with several small rills of water running down in the depressed portions. The snow had not entirely disappeared in the hollows, but in most other parts the herbage was already luxuriant, and flowers were beginning to blossom; in another month it would be a perfect garden. It has a very appropriate name, being called by the Puharies Phoolaldaroo, which means, bank or hill-side of flowers.

I was disappointed in my expectation of seeing

burrell, for a large flock of sheep had been grazing on the hill for more than a week, and the wild animals had been disturbed. Stretching myself on the beautiful carpet of grass where the camp was to be pitched, I awaited the arrival of the Coolies, indulging in a variety of reflections on things past, present, and to come; till, yielding to the somnific effect of the mellowed roaring of the torrent below, and the genial warmth of the afternoon sun, I fell fast asleep, and must have been so upwards of an hour, when one of my attendants roused me up with the intelligence that there was a bear. It was about half a mile higher up the valley, and on the opposite hill-side, now all in shade, busy feeding on a green bank. Fortunately there was a snow-bridge over the river, and without much difficulty we got up within shot, the ground being very favourable for the stalk, as we were out of sight of the bear nearly the whole way. I fired from behind a little knoll, and the first shot rolled it over. It was up again in a moment, and I gave it the other barrel as it went, sometimes rolling, sometimes scrambling down the hill. Without waiting to reload the rifle, I seized the double-gun, and followed as fast as I could; after a chase of about ten minutes coming up to it on the bank of the main stream, when another bullet at a few paces extinguished the little life that was left. In the excitement of the moment I did not notice, when I fired, that there was nothing to prevent the bear from rolling into the stream, which I had the mortification of seeing it do, and in a fair way of being lost, the torrent carrying it down almost as fast as we could walk. After several ineffectual attempts, one of the men managed to get hold of a paw, just in time to prevent its being swept under the snow-bridge, and fastening his waist-belt to it, we soon dragged our prize to shore. On skinning it, we found an old bullet lodged in the neck, which must have been fired at it many months before, as there was no appearance of a wound in the skin.

In the meantime the camp had arrived, and some of the Coolies, who had been spectators of the chase, came running up the banks of the river to give assistance, but we had managed to get the bear out before they arrived. Before going to bed I wrote to Wilson, asking him to stretch and dry the skin for me, and send it the first opportunity to Mussoorie, whither I had forwarded my collection. Fortunately two of the villagers who had come with my camp were to return in the morning, which gave me an opportunity of sending it down; otherwise it would probably have been spoiled, as with the pass before us, we could not afford time to dry it ourselves.

The next march was a long one of sixteen miles to the encamping place at the foot of the pass. This is a little sandy flat, close by a large dirty black-looking glacier, the main one of the valley, alongside which we had walked the last mile of the march. Steep granite rocks rose abruptly from the flat on the north side, and the entire **absence of** vegetation made the place look very dreary; and this appearance was not softened by the only other object near, a small lake of half-melted snow and lumps of ice, which covered one half of the flat. There was nothing to be seen around but glaciers, mountains **of** snow, and bare granite rocks. The men, after arriving, threw down their loads, **and** leaving two or three to pitch the tents, retraced their steps **a** couple of miles down the valley to collect wood, some juniper bushes on the bank side there **affording** a scanty supply, **the** only one within reach. The day had **been** beautifully fine, but as evening closed in clouds began to appear, as if from behind the high snowy hills, and gradually creeping down their sides, **we** were soon completely enveloped. Many were the ejaculations to **the** Deity for fine weather, but fate seemed **to** be against us, and before dark it began to snow. Some of the men found shelter under the rocks, some in the servants' tent, and others I made room for in my own; and while **the** snow continued great anxiety was felt for the morrow. Fortunately it did not last more than a couple of hours, **and** before I went to bed the sky was again clear.

The morning dawned clear and bright, with every likelihood of a **fine** day, and after an early breakfast we started to cross the pass. The tents were frozen as hard as a board, but as the sun was up almost as soon as ourselves, by the time we were ready they were sufficiently thawed to admit of being bundled up. Being rather wet they were much heavier than usual, but I had provided for this by having an extra Coolie to each. I had unfortunately no coloured glasses, but a pair of green gauze, which Wilson had recommended me to send for, were substituted to protect the eyes. A piece was also given to each man. This is a very necessary precaution, as if the day is fine, almost every one who neglects it in crossing these high passes gets snow-blindness. It is said by those who have suffered from it to be very painful, at times excruciating, attended with considerable inflammation, and total or partial blindness. It is not felt at all the day the snow is crossed, but comes on the night following. The men had brought some cakes made of half-dried apricots, considered a good preventive against the " bise," or sick headache, often attending on a few hours' walk in the rarefied atmosphere of these high regions.

On starting we kept for a mile alongside the large glacier, between it and the granite rocks, and then leaving the main valley turned suddenly up the hill, the rocks ceasing, and a steep shingly bank taking their place. It was, in fact, the entrance of a lateral valley. This was the spot where Mr. Bayley lost the road, he continuing right up the main valley; and certainly every one not acquainted with the pass would have done the same. For a mile we had to climb up this steep bank, and very toilsome work it was. The snow which had fallen the night before had nearly all disappeared; but in many places the earth was loose and gave way under the feet, so that at every step one lost half as much as was gained. In other places large stones were equally tiring, one having to leap from one to another or keep getting on and off. It took a good hour and a half to accomplish this mile, for I kept with the men to see that none lagged behind. On reaching the upper edge of the bank we found ourselves on a bed of snow, about half a mile wide, and closed in on each side by steep naked rocks of very sharp outline and very rugged, which rose about 1000 feet above its level. This continued to the head of the pass, nearly four miles, the road being on the bed of snow, which gradually narrowed as we proceeded, till closed by a ridge of granite rock like those on each side, but only free from snow in a few exposed places. The lowest part of this ridge was the crest of the pass. Up the bed of snow the ascent was very gradual, in some places almost imperceptible, and the only obstacles were the chasms in the snow itself. These were numerous, some stretching nearly across the bed, others winding about in different directions. They were from a foot to two yards wide, and so deep that the eye could not pierce the bottom. When one wider than ordinary was met with, we had to walk alongside it till a part narrow enough to cross in safety was met with. Later in the season these chasms would have been far more formidable, for as summer advances they are said to increase in number and size, and some get so wide as to be impassable, obliging the traveller to skirt along them perhaps the whole width of the snow bed. Mr. Bayley mentions having had to bridge several with the tent-poles ere his party could cross. It is these chasms, lyes as they are called by the natives, which constitute the chief danger of a journey across the snowy ranges. The clouds here only discharge themselves in the shape of snow, and from the end of June to September, the rainy season in India, snowstorms are of almost daily occurrence. A moderately heavy fall covers the chasms, so that an ordinary observer would not detect their presence, and the passage across becomes very hazardous. Should any unfortunate individual step on the snow which thus hides the chasms, he sinks through, and his fate may be imagined. Accidents, however, are of very rare occurrence, as, unless absolutely forced to do so, few venture to cross a pass known as dangerous immediately after very bad weather.

After walking along the snow-bed came the last and worst pull, a few hundred yards of steep ascent up the granite ridge which bounded it. I experienced a slight difficulty in breathing, and had to walk very slowly, besides resting occasionally. The Coolies with their loads seemed to feel it very much. They had come along the snow-bed without much more apparent exertion than on an ordinary march, only walking slower and resting oftener; but the ascent from it to the crest of the ridge appeared very distressing. It was certainly not more than 300 yards, but it occupied some of them more than an hour, and they arrived perfectly exhausted. I proceeded with the foremost men, and waited on the ridge till all arrived. It was very cold, and a sharp, piercing wind blew across, its effect doubly increased by the previous warmth the exertion of walking up the hill had produced. It tried one's patience waiting an hour under these circumstances for the hindmost men, who all the while were within hail; but as they arrived, their appearance at once turned into commiseration the slight feeling of anger their tardiness had tended to provoke. A few of the foremost, who arrived with myself and shortly afterwards, were comparatively fresh, and talked and joked in their usual manner, setting up a few stones on the ridge, which they called my "chourie," and for which they said I must make them a present of a sheep or goat, or a few rupees. This is a time-honoured custom when crossing high passes, and they pointed out to me Colonel Markham's, Wilson's, and others, most of which had tumbled down. These men, after a short stay, commenced the descent, together with a dozen sheep which carried our provisions, and which did not appear to feel the slightest effect from the difference of altitude, though carrying upwards of thirty pounds each. Some of the men had not more than forty. Before starting they earnestly entreated me to wait till all had arrived on the crest, in case any might be tempted to give in, for if they did, and were left to themselves, they would probably perish. The later comers, and especially the few last of all, were completely done, and one had but to look in their faces to see their powers had been taxed to the utmost. As they arrived they divested themselves of their loads, and sat down to rest without any attempt at conversation, some being scarcely able to answer when spoken to. Many complained of severe headache and the dreaded " bise." I had partaken of a glass of brandy and some cold tea and biscuit, and felt nothing unusual except the cold; but no doubt there is a great difference crossing a pass with nothing but a stick to carry, and having a load on one's back. I had expected something grand in the way of scenery, but was rather disappointed, as the view was confined by the nearest ridges in all but one or two places. In these the eye looked over a succession of mountain tops clothed with snow, and innumerable glaciers, every ravine and hollow down the mountain sides containing one. It was long after midday when the last of the men got up; the clouds were beginning to collect as on the previous evening, and I was glad enough to quit the ridge. The first few hundred yards it was very steep, as on the side we had come up, but the snow came right up to the crest of the ridge. The men who had loads they could safely roll down set them going from the top, and away they went down the slope to the more horizontal bed of snow below. The tents, my bedding, and some other loads, were despatched in this manner. The men themselves, sitting on the snow, slid down after their loads, and appeared to enjoy the fun, though they shot down with great velocity. Some did it very nicely, keeping as straight and firm as possible, but others had hard work to keep their legs foremost, and one poor fellow was turned altogether when half way down, and went the remaining part head-foremost, causing a hearty laugh amongst his companions. Those whose loads could not be rolled down had to pick their way very carefully, placing their feet in holes cut by the leading men while I was waiting on the ridge. I was inclined to slide down, but when I saw the man turn and go head-foremost, I remembered the proverb, "Discretion, &c." and took the path cut in the snow. There was certainly no great danger, but it looked anything but pleasant shooting head-foremost down an inclined plane of several hundred yards; and besides I had never tried the experiment. After the steep part we got on another nearly level bed of snow, which continued for two miles, and, gradually getting more incline as we descended, terminated in another steep bank to the edge of a vast field of ice which filled the main valley, of which the slope we had come down was but one of many others running down at right angles to it from the ridges on each side. The chasms in the snow were more numerous on this side than the other, and one of the sheep, with its load of flour, had fallen into one of them. Nothing could be done to extricate it, as the chasm was too deep to venture to let a man down with a rope. Two others had, I was told, fallen into another, but it not being nearly so deep, they had been extricated without much difficulty.

The field of snow we had now got on was different from those we had hitherto travelled over. They appeared to be hardened snow, or rather the winter snow was still deep on them; but the vast bed we were now on was dark-coloured ice, with incrustations of earth and lumps of rock in some places, and in others quite smooth and clean, and varied by patches of snow. What, however, rendered it peculiarly striking was that all over the vast bed, which was nearly two miles broad, and several in length, were immense blocks of stone, each perched on a tall pillar of ice. They were of all sizes, many being much larger than my tent. Some, which were flat, had the appearance of immense tables, the supporting column of ice in many instances not being much thicker than one's body, while the slab on it was several yards in circumference. The pillars on which these various-shaped blocks were perched, were from six to nine feet in height, and larger or smaller in circumference according to the size of the stone they supported. Mr. Bayley noticed this phenomenon, and accounted for it very satisfactorily in the following manner:— The pieces of rock, he says, must have been detached from the hill above and rolled on to the field of ice when its surface was nine or ten feet above its present level. From the action of the atmosphere the ice has gradually melted away, except immediately underneath the blocks of stone, where, being sheltered by them, it has retained its former level, thus leaving a column of ice under each. These must have been at first as thick as the stones which sheltered them; but as the sides were exposed to the atmosphere, each column has gradually melted to a slender pillar, and must, from the same cause, continue to waste away, becoming every year longer and thinner, till, unable to bear the weight of the rock, it will be rolled on to the plain, again to become supported by another pillar, formed in the same manner, till the bed of ice is exhausted, or the whole covered for ages by another avalanche from above. Indeed, it is very probable this change had taken place in the interval between Mr. Bayley crossing and myself; for Prince Waldemar of Prussia and suite crossed in that interval, and in the journal of Dr. Hoffmeister no mention is made of the stones being then supported on ice pillars, and the scene is so novel that he could not but have noticed it had the features been the same as when we passed.

Our way was now down this field of ice for nearly three miles, when we came to the junction of this valley with the main one of the Buspa river, the glaciers of each joining and terminating a few score yards below. That of the Buspa was the largest I had yet seen, and, indeed, is one of the largest to be met with in the Himalayas, stretching right across the broad valley, and showing everywhere a bold perpendicular front, several hundred feet in height, and extending more than twenty miles up the valley. The general features were the same as at Gangootree, but the mountains around were not near so grand. Our camp was pitched a few hundred yards below the great glacier, near the river, which, immediately after issuing from its icy bed, was broken into several shallow streams, running in a wide sandy channel. The valley, or rather plain, for it was more than a mile wide, furnished even here a supply of firewood, dwarf willow bushes being abundant — a great blessing for the men, who arrived benumbed with cold, for the afternoon had turned out cloudy and damp, and night was fast setting in before all arrived. No accident had occurred, except to the sheep; but many of the men were suffering from headache, and ere I went to bed I was told that one, who had foolishly taken off his bit of gauze, was complaining of his eyes. I knew of no remedy, neither did the men, and all we could do was to recommend him to keep from the smoke and apply snow. I was very thankful no worse mishap had attended our crossing the pass.

One of the chief sufferers from headache was my cook, who was so bad as to be unable even to attempt cooking my supper; but, thanks to my month's shooting with Wilson, several of my men were now quite at home in the kitchen, and I could easily have dispensed with his services altogether could I have kept my present lot of men. Animals do not appear to suffer at all from the rarefied atmosphere of the higher regions; neither the sheep nor my dogs were the least affected, and the latter gamboled about on the top of the pass, running up and down the hill as at any other time.

Our first work in the morning was fording the river, as it was necessary to cross to get to the road lower down the valley; and the lower we went the more difficult it would have been, unless there was a snow bridge, of which we could not be certain. The water was intensely cold, and, though we were not in it very long, the pain it occasioned made one grin again. The man who had complained of his eyes got quite blind during the night, and was obliged to be led. His eyes were fearfully inflamed and swollen, and he seemed to suffer great pain. He had not completely recovered when I parted with the men a week afterwards.

Two long marches would have taken us to Chitkool, the first Koonawur village, but I made four of it, to have a little shooting. Burrell were very numerous, and I came upon several flocks almost within shot from the path, and succeeded in killing two. Several bears were seen, but on the opposite side of the river, and my travels were near coming to an abrupt termination in an attempt to get at one. I was walking along the second morning ahead of the Coolies, and looking out for a burrell, when a bear was espied feeding on the opposite bank, but too far for a shot from our side. A few hundred yards below the river was bridged over with snow, which seemed firm enough to cross. I ran down to it with one of the shikaries, he carrying the double gun and myself the rifle. It gave way while we were crossing, and both were precipitated into the river and carried down some distance ere we managed to get out, which probably we should not have done at all, had it not, a little below, fortunately spread out into a much wider and shallower channel. How we kept hold of the guns was wonderful; but both did, and the only misfortune we suffered was a good ducking, and having our shooting spoiled till the guns were put in order.

For ten or fifteen miles the Buspa from its source flows in a broad flat valley without much fall, probably not more than a thousand feet in all. The hills on each side are grassy slopes capped with a ridge of snow of moderate height. There are no trees of any kind, as it is above the limits of forest vegetation, but dwarf willow bushes are spread in clusters near the river and over the flat, and juniper extends some distance up the slopes. The valley then narrows and falls rapidly, birch and rhododendron making their appearance, and soon on the left bank form a dense forest. Lower down it again widens, and the fall is less rapid, though still considerable, to Chitkool, the first Koonawur village. Pines first make their appearance six miles above; and opposite the village a fine pine forest extends several hundred feet up the hill side. Six **miles** further **is another village,** Ragchum, and so far the fall is again inconsiderable. The next eight to Sangla it is more rapid, and from thence to its junction with **the** Sutledge about twelve miles, the fall is still greater. Altogether the Buspa has a very straight course of between fifty and sixty miles, and falls in that distance about 8000 feet.

The Buspa valley is one of the prettiest I **saw in** the Himalayas, out of Cashmere. Below Chitkool it varies from a few hundred yards to nearly a mile in breadth; and groves of pines, cedars, walnuts, and apricots, separated by cultivated fields, or plots of rich green grass sparkling with flowers, and little rivulets meandering through all, **make** it a perfect garden. On each side, the hills, clothed for some distance up with pine and birch forest, rise very abruptly, and far into the regions of snow, forming a long line of glistening, fantastic-shaped peaks. In summer the climate is a mean between the dry one of Thibet and the damp one of Gurwhal, and is very pleasant. **In** winter it is said **to** be, and no doubt **is,** very cold, being completely surrounded with snowy mountains, and **the** inhabited part from 6000 to **10,000** feet high. It is **a** very fair place **for** shooting. Burrell are numerous on both sides, from the very head to near the end of the valley. Snow-bears are plentiful, and black ones not at all uncommon. The forests contain musk-deer, and in the lower part, near the Sutledge, are tahr and goral. Snow pheasants are very common, moonalls tolerably so, and chuckores abundant.

At Sangla, I parted with regret with my band of Gurwhal coolies, except the two shikaries, the extreme dearness of food in Koonawur rendering the step absolutely necessary. In Gurwhal we got from thirty to sixty seers of flour for a rupee, while here we only got eight, and a paper was shown to us with the signature of the superintendent of Hill States, authorizing the exorbitant charge. I had been forewarned of this by Wilson, who recommended Sangla as the best place to discharge the men, as from thence there was an easy road to their own country. They had been all the most fastidious person could desire, giving no trouble, and never complaining either at long marches or heavier loads than usual, when I wanted a few to go out with me shooting while the rest were on the march, and we had become more like companions than master and servants. Their pay was five rupees, or ten shillings, a month each, and at parting I made each a present of three rupees, which they had certainly well earned.

The reason given for the exorbitant price of provisions in Koonawur is the comparative sterility of the country; but this, though true in regard to the Sutledge valley above the junction of the Buspa, can hardly be alleged with respect to other districts. The Buspa valley is as productive as any other in the hills at the same elevation, and Chooar, and some of the other lower valleys, are as fertile as any in Gurwhal. If done with an idea of encouraging cultivation, it certainly has not that effect; and in the hill countries, from causes it would not be difficult to explain, it will be found that increasing the price of grain on the spot will rather decrease than increase the amount of land under cultivation. If the Puharies cultivate land to raise grain for sale, they must depend on the real marketable value of the article, and not on the fictitious one the authorities are pleased to put on it. A very good demonstration of the rule may be found in comparing British with Independent Gurwhal. The countries are as much alike as can possibly be, but the price of grain in the former is double, or more than double, what it is in the latter. Yet what is the consequence? Grain is far more plentiful in Independent than in British Gurwhal, or any hill country where the price is kept up by authority; and the inhabitants, though paying higher rents and taxes, are for the most part in better circumstances. Again, British Gurwhal barely raises grain sufficient for its own consumption and that of a few pilgrims and travellers, and a bad season is generally attended with partial famine, while Independent Gurwhal exports a considerable quantity to all the surrounding countries.

From Sangla my traps were carried by the villagers; and, as usual in Koonawur, the porters were nearly all women. This is the custom of the country, and not owing, as might be supposed, to any paucity of the stronger sex. For transporting the baggage of travellers, the mate, or pauree of the village, warns each family in turn to send a member; and even should there be several young men composing it, they always send one of the female members, if any are available. Carrying the loads themselves while the women were unemployed, they would look on as something like putting the horse in the cart, and getting into the harness one's self. I left some very good shooting behind in the Buspa valley, and a few days' sojourn would doubtless have made a considerable increase to my bag; but I was anxious now to push on to the ibex country, as the best time for shooting these animals was fast slipping by.

The first march from Sangla is over the Barung pass into the Sutledge valley. As it is only crossing the angle a little above the junction of the Buspa with the Sutledge, and the ascent is at least 5000 feet, some idea may be formed of the precipitous nature of the country. From the crest of the pass a good view of the Sutledge valley is obtained. It is very different from the green hills of Gurwhal. Nature, besides being in a different dress, looks altogether on a more gigantic scale. The hills rise at once from the river, which is not more than 6000 or 7000 feet above the sea, to 18,000 and 19,000 feet, and the peaks to more than 22,000. The lower part of the valley, on both sides, is composed of patches of dark cedar forest, mingled with grain fields, vineyards, landslips, and immense precipices. Above, **instead of the rich grassy region** found above the forest in Gurwhal, the distant view presents nothing but **apparently dry, arid, brown slopes of bare earth and** rock, capped here and **there** with **a snowy** peak. The extent of country between the forest and the snow is also much greater. The valley, from its turn at **the** confluence **of the** Buspa, **is** entirely **out** of the influence of the rains, and the **character of the** country is gradually approaching that **of the dry table-lands of Thibet.** The climate in summer **is** the finest that can be conceived. This portion of Koonawur is rather unproductive, and in the higher parts the fields all require to be irrigated. Grapes are the chief agricultural produce, and in no part of the world perhaps are finer or better flavoured. There are a great many varieties, and wine and spirit for home consumption are made from them, but the greater portion are dried and exported into Thibet. The inhabitants profess to be Hindoos, but their religion is highly tinged with the Buddhism of Thibet. Those who call themselves rajpoots eat with the Tartars without scruple, though they affect to despise the low-caste people of their own country; everywhere else the Tartars are looked upon as on a par with the lowest castes, or rather as having no caste at all. It is, however, a matter of expediency; the Tartars would be highly offended if they refused to eat with them, and the loss would be all on the side of the Koonawurees, as their trading excursions into

Thibet would then be attended with many inconveniences, and they would lose many a good meal. They certainly deserve credit for thus throwing off the trammels of caste in their dealings with the Tartars, with whom they carry on an extensive trade; but it is a strange anomaly, their still refusing to associate on the same terms of equality with the people of lower caste in their own country.

In their social habits and general character, the Koonawurees are somewhat different from the Puharies of Gurwhal. The passionate love of country and home, such a deep-rooted feeling in the latter, is entirely wanting, and they are rather enterprising travellers, and fond of visiting strange countries. They may be found, as petty traders, between Thibet and Hindoostan, in almost every hill state from Nepaul to Cashmere. The unnatural custom of several brothers having but one wife amongst them is universal; and it reflects little credit on our government, to whom the country is subject, that no attempt has ever been made to induce the people to discontinue the horrible practice. It would certainly be as philanthropical as directing the construction of a new road over all sorts of inaccessible places, taxing the labour of the country to the utmost, when there is already a very good one from the plains to the very confines of Chinese Tartary, quite sufficient in every respect for the present or prospective requirements of the country.

In appearance the Koonawurees are taller, but less robust, than the Gurwhalees, and the men on the whole better-looking; but the women are still plainer, possibly owing to harder work and still more miserable fare. A good substantial meal of even the very coarsest bread is a luxury to the Koonawur women, who subsist chiefly on boiled vegetables and thin gruel, seasoned with dried apricots. The dress of the men is nearly the same, but the women seldom wear anything but a striped woollen blanket, wound round the body in such a manner that the plaits are all behind, confined round the waist by a long belt, and leaving the arms and one shoulder exposed. It is fastened on the bosom with an immense brass brooch, weighing nearly a pound. The head-dress is the same round woollen cap worn by the men.

The next day we crossed the Sutledge, being suspended from a lot of woollen ropes stretched across, and pulled along from the opposite side. The river is here a large and majestic stream, nearly three times the size of the Ganges, and was already very turbid and muddy. Walking up the hill about two miles through fields and vineyards, we got on the old grand trunk-road, a very fair one for such a rocky and precipitous country, and encamped at Powngee, where on the walls of the temple I saw several pairs of ibex horns; magnificent things they looked, and the thought of soon being amongst animals wearing similar made me fairly tremble with excitement. Some of the village temples in Koonawur are very nicely built, and the wood-work curiously and intricately carved. The next march, to Asrung, was a long one of twenty miles, over a high ridge, the Coolies being changed half way. It is in fact two stages, though there is no village on the road, all being lower down the hill. The vegetation above the forest was composed chiefly of odoriferous plants, with here and there plots of grass, and the soil appeared to be everywhere dry and sandy. Near the crest of the ridge I saw several pairs of snow pheasants, and killed one with the rifle. I had almost forgot to mention that, while my traps were being transported over the Sutledge, the Wuzeer, who resides in a village close by, came to pay his respects, and brought as a present a basket of dried raisins and some seeds of the pine tree peculiar to this country, which I saw growing amongst the cedars. He informed me there were two gentlemen residing at Chenee, where a large bungalow has been built, which is generally occupied through the summer by parties from Simla, who think the dry climate will be more beneficial than that of the sanatarium. Chenee is two miles up the hill from the river, and must be upwards of 8000 feet high. The climate is said to be perfect, but drizzling rains are not uncommon; and any place a couple of marches higher up the Sutledge would have been a far more decided change.

The Asrung valley is said to be the best ibex ground in Koonawur, and the number of horns on the walls of the temple fully corroborated the report. Arrived at the village, the tent pitched, and dinner getting ready, I sent for the headman, who came with several others; and judge of my dismay when I found the hopes of having a few days' ibex shooting I had been so long indulging in were to be utterly blasted. He flatly refused to furnish Coolies to accompany me up the valley, and neither promises, threats, nor entreaty could move him in the least. To transport my baggage to the next village, he said, the Coolies would, if required, be ready on the morrow. This was a public duty, and he was ready to perform it, but he was under no obligation to furnish men for a hunting excursion; and he had been told by the authorities he need not unless he liked. What was to be done? I sent my two shikaries into the village in the evening to try to persuade a few men to come on their own terms, intending to leave tent, servants, &c., at the village, and rough it for a few days, but they would not have it at any price. Rather than lose the chance of trying the valley, I at last asked for but one man as a guide, the shikaries offering to carry what few things were absolutely necessary and provisions for a week, but even this was refused. It was evident they were determined to give me no assistance, and were glorying in their power of withholding it. How superlatively provoking! Here I was, close to the ground I had been hunting over in imagination the last fortnight, and for which I had despised some lovely hunting country on the Buspa, willing to pay anything for assistance, and denied it merely to enable the headman to show his independence of a European without official authority; and my vexation increased a hundred-fold by the tantalizing sight of the splendid horns in front of my tent. I halted the next day and sent down to Lipi, a large village lower down the valley, but the result was the same; and after discussing the feasibility of going with only my two shikaries, and coming to the conclusion it would be foolishness to attempt it, I yielded to stern necessity, and gave the order to proceed on our journey. Had the ground been a little nearer, I might have shot over it without assistance from the villagers; but the head of the valley, where at this time of the year the ibex would be found, is two very long marches from the village, and we could not ourselves have taken what things we required and provisions for the time the excursion would occupy.

One reason given by the authorities for allowing the people in Koonawur to charge so high for whatever they supply to European travellers is their poverty; but the refusal of the Asrung villagers to accompany me for ten or twelve days' shooting, at whatever wages they liked to ask, does not impress one with the idea of their being so very badly off.

That evening the camp was taken to Lipi, where the headman, a rather intelligent old fellow, chatted with me till bed-time. He said that the refusal of the Asrung people to go up the valley arose partly from their having been employed at different times by other travellers and not been paid, which had determined them on never going again. I will not insult any English gentleman by supposing for a moment any one would withhold the poor pittance so hardly earned by the hill Coolies, but I would earnestly recommend those who leave this and other money matters entirely to their servants, occasionally to ask, when leaving a village, whether everything has been paid for. It is a well-known fact that plain servants, when travelling in the hills, often keep themselves the whole, or a portion of what they ought to disburse, though not forgetting to charge their masters with it. The blame of course is always laid on the *Sahib logue*, and much ill-feeling towards us is thereby engendered. The old fellow was very sore about the new Hindoostan and Thibet road, which he characterized as a shameful waste of money and labour. "There is," said he, " one quite good enough for all purposes, and here we have been years at work making another, for what you Europeans only can tell; and such a one! Does the Lord Sahib think the rocks are made of soft cheese, that we can cut through miles of it, merely to save a few score yards of ascent and descent? With a reasonable being we might argue, but what — what can be done," continued he, with great earnestness, and tapping a large stone, "what can be done with hard rock?"

This new road was, I believe, projected the year the Marquis of Dalhousie spent the hot weather at Chenee, and no doubt with the best intentions. But for all the trade that can ever pass through the country the old one was certainly amply sufficient, and it must have been strange infatuation to think a better road would produce more traffic, which depends altogether on different circumstances. Besides, as a trading route between India and Thibet, the one through Koonawur is the very worst that could be selected. It is by far the longest; and, whether we look on it as one of the staple articles of import into Thibet, or merely for the requirements of the traders themselves, grain, an indispensable requisite, is very scarce, and, at the price fixed on it by the authorities, is much dearer than in any part of Thibet itself. The route through Kooloo has far greater natural advantages; those through British Gurwhal and Keemaoon greater still; but the almost entirely neglected one through Independent Gurwhal the greatest of all. It is, however, a question whether the trade between India and Thibet can ever be increased to any great extent. The requirement by the latter country of articles that can be profitably exported over the Himalayas is very limited, and of the imports from thence, consisting chiefly of wool, pusmeena and borax, I am inclined to think nearly all the country can produce is already brought. One thing tending to prove that little probability exists of any considerable trade, in excess of what is already carried on, ever being established between the two countries, is the fact, that those who are at present engaged in it find but a precarious subsistence, and most are involved deeply in debt.

From Lipi we crossed another high ridge to Sonam, where I again had an altercation with the villagers. In the route Wilson had given me I was to go from here over the Mannerung pass into Spitee, it being marked four short marches, but they refused to go, and said the regular route was to continue up the Sutledge valley to the junction of the Spitee river, and then up it, which would be several days more. One of their arguments was, I must confess, rather a poser. If we did not ourselves, said they, like to go along the road, why were we obliging them to make it? When I found talking only made them more obstinate, I had the loads all put in front of the Mukeea's house, and putting into his hands a rupee for each, double the usual hire, told him I should start at once myself, and if my things were lost hold him responsible. There was another village on the route a few miles further on, and I proceeded to this, delaying as much as I could on the way, uncertain whether my plan would have the desired effect. Fortunately it had, but whether receiving the money in hand, or knowing himself in the wrong, induced the Mukeea to yield, I could only guess. Probably he pocketed a few of the rupees himself, but whatever influenced him, in a short time the loads were brought up, and the same evening we got several miles on the way.

I said nothing about shooting, but there was a little lateral valley marked on my route as likely for ibex, and this I determined to try. Next morning, with my two shikaries and a villager who had come as guide, and taking a blanket and something to eat in case we should find it necessary to stay out all night, I started early, telling the servants to go on with the camp to the foot of the pass, where I would rejoin them. We kept on the road a little way, and then striking off up the hill, crossed the ridge forming the angle between my valley and the main one, and a little after noon got to the ground. This was easier than going by the river, for the road in one place led a considerable way up the hill-side, and as we could see the course of the valley, it was evident by crossing the ridge we were cutting off a considerable angle. It was left entirely to my own discretion, as the villager declared his total ignorance of the place I wanted to go to, and said he did not think any one had ever been there. We were now near the head of the little valley, but the first sight did not appear very promising. One side was very steep, and entirely destitute of vegetation, being composed of bluff inaccessible rocks and narrow gullies of loose earth and stones, like the dry beds of as many rivers raised from their horizontal to nearly an upright position. Our side was a much gentler slope, still very barren, but in a few places covered with grass and shrubs. Both ridges were tolerably free from snow, except in the very sheltered places, but there was a good deal at the extreme head of the valley, and several snow bridges over the little river. The information I had got from Wilson of the habits of the ibex was now of infinite service. On looking about where the grass was most luxuriant, we found very fresh traces of ibex, some of the dung being scarcely dry, and there being no likely places on our side, it was more than probable those that came here to feed retired during the day to the rocks on the opposite side. We chose a favourable place among some large stones, and sat down quietly to watch. With a couple of cheroots and an hour's doze, the time slipped away, and the sun at last sinking behind the steep hills, the side we were watching was left in shade. I had looked over it several times with the glass without making any discovery, and another hour passing without any animals appearing, our hopes gradually sunk; but at length I had the extreme satisfaction of seeing a lot of ibex appear as if by magic in one of the gullies near the top of the ridge. The ground was of a dark red colour, and the ibex showing quite white, they were plainly distinguishable with the naked eye, though at a great distance from us. There were five of them, and the glass revealed all to be magnificent old males, with splendid horns. What an evening of excitement was before me! It would be hard to find the man with whom I would just then have exchanged situations. For some time the ibex moved very slowly, though coming gradually lower down, and I began to fear they would not cross to their feeding ground till too late. Soon, however, they moved faster, and at last fairly came down at full gallop, throwing up a cloud of dust in the narrow gully. As they approached the stream the swell of the ground on our side hid them from view, for we were nearly 200 yards up the hill-side, but it was evident they were making for one of the snow bridges, which they would cross to come up to the grassy slopes. We had previously calculated all the chances, and running quickly a hundred yards further to our right, we were again ensconced amongst some large stones which the ibex would have to pass. My heart beat so just now with the excitement and the running, that had they come up at once I should certainly have made a mess of it, but whether they had stopped at the river, or were moving very slowly, half an hour elapsed ere they made their appearance. I could only see about half way down to the stream, and dare not expose myself by going to look, for fear I might be seen, and the intense excitement and suspense were almost painful. At last the majestic head and horns of one appeared, and in a few more seconds all were in sight, coming slowly up the slope a little to our right, and they would pass within thirty yards. They were even now within 120. I was laid with one man behind a stone which fully concealed us, the rifle was slowly presented over another rather lower which leaned against it, and I had a fair scrutiny of the five noble beasts as they came slowly forward. They were now within eighty yards, and coming nearer and nearer. Shall I fire, or let them come on? The stock is to my shoulder, the barrel resting over the stone, and my elbow on the ground. I cannot miss such a deliberate pot, and they may discover the danger. The sight bears against the shoulder of the second, which appears to be one of the largest, and it is now within sixty yards, and a raking broadside shot. The trigger is pressed, the deadly messenger speeds on its way, and the noble ibex is floundering on the ground. The second barrel is fired at one of the others as they go off at full speed across the flat, but the singing of the bullet as it glances from a stone tells it has missed. But what of that?— one is down, and perfectly satisfied I ran up to the prize, and surveyed with intense satisfaction the splendid animal. The ball had struck him in front of the shoulder, and passed out at the opposite loin, a sure and fatal shot. He was a very large one, and I have nowhere seen a finer pair of horns than the one this, the first I had ever shot at, possessed; they were measured when I got to camp, and found to be forty-five inches in length, and thirteen in circumference. The skin was of no value, as a great portion of the winter fur was gone, and it came off in large flakes, leaving only a little very short hair underneath. The stuffed head, however, made a magnificent addition to my collection.

It was now getting late, and time to think about where to pass the night; and as soon as the ibex was skinned and cut up we got to the river, and went down it some way in hopes of finding wood. Its only shape, however, as far as we got, was in prickly bushes, which yielded none thicker than one's finger, and a few stunted willows; but the ground being too dangerous to venture over in the dark, we chose a snug corner, and collecting as much as we could, prepared to bivouac. With what I had brought, and the kidneys, and a portion of the heart and liver of the ibex roasted in the embers, I made a very good supper, and the men ate to their hearts' content. Roasted in this manner in small pieces on the embers, the flesh, though very lean, was palatable, and much better than when cooked in any orthodox way. It did not turn out nearly so cold as I expected, and wrapped in my blanket I slept very comfortably till near day-break; and as soon as it was light enough to see we started for the camp, which we reached about 11 o'clock, finding our valley a horribly awkward place to get through, the banks being in many places almost perpendicular, and composed chiefly of loose stones and shingly rock.

It was too late to think of crossing the pass, but at the suggestion of the guide, the camp was taken a few miles further up, each Coolie taking a little wood, which materially lightened the labour of next day. The little flat we encamped on was under the last great ascent, and probably 15,000 feet high. Not a vestige of vegetation was near us, but the scenery was very different from that near the foot of the Nela. There nearly all was snow and steep granite rocks, and every ravine contained a glacier. Here the prevailing characteristics were steep shingly slopes, rugged masses of bare rock, and narrow gullies of loose earth and stones. The hills, though higher, were comparatively free from snow, and these gullies in similar situations on the southern face of the Himalayas would have been filled with glaciers. There was one in the main valley — in fact our camp was pitched on it — but it was so deeply covered over with earth and stones, that, but for the ice showing itself in a few places on the steep sides, it would not be noticed or distinguished from the other slopes and ravines. We were in the sterile region between the limits of vegetation and perpetual snow, which is of greater extent the further we get, towards Thibet.

The ascent to the crest of the Mannerung pass is steep and a very trying pull. The first part is up the hill-side, over rock and shingle, and the rest up a narrow ravine or hollow, the greater part of which is snow. There is no gentle slope, or a few score yards of level ground, which would be a great relief, but all is one continuous ascent of, from where we were encamped, four miles.

We arrived at the summit soon after noon, and notwithstanding the greater elevation, the Mannerung being 18,500 feet above the sea, neither the Coolies, myself, nor servants, were half so much distressed as on crossing the Nela. This I attributed a great deal to our having come so far up the evening before. One half the Coolies were of the gentler sex, and I really felt ashamed as I saw them toiling up the steep ascent, but there was no help for it, and far from being less capable of the severe exertion, they appeared to feel it even less than the men. It was some comfort to think that all my loads were very light, 40 lbs. being the maximum. One buxom lass particularly attracted my attention; she laughed and joked nearly the whole way, and seemed to be chaffing some of the rest, but as she spoke in the Koonawur dialect, High Dutch to me, I lost the benefit of her lively discourse.

There was a little round space free from snow on the ridge, and I threw myself down for a rest after the fatiguing pull, but in a few minutes was very glad to jump up again. The shingle was so hot I was fairly roasting. Surprised at such an unlooked-for thing in a place where one would expect it to be almost freezing, I had the curiosity to take out my thermometer and lay it down on the shingle, where the sun's rays fell directly upon it. It went up to 130°. This I found to be often the case in Thibet on the highest hills. In certain situations, though the air is quite cool, the stones, particularly the black ones, get so warm that it is very unpleasant to sit down on them. Amongst the shingle I found several small fossils, and having some time before been conversing with my shikaries about the deluge, and the waters having covered even these high hills, I directed their attention to the circumstance as proof of what I had told them. I am not, however, certain whether I succeeded in persuading them that these were really the remains of marine animals, for Blackey will often pretend to believe if he thinks it will please 'master; and though I doubt whether mine had heard the line of Sadi,— " If the king at noonday says, It is night, declare that you see the moon and stars," it would not have been difficult to make them profess belief in the same fossils being the fingers and toes of the old man of the sea, who clung so lovingly to Sinbad's neck, and whose body was doubtless after death committed to the deep by that renowned sailor.

From the pass there is a fine panoramic view of the Spitee valley, and the hills at its head and on each side. A strange expanse of rugged barren hills, sterile slopes, and as sterile looking ravines. The descent was for a couple of miles on a glacier, the termination of which was so steep that we wandered about for some time ere we found a place to get down. The vegetation seemed to extend higher on this side (the north) than the other, and soon after getting down to it we encamped near a small lake. Wood was very scarce, but this would now be the rule in the country I had got into. We had passed some very likely-looking ground for ibex, but there were no traces of them, and the Coolies declared they had never seen any on this side. A pair of snow pheasants were the only things I saw crossing the Mannerung.

The next morning at breakfast time we got down to Manna, the first village in Spitee, and I found that I should, as I had much feared, be at a loss for an interpreter. Wilson had warned me of this, and I tried hard to get a man in Koonawur, but though they can all speak the Tartar language, I could not prevail on any one to accept service. We did well enough this day while the Koonawur Coolies remained, but when they left we were in what a Yankee would call "a pretty considerable of a fix," for our new friends could not speak a word of Hindoostanee, and we were just as proficient in their language.

CHAPTER IX.

THE Spitee valley, with another called Penee joining it, fell under our rule, with Kooloo and Lahool, on the cession of the Jullunder Doab, after the first Seikh war, thus for the first time including Tartars as Company's subjects. A full description of it may be found in Moorcroft's Travels. We got on better on our journey through than I anticipated without an interpreter. My men learned the names of the articles daily required, and the villagers came themselves to transport the baggage, but, as may be expected, some laughable mistakes occurred. As well as I could judge, the people appeared in tolerably comfortable circumstances, and very glad at the change from Seikh to British rule. The aspect of the country was to me very sterile, but no doubt to one accustomed to the dry arid regions beyond the Himalayas it would have appeared as comparatively fertile. The river, one of the head streams of the Sutledge, runs in a wide sandy channel, in which are occasional groves of willows and plots of grass. In a few places the hills rise at once from the river, forming a narrow gorge; but in general a gentle slope, in many places reduced to nearly a level plain, extends from a few hundred yards to a mile on each side. This is a sandy track, in most places giving birth only to a few thistles and scattered tufts of coarse grass; in others covered with rose-bushes and other prickly shrubs, and where a stream from the hill above can be made available, portions are irrigated and made into fields. Wheat, rye, barley, and buckwheat are the grains cultivated, all being sown in spring, and the crops are very luxuriant, equal to those of any other country. There are no trees, except a few fine poplars and willows planted near the villages, and a great portion of the summer's labour is collecting fuel for winter. Where willow is scarce, the rose-bushes and other shrubs are cut while green, and stacked on the roofs of the houses to dry. On the hills, a scant but remarkably nutritive vegetation on the more favoured spots affords sustenance to the sheep, goats, yaks, and ponies the people possess, but the greater portion is entirely barren. None of the peaks are of extraordinary height, the generality being from 18,000 to 21,000 feet. The valley is between 13,000 and 14,000.

Four days took us to Keewar, the last village on the Ladak route, where we met a party of three travellers, officers of the Company's army, *en route* from Cashmere to Simla. We could not give each other much news, for it happened their last papers from the Punjaub, and mine from Mussoorie, were of the same date, but we spent a very pleasant evening together. They had not done much in the way of sport, indeed did not profess to be sportsmen, but, like most others who shoot at all, had killed a few bears in Cashmere. Besides a Sepoy from Ladak, whom the governor of that place had sent with them, they had two other men who spoke Hindoostanee sufficiently well to interpret; and on my mentioning the fix I was in, an arrangement was soon made by which one of them was transferred to my service. This was very fortunate, as without any means of communion with the people I should either have had to forego my shooting altogether while amongst the Tartars, or send to Ladak for an interpreter.

When we were to start in the morning an altercation took place, or rather was renewed, for it had been in discussion the evening before, whether my traps were to be transported over the Parung la into Rupsha by the Spitee people or by the Tartars who had come from that place with the other travellers. The latter contended it was the duty of the former, which in reality it was; but as soon as I thoroughly understood the bearings of the case, I settled it by showing the leader of the Rupsha band my loads, now reduced to sixteen, and putting into his hand twenty rupees, as hire for ten days, telling him I would gladly pay whatever else was necessary while I remained in his country. It would have been fairly throwing money away on his part to have refused, as, employed or not, they must go back to their own country. My traps were accordingly transferred

T

to them, and soon packed on their yaks, and I was offered a pony to ride when I felt inclined.

The animals being tired, at the request of the chief, who appeared an intelligent, obliging man, I made a short march of a few miles, and in the evening went out and killed a female ibex, out of a flock of some twenty, found a couple of miles from camp. The next march was also a short one, to the foot of the pass, and I went out in hopes of seeing male ibex, but could find no traces of them. Crossing the Parung la in our altered way of travelling was an easy matter, though it is one of the very highest, being fully 29,000 feet. Commencing at nearly 16,000, the ascent was not much felt, and I rode part of the way. There was very little snow on this side, and the road was over shingle and barren rock. The first part of the descent was over a bed of snow, nearly level for a mile, and then down a narrow and steep ravine into a valley, compared to which the Spitee one was a perfect garden, and down which we continued travelling two days. The hills on each side were the utmost one can conceive of sterility. There was very little vegetation either on them or in the valley, and no traces of wild animals, and scarcely even a bird was to be seen. As nothing else was to be done, I tried to pick up a few words of the Tartar language, and, with the help of the interpreter, conversed with the chief, and got what information I could about his country, and the one I intended to visit further north. The Rupsha

Tartars I found a very willing, good set of men, and we were soon very good friends.

Emerging from this sterile valley we came into a much wider one, or rather a large plain, some parts of which were swampy, and grass luxuriant. Here were some large birds, which I could not make out, but on shooting one, found they were a species of eagle. Ten miles further on we came to the banks of the Choomarera lake, which fills the upper part of this valley. It is a fine sheet of fresh water, about twenty miles long and five or six wide, and its clear blue waters impart a certain charm to what would otherwise be a dreary scene. There were a few wild ducks and geese, and flocks of a kind of gull, all very wild; and here I first saw the wild horse, walking up to about 300 yards of a couple, but they would not allow of a nearer approach. I looked into the lake for signs of fish, but saw none, and the Tartars assured me there were none in it, a rather unaccountable circumstance, as I found some in a small stream running into it. My interpreter had been describing the lake to me the day before, and amongst other things said the water boiled up when any one approached it. This rather puzzled me, till I found he alluded to the waves dashing on the shore, which he did not seem to understand was occasioned by the wind. May not many other improbable stories of strange countries told by ignorant people be capable of quite as simple a solution. The hills around are of moderate height, with the usual look of utter sterility the Thibetian hills present, and of a gentler slope and more rounded outline than those we had hitherto met with. A few peaks were capped with snow. The Choomarera lake is nearly 15,000 feet above the sea.

For two days we travelled along the banks of the lake, and then leaving the Ladak road, crossed a low hill, and passing another small sheet of water, got to the head of a stream running down to the Indus, being guided by a sketch map Wilson had made for me. A few wild horses, and now and then a hare, and a few marmots, were the only wild animals met with. To enable me to roam over the country with more facility, I determined now to send my two plain servants with the heavy baggage to Ladak, to wait for me there; and on selecting whatever I thought necessary, I found I could manage very well with five loads, including one of the tents. As these could be carried by two yaks, I found myself quite as comfortable as I could wish in such a country. Shortly afterwards we passed the Pooga borax mines, and I called a halt and went up the valley to examine them. The borax is found at the bottom of the valley, which is about four miles long, near the little stream that runs through it, and appears on the surface of the ground in the little open places between the tufts of grass. The dirt on the surface is scraped off, and the borax lies beneath from one to three inches deep, in appearance like damp discoloured lime. It is collected and dried in the sun, and transported into Kooloo and Koonawur by the traders of the two countries, from whence it finds its way into the plains. The supply, though limited in quantity, is inexhaustible, as it is renewed yearly in every place from which it is taken. The Tartars themselves never collect any, but receive something from the traders for allowing them to do so, as the mines belong to Rupsha. There were a great many people of both sexes at work collecting, and from inquiries I made, some 5000 or 6000 mounds of the crude borax must be taken from this place every year. In the stream fishes were plentiful, and while walking back to camp a large hawk pounced on one about two pounds weight, and was bearing it away, when a shot from the rifle caused it to drop the fish, which I had to supper. From this place we followed the stream, through a narrow valley full of willow bushes, for about ten miles to the Indus, encamping at the junction.

A long march up the solitary banks of the river brought us opposite Neema, where the Rupsha Tartars were dismissed and the yaks changed. To-day I noticed a very remarkable phenomenon. I was walking quietly along about a mile in front of the men on a perfectly level plain, which extended from the river to the low hills, when I thought I heard voices a little distance behind, and turned round to see who it was had come up. Much to my surprise there was no one, and the voices I heard were those of the men, which, from some peculiarity of the place, were distinctly heard this amazing distance. I walked on, and for a mile continued to near the men conversing as plainly as if they had not been more than twenty yards distant.

Rupsha is an elevated district in the Ladak provinces of Goolab Sing, inhabited by a tribe of wandering Tartars, who have no villages, but live always in tents. The ground is everywhere too high for cultivation, and they are entirely a pastoral people, rearing large flocks of sheep, goats, and yaks, and bartering the wool and other produce for what grain they require. The general features of the country are low, rounded, stony hills, the valleys between sometimes narrow, and sometimes forming undulating plains many miles in extent.

We crossed the Indus on a raft supported on inflated skins; but the river was fordable, as the raft was pushed across by two men, walking sometimes up to the neck, and sometimes not above the knees. The current did not seem to run more than two miles an hour. We then had a march down the other bank to nearly opposite the place where we first came to the river; and then crossing for three days a very irregular range of hills, about 18,000 feet in elevation, inhabited by another tribe of pastoral Tartars, we came to the Chooril lake. This is said to be eighty miles long, and where we traversed its banks it is from three to four wide. The water is slightly salt and beautifully clear. The lake is at an elevation of little more than 13,000 feet, and a few small villages and grain fields occur at intervals along the bank. Just before reaching it there was a wide swampy plain, where the grass was very luxuriant, and on it I saw a very large blue bird, apparently of the heron tribe, but much larger than any I had ever seen of that family. I tried hard to get a shot, but it would not allow me to approach nearer than 200 yards.

Skirting along the bank of the lake for ten or twelve miles, and rounding its western end, and then for six or seven miles up a stream that ran into it, we found another tribe of pastoral Tartars, and I pitched my camp near them. These were the last we should meet with owning allegiance to Goolab Sing; and to them I had to trust to take me to the ground Wilson had recommended me to shoot over. The hills here were marked in his sketch as good for *Ovis Ammon*, and I determined to spend a few days in search of them before proceeding further. The first thing was to get on good terms with the Tartars, so as to secure their hearty co-operation; and I found no great difficulty in doing this, for they appear to be a good natured, obliging race. For a trifling consideration they agreed, while I remained to hunt near, to furnish me with a couple of men and a fresh pony every day; and to my inquiries about Ovis Ammon, replied we should assuredly find some, but that they were very hard to get at. There were about twenty families of Tartars encamped at this place, and when at home I spent a good deal of my time amongst them. At first they were rather timid, but we soon got quite friendly, and they always gave me a kind welcome; though, if the truth must be told, I am afraid my visits were to them rather troublesome. When I approached, the first thing they did was to drive away all the dogs, and very often some calf tethered near the tents, affrighted at my appearance, would break loose and scour away over the plain, followed by the children. Their tents were made of black woollen cloth, rather low, and open at the top to give exit to the smoke. Much ingenuity was shown in the way they were made and pitched, so as to make the most of the slender sticks which served for poles. The women appeared to be always busy, either engaged in domestic concerns or weaving. Their dress consisted of a long woollen coat, striped red, blue, and yellow, and confined round the waist by a red woollen belt. All were without head-dress, and wore their hair parted down the forehead, and falling over the shoulders in a great number of small plaits. The men wore a long woollen coat of red or undyed wool, and cloth boots secured with a garter below the knee, but no unmentionables. Some few were bareheaded, but most wore the black Ladak woollen cap hanging down on one side. This is the general dress of the Tartars, except that in the Chinese territories the men wear hats more like a wideawake, if they cover their head at all. Their ornaments are chiefly turquoise and coral, and some of the women wear for bracelets enormous sea-shells.

In the little stream that ran past the camp were lots of fishes, and I soon found out an excellent way of catching them. Selecting a spot where the stream was very narrow, I took one of our baskets and held it down in the water, sending a couple of men to wade down from a little distance above, making as much row as they could. The fish came before them in a shoal, and when a good many had got into the basket I lifted it sharply up, securing sometimes twenty or thirty at a time, from a few ounces to a pound in weight. They were a species of trout, and excellent eating. Strange to say, the Tartars look on fish as unfit for food, and never eat of it.

I remained here shooting—trying to shoot would perhaps be nearer the truth—for more than a week, having a day's rest occasionally, for it was very hard work. The first day I went out very early with one of my shikaries, the interpreter, and two Tartars. The hills were not very high, and I could ride in most places. We went for five or six miles up one of the numerous valleys, low, gently sloping hills on each side, and the dry bed of a watercourse at the bottom. Seeing nothing in this, we crossed the low range of hills at the head into another similar valley, and soon espied five animals which the Tartars pronounced to be Ovis Ammon (naheen). They were upwards of a mile from us on the open hill-side, and the question now was how to get at them. The Tartars could suggest nothing, so the stalk was left for myself and shikaree to manage. Leaving them with the pony we retraced our steps a little, and getting over the ridge we had just crossed, went behind it till directly over the animals; but on descending the slope till they came in view, we found they were still 500 yards off. I looked at them through the glass and made them out to be females, and after a careful scrutiny of the ground thought I saw a way to get a tolerably decent shot. A little further on was a slight depression in the ground, running from the ridge right past them, and if we could get unseen down this we should be within range. For a little way we went on all right, but soon found that even when crawling on all fours we were sometimes unavoidably in sight. There was no other way, however, and on we went, though progressing very slowly. For a dozen yards or so we would be completely screened, and then for a few more partly or wholly exposed. We had passed several of these places, and I began to have hope, but it was of no use; when about 400 yards off we were seen, and the naheen set off at full gallop, going like racehorses for half a mile, when they stopped a little, and then off again over the next hill. This was only what I expected, for Wilson gave me one decent shot out of every three, and one good one out of every half dozen attempts at stalking. Some hours afterwards we found another lot, and as there was no chance of a stalk I attempted a drive, but they went off in a quite different direction from that where I had posted myself.

The second day was not attended with any better result. We found a large flock of females in one place, and three fine old males in another, but in both cases, from the open nature of the ground, the stalk was a failure. On our return home we came across a troop of wild horses, and at the earnest request of the Tartars, I shot one, though not without difficulty. After several ineffectual attempts to get within decent range, and following them two or three miles, I fired at 250 yards and broke the leg of one, which we did not get till after a long chase and three more shots. The Tartars eat the flesh of the wild horse, and as they cannot afford to kill many of the domesticated cattle, the skins are always very acceptable to make leather for their boots.

It is the open character of the ground more than the natural shyness of the animal that makes Ovis Ammon shooting so difficult. Here, and in almost all other places where they are found, the hills are of a rounded form, something like the moors in the West of England, but almost as destitute of vegetation as the king's highway, and in most places an animal has a clear view several hundred yards in every direction. There are of course places better adapted for stalking, but one may wander about for days and not be fortunate enough to meet the game on them. In pursuit of such a magnificent beast, however, to a thorough sportsman this difficulty only increases the excitement, and day after day, from morning till night, he will pertinaciously tramp over these barren hills, content with one good chance in a week. The sight of an old ram will instil fresh vigour into his flagging energies, when several blank days have almost disgusted him with the hard work; and when perseverance is at length rewarded, and he runs up to a fallen beast, lifts up his enormous head, and surveys the ponderous horns, he may rest assured that he has gained the highest step in the art of deer-stalking. Unless by some extraordinary good fortune they are come upon in a place favourable for stalking, the Ovis Ammon is undoubtedly the most difficult of all animals to approach.

The third day I was more successful. A flock of fifteen females was discovered near the top of one of the long low ridges, and when I ascended from the opposite side and looked over, I found myself within decent range, as I thought, about 120 yards; but on stepping it afterwards, I found it 160. How carefully I presented the rifle, lying at full length on the rounded crest, and selecting one of the nearest, fired at its shoulder. All were off at full gallop in a moment; and springing up, I fired the other barrel almost at random into a cluster of five or six, before they got very far, and luckily hit one in the neck, rolling it over dead. Eager enough to see what they were like, I ran up, and found, instead of a female, a young male, probably a lamb of the previous season. Going to the spot where the first one had stood, and following the direction I fancied it took, we soon found blood, and so plentiful, there was no difficulty in tracking it onwards. About a mile from the spot, we found the animal standing alone on the hill-side, but it also saw us, and was off again at a very respectable pace, and led us a chase of at least five miles ere I succeeded in getting a second shot. At last we saw it lie down, and I managed to creep up within eighty yards, and shot it through the neck as it was getting up. It was a fine old female, with horns twenty-six inches long ; a very good specimen, if I could get a male to match. Leaving the Tartars with the pony, to take the two to camp, I went home with the shikaree in another direction, and we came across five old rams ; but I was almost beside myself to find I could not get nearer than 300 yards. I waited for a long time behind the stone I had crept up to, in hopes they might feed in my direction, and not daring to venture further ; but as there seemed no chance of their doing so, and it was getting late, I tried a shot. I had practised a good deal at the camp at long ranges, and shot pretty well, but it is very different firing at a mark 250 or 300 measured paces, and at an animal which you think is that. I put up the sight for 250, thinking that was about the distance, but the ball struck low, and on stepping it, I found the animal I fired at was 315 paces. The difficulty of judging distances correctly in these regions, is one great obstacle to shooting well at long ranges; and the gunsmith who invents a rifle to shoot point blank 200 yards, will confer a much greater obligation on the sportsman than those who make rifles to shoot 1200 with high sights.

Two more blank days followed; but the next I managed to circumvent three fine old rams, and got an excellent shot. The ridge below which they were feeding was rocky in most places, and as the Ovis Ammon avoids such, it was probable they would, when disturbed, cross it at one of the open parts. I posted myself in one of the most likely, and the Tartars went round and showed themselves in the opposite direction. As luck would have it, the animals came right up, a magnificent old fellow leading, and offering a splendid shot at not more than eighty yards. At the crack of the rifle it plunged forward a few paces, and rolled over; and in all my experience of shooting, I certainly never felt such intense satisfaction as when I saw it do so. Its companions went off at such a pace that I did not get a second shot. Running up to the fallen one, I gazed with delight on the long-coveted prize. It was indeed a magnificent beast, and though not perhaps one of the largest, as good a specimen as a person could desire. The horns were twenty inches in circumference, and three feet eight inches round the curve.

I had now been here ten days, and had hunted six, and hard days' work they were, for, except on the last, we were never home until long after dark. I considered I had been extremely fortunate in getting three specimens of Ovis Ammon, and one such a fine ram, and now decided on going on, after one more day's halt, to allow the Tartars to get ready, while I carefully preserved the ram's head. We had been very comfortable at this camp, and wanted for nothing, the Tartars supplying us with everything we could require; while, in addition, the flesh of the wild sheep was excellent, and the stream at the tent door afforded a dish of excellent fish obtainable at any time in a few minutes.

CHAPTER X.

The country where Wilson had directed me to go to in search of the Thibetian antelope and wild yaks was four or five days' march further north, and as it was uninhabited, it was necessary to take supplies with us for the whole time we might be away. The Tartars managed this, and we started with four yaks and about a dozen goats, including two milch ones, which the chief added that I might have the luxury of milk to my tea and coffee daily. As a favour he begged I would dispense with a pony, saying if I rode the same one every day over the stony hills, where there were no roads, it would get lame, and be more trouble than service. Three Tartars, the interpreter, the two shikaries, and myself, formed the party. Crossing the hills I had lately shot over, we got into a valley which led to a tolerably large river, running in a wide sandy channel, which I saw by the map was a branch of that joining the Indus at Iskardoo. The boiling point of water gave an elevation of little more than 13,000 feet, but this valley, for the first day's march we went up it, was the most sterile I had yet seen. There was scarcely a blade of vegetation to be seen either in the valley itself or on the hills on either side; all was one barren waste of rock and sand. On the evening of the fourth day we got to the ground, and I had the pleasure to see a flock of antelopes on the spot where we intended to encamp, but having neglected to keep ahead, they **saw us, and were off.** In form and carriage they were much like the black buck of the plains, but altogether of a pale fawn colour. The country was a succession of low rounded hills, with wide plains between; the whole very barren, except here and there damp places near the watercourses, a few hundred yards in extent, where the grass was very luxuriant. These were the places where the antelopes came to feed, and where we might expect to find them morning and evening.

My first day was a blank, though we found no less than five different lots. They were very wary, and our not knowing the ground was much against us. We walked up the ravines in which the grassy places were, instead of stalking to them from above, for the chance of antelopes being on them; but our failure had the good effect of showing us what we ought to have done. Next day we were more careful, and having noted **the** best way of getting a view of each feeding-ground, unseen ourselves, I soon got a shot. One of the nearest was not more than a mile from camp, in a ravine which bordered a wide sandy plain, and so depressed that nothing on it could see us moving on the plain until within range. Creeping cautiously up and looking down on it I saw three antelopes **a** few hundred yards further on; and drawing back, and walking that distance on the plain, I came directly over them, and creeping again to the bank, got a splendid shot, knocking over a fine buck. Its two companions, at the crack of the rifle, which from the high wind I fancy they could but just hear, rushed forward a few paces, and then stood as if bewildered, offering another fair shot, which brought down a second. The remaining one, after another sudden start, stood again, and thinking it too far for the smooth gun, I proceeded to reload the rifle as quickly as possible, while I was doing so the antelope actually coming back a few paces. I was just about putting on the caps when it turned and went off at a race-horse speed; a few more seconds, and I should probably have bagged all three. Highly elated I went down to examine my prizes, when, to my utter amazement, the first one jumped up and was going off at a slashing pace, when a lucky bullet put a sudden stop to its career. On examination I found the first had done little more than graze it on the back, not low enough to injure the spine, though it must have touched some nerve so as to completely paralyze the animal. It was fortunate I had kept the rifle in my hand, or I should most likely have lost this antelope, which turned out the finest I got, having horns twenty-eight inches long, those of the rest being from twenty-five to twenty-seven. I sat down and surveyed with great satisfaction my first two antelopes, rendered doubly acceptable from the thought that they were amongst the first that had fallen before the **rifles** of English sportsmen. Wilson was, I believe, the **first to find** and bag one, which he sent to England, skin **and** skeleton, for sale by auction, but the sum it realized did not cover the expense **of** transit. This, he told me, had deterred him from **making** an attempt to reach the country of the unicorn antelope, described in Huc's Travels through Tartary. We remained at this camp three more days, and bagged two more bucks, but, **strange** to say, amongst some scores of antelopes, never **saw** a doe. There appeared to be no other animals near, but old traces **of** wild yaks were numerous, and the place appeared **to be** one of their winter resorts. Moving the camp some twelve miles further eastward, I hunted over the fresh ground three **days,** and got four more antelopes,—three bucks and a doe,—but with the exception **of** a few wild horses, saw no other animals. **The** ground was of the same character, low stony **hills and** wide plains, almost entirely destitute **of** vegetation, except the rich grassy **plots** in the damp places, little specks, indeed, compared with the vast wilderness of sterility around, but rendering the **finding** of game comparatively **easy,** as the antelopes **were** sure to be found on them morning **and** evening. Further eastward we came to a plain, extending to the verge of the horizon, which seemed to be the commencement **of** the great plains **of** Chinese Tartary. It was a perfect desert, without a vestige of vegetation. **A kind of** mirage was always present in the atmosphere soon after sunrise, appearing like a thin, glass-like transparent fluid, flowing swiftly past, a few feet from the ground.

We now returned to the river below our first camp where it made a turn from the north, and proceeded up it for two days, when we found ourselves near its sources, several streams coming from high snowy mountains on the west, and others from low rounded hills on the north and east. According to the latest maps, we were on the Karrakoram range, but it is marked down as a continuous high snowy one to a point much further eastward. The valleys here were narrower, and more fertile than those we had left, the banks of the streams being almost everywhere covered with grass, and we soon saw we were now in the yak country. Footprints and fresh dung were everywhere plentiful; those of the antelope were also numerous, and the ground being tolerably favourable for stalking, everything seemed to promise a first-rate shooting region.

Having pitched upon a nice place for the camp, I waited for morning in a state of pleasing anticipation. What kind of customers would the yaks be? To judge from the domesticated ones, they ought to be among the noblest of animals. What would they be in reality? Would they charge like the buffalo or turn out timid? Were they wild or otherwise? On these subjects I knew nothing, for Wilson had refused to enlighten me (and indeed could not in a satisfactory manner, as he had only killed one), saying that from his own experience he was sure I should enjoy the trip much more if I remained in ignorance until I got amongst the animals myself. In this supposition he was certainly right, for in sporting a great deal of the excitement lies in expectation and uncertainty, and I should not have experienced half so much as I now did, had I been fully informed of what the next few days revealed. Were I writing only to direct other sportsmen, I should certainly follow his example and leave them in the same state of speculation, merely saying I found the yaks and killed so many; but other readers, if these chapters are interesting enough to command any, may complain of the omission, so I will relate events as they took place.

Morning dawned on the solitary hills where, for scores of miles in every direction, we were probably the only human beings, and with rifle and gun well cleaned and carefully loaded, we started on what I had been so anxiously looking forward to,— my first hunt after wild yaks. Proceeding up the stream on the bank of which we were encamped, continually meeting with traces old and new, and as every fresh portion of ground came within view, fully expecting to see some of the huge beasts, half the day passed and we got to the head of the valley without having seen one ; all was blank, though it was evident they had been there the preceding day. After a little refreshment we ascended the hill on our right, and now looked down into a similar valley, but from the fall of the ground, gradual at first and then rather steep, could see but little of the bottom from the ridge. After a careful scrutiny of what was within view, without any discovery, we descended the slope, fresh portions of the grassy banks of the stream coming within sight as we went on. There they are at last; four large black objects a couple of miles lower down, and no glass is needed to tell us what they are: there is nothing else in these regions for which they could be mistaken. One of the Tartars intimates by signs, that as the wind is blowing down the valley it will be necessary to go round along the hill-side and stalk from below, and tells the interpreter to explain to me that if they get the least scent of us they will be off at once and not stop for miles, which by the bye they had told me twenty times before. We accordingly made the round, and the spot being very favourable, got within range without difficulty. The flat grassy bottom of the valley was not more than sixty yards wide, and the hills rose rather steep on each side. The yaks were quietly grazing near the stream, and I was a little lower down, behind a knoll a short distance up the hill-side; the range not being more than eighty yards. There was little perceptible difference in size, and taking the nearest, I fired at its shoulder. All made a sudden start, the stricken one stumbling forward a few paces, and I gave it the other barrel almost at the same moment. The four rushed across the little stream, and went **up the opposite hill-side at what appeared** to **be a trot, but they got over the ground** at an astonishing pace for **such** short-legged, ungainly looking creatures. The wounded one soon lagged behind, and I saw that he was done for. He soon subsided into a walk, and at **last lay** down, and ere we got up to him was dead. **The two bullets** had struck him in the shoulder, a **few inches** apart.

I had felt a shade **of** disappointment from **the** first moment I saw the animals, and this **was not** dispelled on a closer examination. I **saw at once** that I should **not** trouble myself much more about the yaks. Wilson was right. **If** I had known exactly what they were like, **I** certainly should not have experienced half the **pleasure I** had felt during **the** journey, when thinking **of** what was before me. Somewhat larger in body than the domesticated **breed, and** with **horns** thicker, but not longer, in **all** other respects **they were** exactly similar, and scarcely carried with them the idea of game. There was nothing worth carrying away **as** a trophy, and though glad that I had killed **one**, I felt as if I should care little about killing another. The long hair being **at** this season of **the** year nearly all gone, the skin was **so** indifferent as to **be** useless for a collection, and **I** contented myself with the skull, which I thought I might as well keep, though it would have been hard to distinguish it from that of an English bullock. Winter, or early in spring, would be the time to get one as a perfect specimen of what the animals are, when the long shaggy hair trailing almost to the ground must give it a noble appearance.

There requires something in an animal besides its being wild to give excitement to the chase when the sportsman is alone in an uninhabited wilderness; something noble to carry away as a trophy, or in the nature or habits of the beast to render its capture desirable. It must either be shy and wary, or savage and powerful, so as to call forth skill or daring. Wild horses for instance, met with so frequently, scarcely attract the sportsman's attention in these regions. One may perhaps be killed on his first arrival, but afterwards he passes without thinking of them as objects of pursuit.

Next day two of the Tartars went with a couple of yaks to bring away the skin and flesh of the wild one. It was excellent beef, and much to the disgust of my two shikaries I made several meals of it. Since I parted with my servants, and they had cooked and done all for me, they had gradually thrown off a good many of their Hindoo prejudices of caste, but the yak's beef was too much for them, and for a time freshened them up to their pristine vigour. In the meantime I went out in another direction and found a couple of yaks, which I tried to walk up to without stalking; but they saw me when four hundred yards off, and started away at a slashing pace, and in a short time after I saw them crossing over the ridge at the head of the valley, some five or six miles away, which distance they must have gone without once stopping. Some time after we found a flock of antelopes, and I got another fine buck.

I had not an opportunity of seeing whether a yak would charge, but from what I saw of them am inclined to think not as long as there existed a chance of escape; and the open nature of the ground would in almost every case afford this. The most exciting way of hunting them would undoubtedly be on horseback with the spear; but the country they inhabit being so remote, it is not probable this will ever be tried.

From the furthest ridge we reached on the northeast, low hills and undulating ground stretched to the distant horizon, and I should much have liked to have penetrated a few marches further for the chance of meeting with other animals, and the charm of exploring a totally unknown region. This, however, was impossible without a further supply of provisions, and the Tartars said we might possibly meet with some wandering tribe who might not scruple to rob and murder us. They denied all knowledge of the country, and whether it was inhabited or not, but said it was considered unsafe even for them. At rare intervals they brought their flocks to graze about the country we had shot over, but never ventured further.

I got another antelope on our way down, in rather a singular manner. Seeing a lot in a wide plain, I stalked to behind a large stone about two hundred and fifty yards from them, and there being no chance of getting nearer, fired a shot. They trotted off a little way and then stood, when, to my great astonishment, an old buck came back, and stopping at intervals walked up to within eighty yards of the stone, affording me a splendid shot, which laid him low.

We had seen several skulls of Ovis Ammon, but no traces of the animals, and this portion of the country was probably only visited by them in winter. I went up one day towards the snow on the west, but saw only a flock of burrell. Hares in some places were numerous, and I saw some snow pheasants which appeared to be somewhat different from those on our side of the Himalayas, being much redder in colour. Unfortunately the gun was loaded with ball, and I missed one I fired at with the rifle. One day, while after the antelope, I saw what appeared to be a large yellow wolf, but too far off to determine exactly what it was. From what the Tartars said, the surmise must have been correct.

We got back to the Tartar encampment, which had been removed into another valley, having been away twenty-six days. Not a single shower had fallen since I left Spitee, and the sky was rarely obscured with even a passing cloud. The climate of these elevated regions is the finest it is possible to conceive, wonderfully bracing, and makes one feel equal to any amount of exertion; but the absence of shade is often felt as a drawback. The last march, in not being more than ten miles, and half a dozen more or less being of no consequence, now that I had got so accustomed to walking, I made a round over the hills where I had killed the Ovis Ammon, and found a lot of females. A lucky long shot knocked one over, as I thought dead, but before I got up to it, it got up again and went off at a pace I have rarely seen equalled by any animal. I was not so lucky as with the antelope, for I fired both barrels and missed, and saw no more of the sheep. Noting this circumstance brings to my mind a somewhat similar but more laughable occurrence of this nature which Wilson related to me. He was encamped near the head of the Tartar branch of the Ganges, where the Ovis Ammon is occasionally found, and happened to remain at home, having sent his man out with his double rifle to try and shoot a burrell. In the middle of the day a couple of female Oves Ammon were seen walking across the hill-side above the tent, and as they appeared to be undisturbed, and not likely to go far, he started in pursuit with the only other gun he had, a light pea-rifle, and after following some miles saw them lie down to rest. Leaving a man who had accompanied him to watch, he made a round above, and stalked them nicely to within eighty yards. At the shot they both jumped up, but stood as if uncertain whether there was any real cause of alarm; reloading, he took another deliberate pot, when the one he fired at sunk gently down, the other keeping its erect position.

He took two more shots at this without any
apparent effect; it never even moved, and he had
no more bullets. Drawing quietly back, he went
round to the man, who congratulated him on
having killed one, and sent him to camp for more
balls, and some of the other men to carry the sheep
home, making sure of getting both, and remaining
himself to watch and cogitate on the singular
circumstance of one of the very wildest of animals
allowing four shots to be fired at such a short
distance without taking alarm. For an hour the
sheep were quite still, one stretched out to all
appearance dead, and the other standing alongside.
The latter at length began to graze, and several
times left and returned to its fallen companion,
which never moved, or even lifted up its head, for
more than two hours, when the man with two
others arrived. Wilson loaded his rifle, and now
leaving them to watch, went round again to polish
off the second sheep. From the nature of the
ground he would not see it again until he got to
the place he had shot from; and before he reached
it, the supposed dead one got up as if unhurt,
walked to its companion, and both went slowly off,
and unfortunately in such a direction that they
saw him before he was within range, and scouring
over the hill, were soon out of sight. He could
scarcely believe they were the same, and went up
to the spot where one had lain so long as if dead,
to make certain of the fact. After much thought
he came to the conclusion that the one supposed

to have been killed, had, by a strange coincidence, sunk down to sleep at the moment he fired, and remained so all the time; neither of them, from the strong wind blowing, having heard the shots, and their jumping up at the first being occasioned by the ball striking the ground near, while the others, fired while they were erect, passed by without striking, and did not disturb them at all. Missing four successive shots with a rifle which at the distance was perfectly true, he could only account for by supposing, either that the wind had more effect than usual on the course of the light bullets, or that some optical illusion in the line of sight destroyed the aim, which he affirms does sometimes happen in the hills, particularly in the light atmosphere of Thibet.

Having now, as I thought, spent a sufficient part of my holiday in these regions, and seen whatever they had to offer to the sportsman, I left my Tartar friends, and passing through a little district called Tangee, on the west of the Chooril lake, and then crossing the hills, on the fourth day came again on the Indus, about twenty miles from Ladak, at which place I found my servants very anxiously awaiting my arrival. The authorities were very attentive and obliging; the Thannadar, Bustee Ram, who is governor of the province, and though not a military man, commander of the fort, being assiduous in his endeavours to render my visit agreeable, and himself accompanying me round the place. The town is much smaller than

I anticipated, and contains only a few shopkeepers, and the dependents and followers of the present authorities, the garrison, and the family of the ex-rulers. There were a few Yarkund merchants, and some traders from Kooloo and Koonawur; but the number of these who visit the place is decreasing every year, and I was told that the trade of the place had diminished greatly under the Seikh rule, and was now but the shadow of its former self. Among the articles I found for sale were china ware, musk, and a very fine cloth made from shawl wool, something like merino, but much softer and stronger. The dealers showed an evident disinclination to expose their wares, and there were doubtless many things I did not see. From the universal custom of the Ladak and Tartar women wearing turquoise ornaments, I expected to find some good ones for sale, but was quite disappointed; I could not find one worth purchasing. One article of trade is opium, which is brought from the hills near Simla, and disposed of to the Yarkund merchants, who give in exchange silver and churrus, the well-known intoxicating preparation from the hemp plant, used throughout the East; that of Yarkund being considered very superior. It is brought in large solid cakes weighing nearly half a maund each. At one of the shops I was shown a black fox skin, at least I judged it to be of that animal. It was certainly the handsomest fur I ever saw, and the price asked for it, twenty rupees, showed how highly it was prized even here.

The owner was about cutting it into strips an inch wide, for each of which he said he would get a rupee. These strips are used as borders to the little semicircular piece of cloth which the women wear attached to the hair as a covering for the ears, but apparently more for ornament than protection against the cold.

There is little or nothing to interest the ordinary observer in the town of Ladak. A new wide street, or rather square, to serve as a bazaar, has been added by the present Thannadar. The old ones are narrow and dirty, and present nothing but blank brick walls, and a few doors and windows. The residence of the last native sovereign, where his son, a boy of fourteen years of age, still resides, is a little above the rest of the town, on the hillside, but presents nothing remarkable, being a confused mass of plain, unadorned brick buildings. On the roads leading into the place are the never-failing heaps of stone and the rough walls, on which are piled slates and slabs inscribed with the mystical sentence held so sacred by the Thibetians, but of which they themselves appear not to know the meaning. Go wherever you will in their country, — into the villages, along the roads, and even into places far removed from human habitations, — you find these piles of stones and inscribed slabs. Most contain only the mystic sentence, in some cases rudely, and in others elaborately carved, and often coloured, the characters from a couple of inches to half a yard in height; but others contain a lot of writing besides. One long wall on the right of the main entrance into Ladak supports many thousands of these inscribed slabs. To the natural inquiry, of what use the universal repetition of a sentence without meaning, they reply that it contains something peculiarly sacred, and propitiates the Deity.

Like all other Tartar towns and villages, Ladak looks well at a distance, but utterly disappoints on a nearer view. It is built at the base of a low range of hills, on one side of a wide well-cultivated valley, a mile from where it debouches on the Indus. The fort erected by Goolab Singh's general, Zoorawur Singh, whose career terminated in the disastrous expedition for the subjugation of Thibet, stands in the fields a few hundred yards from the town, and is a gingerbread structure, strong enough for defence against foes without artillery, but would be knocked down by a few rounds from the lightest guns. It is garrisoned by a few hundred of Goolaub Singh's Hindoo troops, and defended by some twenty guns, six and nine pounders.

The Kardar, whose exact position I could not ascertain, but who is some officer employed under the Thannadar in the revenue department, and the highest native functionary in the province, is a native of Ladak, a fine, jolly, good-humoured fellow, and a fair specimen of a Tartar gentleman. As there were no prejudices of caste on his side to curtail our social intercourse, I surprised him by an unannounced visit to his house, half a mile out of town. This was, I could see, an unusual and unlooked-for circumstance, but he gave me a hearty welcome, ushered me into a snug carpeted little room opening out into a flower-garden, gave me a repast, which I partook of under the condition that he would join in it, of cakes, kabobs, and dried fruits, with tea and beer; and with the assistance of the interpreter we chatted for some time about his country and its productions. Without any apparent discomfiture at the unexpected visit, he seemed pleased and gratified with it, and showed a great deal of natural politeness in the manner he received me, at the same time appearing perfectly at his ease,—a rather uncommon thing in meetings between Asiatics and Europeans, where there is generally more or less of constraint on one or both sides.

The direct route from Ladak to Cashmere leads for thirty miles down the Indus, and then crosses the hills, and is twelve days' march. There are several other but longer routes, seldom traversed by Europeans; but as none promised anything extraordinary, I decided on taking the direct one. Wilson had recommended this for shalmar, a third species of wild sheep, and the one through Zanskar for ibex. As I went on, the country became a little more fertile. Grass was more plentiful, both in the valleys and on the hills, and wild-rose bushes not uncommon; and in addition to willow and poplar, the only trees above, magnificent mulberries flourished near the villages. On the evening of the second day a Tartar lady came to pay her respects, being, as she said, the official of the place, or rather holding the situation for her husband, who had been taken prisoner by the Thibetians in the unfortunate Seikh invasion, in which he had been compelled to take part, and was still kept by them in durance. The lady, a corpulent, middle-aged body, attended by several female domestics, superintended the delivery of what was required for the camp, and seemed to be much respected by the villagers. She informed me she was in treaty for the ransom of her lord and master, and expected shortly to hear the result of her offers. As in duty bound, I condoled with her on her misfortune, wished her success, and regretted the utter impossibility of myself or any other European being able to assist her.

At another village, a fat lama came to pay his respects, in the absence of the kardar. He was one of the merriest, jolliest fellows I ever met with; seemed to be made up of good humour, and must have weighed twenty stone at least. One of his peculiarities was using a pocket-handkerchief, not for his nasal organ, but to deposit his spittle in it when obliged to expectorate, which probably, from his redundancy of flesh, was very frequently the case, though I must do him the justice to say he always turned aside when the fit came on. This being so different from the habits of his countrymen, I waived the indelicacy of the question, and asked him **the reason,** when he told me that, **as** the action was **a mark** of contempt, **it was showing** a great want of respect to our mother earth, from which we derived all things, to expectorate on the ground; and that a certain class of lamas, of which he was an unworthy member, **never did** so.

Crossing the **Indus,** which now, by the addition of the Zanskar river, was a mighty torrent, **on a** substantial wooden bridge, over the only place where one could be made, and on which **was a** guard of soldiers living in a house, a chamber of which it was necessary to go through to cross, we commenced to strike across the hills, and encamped near the large monastery of Lamayoura. The next march was over low rounded hills, where **the** rifle was again brought into use. **Shalmar were abun-dant,** and I halted a couple of **days to hunt.** These animals **are a** species of wild sheep,' a little larger than the burrell, with horns like the domesticated ram, but having only one curve. They were not very wild, but when fired at they invariably started off at once at full **speed,** seldom giving the chance of a second shot for several hundred yards or **a** mile, when they would suddenly stop and begin **to** graze again as if nothing had happened. **I got two** males and a female to add **to my** collection.

Nothing worthy of remark occurred while hunting here, **or** during our progress through Soroo and the Drass **valley,** to the Bultul pass, leading into Cashmere. Vegetation became every march more abundant; and we were now on hills clothed with luxuriant grass, and again saw birch and rhododendron. I was encamped on a flat where the grass was up to the knees, and hundreds of marmots were whistling around, and in every direction could be seen, standing erect at the mouth of their holes, or running backwards and forwards near them. These were of a much redder colour than those I had seen in Thibet, and the fur, I found, was very coarse. A little before dusk a snow bear made its appearance on the flat across the river, and putting up the sight for 250 yards, I took a quiet shot, and much to my own surprise, I must confess, killed it the first shot. It walked away a short distance, and then lay down and remained motionless; and after firing two more shots, which were unheeded, I crossed on a pony, and found it dead. It was one of the longest shots I made during the trip.

The ascent of the Bultul from the Drass side is so slight as to be almost imperceptible. The fall from the crest to the Drass fort, nearly twenty miles, is not more than 2000 feet. It is, in fact, more like a level narrow plain between high hills, along which you walk till the abrupt descent on the Cashmere side commences. The pass is open all the year round, being little more than 11,000 feet high, but is of course covered deeply with snow in winter, and people who cross then not unfrequently lose their toes from frost-bites. From the pass you look down into a pine-covered valley, with green hills on either side, something like the old scenery on the Ganges where I shot with Wilson. The Cashmere valley itself is not within sight, being four marches further, but this one leads to it. The scene, ordinary enough in itself, was charming in comparison with the barren hills and wastes I had so long been travelling over. In the evening we got to Soonamurg, and in three more days I found myself at the capital of the far-famed valley, encamped in an orchard near the houses built by the rajah for the convenience of European visitors, and again amongst my own countrymen. The houses, seven in number, were full to overflowing; and many later comers were, like myself, encamped in the gardens.

In a hurried journey through any country, particularly when unable to converse with the inhabitants but through a second person, one cannot expect to glean particulars sufficient to be enabled to describe it properly; yet I may as well endeavour to show what idea my journey through gave me of Ladak and Goolab Sing's Tartar provinces.

The history of the country I am not competent to touch upon. All who are acquainted with modern eastern geography know as much as myself: that not a great many years ago it was an independent state; that, after a fruitless attempt on the part of its sovereign to be allowed to place himself and country under British protection, he was obliged to submit to the Seikhs without an effort at resistance; and that on Goolab Sing's being guaranteed the sovereignty of Cashmere and other hill countries, Ladak was included amongst them.

The country itself being so high, the hills do not appear to attain any remarkable elevation, except a few peaks on the Karrakoorum range, which forms its northern boundary, and others on the ranges which separate it from the Indian Himalayas on the south. Between these ranges, which are about 120 miles in direct distance apart, the hills are almost all below the limits of perpetual snow; but it must be remembered the limit here is much higher than on the Indian side. The ranges average from 16,000 to 19,000 feet, the valleys being from 9000 to 13,500 in the agricultural, and from 13,500 to 15,000 or 16,000 in the pastoral districts. In the lower or western part of the country the hills are often rocky and precipitous, and the valleys narrow; but as we advance eastwards the hills become of a more rounded form, with much less rock, and the valleys are wider and often form extensive plains. The great characteristic is sterility; hill and valley on the whole presenting an expanse of stony or sandy waste. From any commanding eminence the eye looks over a succession of barren mountain ranges, of different shades of brown, red, and yellow, with here and there a snowy peak towering in the distance; and unless some portion of a cultivated valley, with its fields and villages, forms part of the scene, all appears utterly devoid of vegetable life. This is more particularly applicable to the northern and eastern parts, where, to an eye accustomed to the green hills and dark forests of the Indian Himalayas, hill, valley, and plain appear at a distance irreclaimable desert.

The habitable portion of the country may be divided into two parts, the agricultural and pastoral; the former including the valleys to an elevation of 13,500 feet, and the latter the table-lands and valleys above that elevation. The latter are chiefly in the eastern part, and in a manner distinct from Ladak, of which they form dependencies.

The country, as may be expected, is very thinly populated. In the agricultural districts, where most fertile, the villages are generally many miles apart, and there are often wide tracts of sandy waste between. They are mostly in the valleys, though occasionally a little way up the hill-side, and round them are clean, well-kept, and often large fields, surrounded with stone walls, and irrigated by canals from the nearest stream, these being often several miles in length. Groves of tall poplars and willows are very general accompaniments, either round the village or along the canals. These are all planted, there being no indigenous trees, except here and there copses of stunted willow along the banks of the streams. The houses are generally of two or three stories, built of large sun-dried bricks, with flat roofs covered with earth. Large timber being so scarce, the doors are frequently made with a number of willow sticks, about the thickness of one's wrist, laid side by side, and secured at top and bottom with a cross-piece. At a distance a Tartar village has a rather clean, imposing look, the houses being high and large, whitewashed outside, with broad borders of red, blue, or yellow painted round the doors and windows. Their being generally built on rising ground, with the absence of wood and other screening objects, sets them out in bold relief. The monasteries are large, imposing buildings, almost invariably perched on a rock, and, there being little else to catch the eye in the unvarying expanse of brown hill around, are striking objects.

The inhabitants of this portion of the country are, with the exception of the religious communities, engaged exclusively in agriculture. The products are wheat, rye, barley, and buckwheat, and a kind of lucerne, cultivated as fodder for the cattle. Nothing grows without irrigation ; but wherever that is resorted to, the soil is very productive, and in no country are finer crops met with. On the banks of the streams, where they do not run in deep channels, the ground is carpeted with short but rich green grass ; but where the liquid element is wanting, from the dryness of the climate and the small quantity of rain that falls, vegetation is very scanty.

The people of Ladak, except in the Drass valley, are Tartars, and follow the customs of that race. A great feature in their social economy is the number devoted in one way or another to a religious life, and living in celibacy. In all Tartar families the second son is made a lama, and the third a tola, both being forbidden to marry, and in a manner obliged to renounce the world, having no interest in their father's property at his death. This accounts for the number of monasteries, which at first, in so poor a country, appears somewhat puzzling. The Ladak Tartars are a little tinged with the vices of their neighbours the Cashmerians, in the distant provinces very slightly, and in the Tartar character there is much that is amiable. They have a great regard for truth, are faithful to their engagements, and are hospitable and humane; retired and modest in demeanour, with a considerable share of natural politeness. From the salubrity of the climate, and their frugal way of living, they are little subject to disease; but the constant glare is injurious to the eyes, and weakness of those organs not uncommon. In their diet they are very simple. Bread is seldom, and amongst the pastoral people, never made. The corn is parched before being ground, and made into gruel, or mixed with cold water, milk, or tea. The Tartar method of making tea is very different from ours. A very strong decoction is first made by steeping the tea with a little soda in a small quantity of hot water. A cupful of this is then poured into a vessel of boiling water, a lump of butter added, and the whole put into a kind of churn, and violently agitated for a few seconds. This mixes the butter with the tea, and gives it a peculiarly soft, but, to our palates, very sickly taste. Tea is a favourite beverage amongst the

Tartars, and is partaken of several times during the day. Those who cannot afford to use the real article substitute for it the bark of the yew tree, a great deal of which is brought for the purpose from the Indian side of the Himalayas. The tea comes from China by way of Lassa, and is generally of very inferior quality. It appeared to me to be the large coarse leaves, with a good deal of the small stalks, compressed into a brick, and has almost always a musty flavour.

Spirituous liquor is unknown, but a kind of beer, made from fermented grain, generally rye, is regularly used by those who can afford it. The grain being unmalted, and no bitter added, it soon becomes sour, and will not keep many days. In taste it is not unlike the palm-tree toddy of India. A common Tartar meal, amongst ordinary people, is something in this wise. A large vessel of hot tea is the first course, of which every one drinks several cups; a bowl or bag of satoo, the flour of parched grain, is then produced, of which every one takes a handful, and mixes it in his cup with a little tea left in it for the purpose, and this finishes the repast. Milk, or butter-milk, is often served with the satoo in place of tea, and amongst the pastoral tribes is most common. When flesh is used, the broth serves as a substitute for tea, and the meat, which is cut into small pieces before being boiled, is eaten by itself afterwards. The Tartars eat and drink out of little wooden saucers, each person having his own, which he almost always carries about with him in his bosom. Some eat with their fingers, **but** most use a small spoon of brass or **wood,** also carried about with them wherever they go, attached by a string to the girdle.

A considerable portion of the **eastern part of** the Ladak territories is high table-land and valleys above 1400 feet, inhabited exclusively by pastoral tribes, who dwell in tents, moving about from place to place, each tribe within its own district. They cultivate no ground, but depend for subsistence entirely on the produce **of** their flocks and herds. Amongst them the observing traveller has **a** fair opportunity **of** seeing what Tartars really **are, as** they retain, in **all** its simplicity, the primitive character, as well as the habits, of that portion of the human family, probably little or **at** all changed from the earliest ages of the world's **history.**

Of domesticated animals the most deserving of notice **is** the yak, called in some works on natural history the long-haired or grunting ox, and is to the Tartars what the camel is to the Arabs. In body it is the size **of** a middle-sized English ox, but stouter, and the legs are much shorter. **The** usual colour is black, with a white line down the back, and a white tail, but many are entirely black, and some of a yellowish brown. **The hair, except** on the back, is long, and if allowed **to grow would** almost reach the ground; but the great characteristic of the animal, as differing from the common ox, is the tail, which is like that of the horse, though more bushy, and **the** hair is much finer and more abundant. When a yak is killed, the tail is cut off and hung up to dry, and they form one item of export in the trade with India, being, as chowries, much prized there by the native princes and nobles. To the Tartars the yak is invaluable; it is an excellent beast of burden, carrying heavy loads over ground where no other large animal could; the hair clipped yearly makes a strong cloth for tents and bags, the milk of the females is very rich and abundant, and the flesh is excellent beef. It is very hardy, proof against the severest cold, and finds subsistence and thrives on high sterile hills where horses or common oxen would starve. It will travel several days without food, and apparently without much decrease of strength,—an invaluable quality in countries where on some routes days are passed without meeting with vegetation.

The common horned cattle are of a small breed, and are kept chiefly in the lower agricultural districts; in the higher and pastoral, yaks being better adapted to the country and climate. A cross between the two produces a jooe, a very useful animal either for burden or the dairy.

The breed of horses most common in Ladak is a middle-sized pony, without any particular quality to recommend it. It is not a horse-breeding country, and those who wish to have good ones get them from Yarkund or from Balk. Asses are common, and of a much better breed than those of India; and remarkably fine ones are sometimes brought from Yarkund. I saw one of these, of a milk-white colour, nearly as large as a horse, for which 150 rupees were asked.

The Tartar sheep is distinguishable by its small head and long slender legs, and is of the short-tailed breed. The wool is very long and soft. The goats are of several varieties; some are very large, and many have very singular-shaped horns, from erect spiral ones, like the markhoor or antelope, to curved ones, like the ibex. In some the horns cross, or are twisted round each other, and one variety has four horns. The shawl-wool goat is a very diminutive species, seldom more than twenty inches high. The shawl-wool is the down or soft fur underneath the hair, and is taken out with a comb. Almost all animals, wild and tame, in these regions, have more or less of it, but none in such quantity, and of so fine a texture, as this little goat, from which alone is obtained that used for the manufacture of shawls and other fine cloths. Most of the shawl-wool used in Cashmere comes from Thibet, but a good deal is produced in the pastoral districts of Ladak.

The Thibet dog is a fine and powerful animal, something in appearance like the Newfoundland, but, except amongst the pastoral tribes, a genuine one is seldom met with. Those of Ladak have been spoiled by crosses with inferior breeds.

The wild animals found in Ladak and its dependencies are the yak, horse, three species of sheep, two antelopes, and the ibex; the white leopard, wolf, fox, wild dog, brown bear, marmot, and hare. The yak, common in the interior of Thibet, is confined in Ladak to the one remote corner where I hunted it. The horse is very common in all the pastoral districts; it is generally called the wild horse, though evidently nearly allied to the ass tribe. It is of a light reddish fawn colour, with white belly and breast, a black mark down the back, a short erect black mane, and the tail of the ass. The head is very large, and the ears long, but the body is very symmetrically proportioned. It is found in parties of two or three, and where not much disturbed, in troops of twenty or thirty. They are not very shy, and will generally allow a person to approach openly to within 250 or 300 yards, when they trot off out of harm's way.

Of the sheep, the first is the Ovis Ammon, of which a good idea may be formed from what has been already said about it. The ram is nearly as large as the red-deer; the legs are long and slender, the hoofs and knee-joints large, giving it a rather lank, ungraceful appearance. The general colour is a reddish grey, deepening on the back and shoulders; the hair about the neck and breast is white and long; the rest is short, crisp, very thick set, and brittle, as in all the wild sheep. The head is long, and the muzzle rather sharp. The horns of a full-grown ram are from eighteen to twenty-four inches in circumference, and from forty-six to fifty-four round the curve; those of the female from eight to ten inches in circumference, and from fourteen to twenty-two in length. This majestic sheep is common on the hills of Thibet, and is met with on those of the pastoral districts and eastern part of Ladak. It seems to avoid both rocky ground and the flat plains, and confines itself to the rounded and gently-sloping hills, from which we may infer it is a distinct variety from the Rocky Mountain sheep of America, which is described as similar in appearance, but said to select the wildest and most rugged cliffs as its habitat. There is, perhaps, no wild animal more wary or shyer of mankind than the Ovis Ammon. It is possessed of the most acute power of vision, seldom allows a person to approach openly within a mile, and it requires the utmost caution to get within shooting distance, unless particularly favoured by the nature of the ground. In summer the males, though keeping on the same ground, are always found separate from the females. The speed of these animals, considering the weight of the immense horns, is astonishing, and it is questionable whether any other animal could go over the same rough ground at the same pace.

Another species of wild sheep is the shalmar, found on the hills in the agricultural districts. It is said to be a common animal in the countries more to the westward, but in Ladak is found only in two or three places. Either the same, or a species exactly similar, is found on the first range of low hills near Bimber, in the Punjaub. Most sportsmen consider it the same, but the very wide difference of climate in the two places would lead a naturalist to infer it must be a different variety. The shalmar is not more than half the size of the Ovis Ammon, of a yellowish grey colour, with the usual short, crisp, thick-set, and brittle fur. The horns of a full-grown male are about fourteen inches in circumference and from twenty-four to twenty-six round the curve. In habits it something resembles the larger sheep, but is not nearly so shy or wary, and its rambles do not extend over nearly so great an extent of country. Like it, it seems to prefer rounded hills and slopes to very rocky and precipitous ground.

The third species is the burrell, of our side of the Himalayas, which is also common in many parts of Ladak, and throughout Thibet. A description of it will be found in Wilson's " Notes on the Wild Animals of Gurwhal."

In the remote corner on the north-eastern frontier, to which I have already introduced the reader, and in the Ladak territories there only, is found the large Thibetian antelope. It is about the size of the Indian antelope, of a pale fawn colour, with elegant black horns, from twenty-five to thirty inches in length. The fur is thick and brittle, like that of the wild sheep, but finer. A distinguishing feature is the thickness of the muzzle, and it has two large orifices in the groin several inches deep. Little more of its habits is known than that it frequents the most retired and undisturbed parts of the country, inhabiting the low rounded hills and elevated plains in the high arid regions of

Thibet. The smaller antelope is also a **rare animal** in Ladak, though common a little further in Thibet. It has short black horns, about nine inches in length. In my excursion I did not meet with any of this species.

The Himalayan ibex is now well known, and is a noble animal, and sought after with avidity by all sportsmen who ramble far into the hills. It is found in Nepaul, and again in Koonawur, **but there** are none in the intervening countries, in Keemaoon, or in British and Independent Gurwhal. **Westward** from Koonawur it is found all along the range as far as the sportsman or naturalist has penetrated, and in Ladak is common in all districts where the hills are rocky and precipitous. It is one of the largest animals of the goat tribe : the colour is a dirty white, inclining to reddish brown on the shoulders, the hair short, thick set, and brittle, like that of the wild sheep, and it has a long black beard. The horns curve backwards very gracefully, and are from forty-two to fifty inches in length, and from twelve to fifteen in circumference. It inhabits high and rocky hills, and is one of the most surefooted of beasts, traversing with the greatest ease, and often at full speed, the faces of almost perpendicular rocks and precipices inaccessible to most other large animals. It is very shy and wary ; but the ground where it is found being very favourable for stalking, it is not, generally speaking, a difficult animal to shoot, though its pursuit is attended with great toil, some danger, and requires a fearless and experienced cragsman. In summer the males keep entirely separate from the females, and resort to the high regions near the limits of vegetation, lying concealed during the day amongst the cliffs, coming out to feed in the evening, and retiring again at sunrise. In winter they are driven down by the snow to the inhabited districts, where they remain until spring is well advanced.

The white leopard, or ounce, is found in Ladak, but here, as everywhere else, it is a rare animal, and seldom met with. It is confined to the high and cold regions near the snow. In size it is the same as the common panther, but its tail is much longer and thicker. The colour is a greyish white, with black spots, and the fur is thick and very soft. No living specimen, and very few perfect skins, of this beautiful variety of the feline race, have been secured for the menageries or museums of Europe.

The wolf found in Ladak and Thibet is of a yellowish colour, with a very fine soft fur. Nothing is known of its habits, except that, unlike others of its tribe, it is a solitary animal, never collects in packs, and is almost invariably seen alone. The fox is as large as our English variety, of a yellowish grey colour, with black ears; it is very rare, and seldom met with. The wild dogs are apparently of a distinct kind from those of the Indian Himalayas, being rather less, and not so red; they are also very rare, but, like all their race, very destructive. The hares are nearly as large as English ones, but have shorter ears. The colour is yellowish grey, but in winter changes to bluish white. There are three kinds of marmots; one very rare, of a dark brown colour, with very fine soft fur, and another of a lighter colour, with coarse fur, common in the pastoral districts of Ladak and throughout Thibet. The third is a reddish yellow one, also with coarse fur, very numerous on the hills between Ladak and Cashmere. The marmots are about the size of a hare, but are very round and bulky animals, with short legs, and always exorbitantly fat. They live in colonies, each pair having their own burrow. In the day they never venture far from their retreat, but may be seen all day long, at frequent intervals, standing erect at the mouth of their holes, or running about near.

The brown bear, found throughout the higher Himalayas, is included in the animals of Ladak, being met with on the Ladak side of the hills separating the country from Cashmere. From the difference in colour of different individuals, and at different seasons of the year, some have supposed there are two or three varieties of the brown bear, but it is now well ascertained there is but one, common on the high hills all along the range. A description of it has been already given in a former chapter.

In a country so entirely destitute of wood, birds, as may be expected, are very scarce. Of *gallinaceæ*, the only kinds met with are the snow-pheasant, chuckore, and a large variety of the pin-tailed grouse. On the lakes wild fowl are abundant, but the species are limited, there being apparently but one kind of goose and three of ducks. Of small birds there are few except sparrows, larks, and a few of the finch tribe. The hoopoe, which seems to inhabit every country under the sun, is as numerous in Ladak and throughout Thibet as on the plains of India. The birds most noticeable by an ordinary traveller are: a magpie, not unlike our English variety, seen near the villages, and a large and glossy-plumaged raven, seen about the camps of the pastoral tribes, and a pair of which I found almost always made their appearance whenever I killed and cut up a wild animal.

CHAPTER XI.

It was early in September when I reached Cashmere, and the remainder of the month was spent about the city and visiting different portions of the valley. So many accounts of it have been given, that the reading portion of the civilized world must know pretty well what kind of a place it is. For those who do not, a brief outline is all I dare venture to attempt, conscious of my inability to give a full and particular account. The valley may be about one hundred miles long, and from thirty to fifty broad, and is surrounded on all sides by high mountains; those on the south and east forming a compact ridge, rising nearly to the limits of perpetual snow, and sloping at once into the valley, while those on the north and west run up in long irregular ridges to the snowy mountains. The streams from the hills round the east corner unite soon after debouching into the valley, and form the Jhelum, which runs through it; a pretty clear, smooth, gently-flowing river, navigable for ordinary river boats till it enters the hills which shut up the valley at the south-western corner. From any commanding hill near you get a very good view of nearly the whole valley, particularly from the

Haramook Mountain, the bluff end of a long range twenty miles north of the city. The valley itself is nearly level, and the greater portion of it cultivated. Except a tract of swampy ground between the city and the south-western extremity, the parts not cultivated are covered with low jungle, which changes to forest as you approach the hills.

Serinuggur, the capital, is situated near the middle of the valley as to its length, but very close to the hills on the north side; the Jhelum, which runs through the city, flowing all along much nearer that side than the other. It is a large place, and with the five bridges spanning the river, has, from a distant hill, a rather imposing look. There are many dirty cities in India, but I really think Serinuggur equals, if it does not surpass, in this respect, the very worst that could be picked out. Those who wish to carry away with them a favourable idea of the place, had better content themselves with what they see from their boat as they while away on the river or lake the summer's evening. Viewed thus, the charm that poesy has thrown over it may still be kept up; but if you wish not to dispel it, keep on the bosom of the really pretty river, or go up the canal to the lake, and read "Lalla Rookh" while gliding over its clear, pellucid waters, but venture not an exploration through the streets of the city, or even the canals that wind through. The houses Goolaub Singh has built for the accommodation of the

European visitors are on the north bank of the river just before it enters the city, and certainly no better spot could have been selected. The avenues of plane and poplar trees near, and the long rows of the latter on each bank of the river, give the spot a pretty appearance. The Maharajah's palace or fort is one of the first buildings as you enter the city, but presents nothing worthy of remark, showing from the river only high walls and a few open balconies. You have passed the first bridge, and now find the river crowded with boats, but you go through to the open country beyond without having seen anything particularly interesting. Hurree Perbut, the round hill close by, surmounted with its fort, attracts your attention, and you think what mincemeat the guns would make of the city if turned against it. You have now been through the best part of the capital of Cashmere, and what is there to look at? When you come to ask yourself the question, absolutely nothing. High brick houses on each side, without any regularity, and without even an attempt at frontage to the river, many having their gable-ends to it; a mosque or two, or temple without much architectural pretension; and the narrow dirty entrances to lanes or streets, sometimes flights of wooden steps forming a landing-place, but generally nothing but the natural bank. There is nothing to be seen in the country beyond; so return, and go up to the lake, if you are not for the present sickened of sight-seeing by an object which would nowhere be a pleasant thing to contemplate—the shriveled-up body of a malefactor, which has been fried in oil, and suspended in a large cage on the top of high poles, to terrify other evil-inclined persons. There are several of these gibbets about the city, and disgusting as it may be, it is likely enough the exhibition has something of the desired effect.

Up we go through the narrow canal, past houses and gardens, frightening large flocks of geese and ducks, many of which belong to the Maharajah, and emerge on the lake or dal, a fine sheet of clear, pellucid water, but some portion hidden by tall reeds and floating gardens, on which melons, cucumbers, and grapes are cultivated for sale in the city. You stop a moment perhaps to look at the little plane-tree island in the middle, "the Isle of Chenars," or to admire some of the magnificent lotus-flowers, and glide on over the transparent water, with the hills round one side, and on the banks the old summer-houses and gardens of the Delhi emperors, and think of the time when Cashmere was in its glory, and "the magnificent son of Akbar" did perhaps retire from the cares of empire for a while, to wander with some "light of the harem" through the Happy Valley. Still, if you are asked the question, there is nothing to be seen; but for all that, there is a great charm over everything, the first few times one gets into a boat and shoots rapidly through the city, or takes a turn on the quiet and peaceful lake; conjured up, doubtless, by poetic feeling. and the soft balmy air of a Cashmere summer's evening.

But,

"The love-lighted eyes that hang over its wave,"

where are they? As you shoot down through the city with the current, the motion of the boat is too rapid to allow of more than a momentary glance at the damsels whom you pass, some in boats, but most come down from the city for water, and perhaps to loiter a few minutes to breathe the pure fresh air of the river, and gaze on the busy world. As you return, the boatmen are perhaps a little tired, and the stream being now against them, they will give you plenty of time if you don't hurry them. So just shove the boat a little nearer the shore, and as you pass them see what the fair dwellers of the Happy Valley are like, those at least whose charms are not hidden, through Moslem or Hindoo jealousy, by the impenetrable walls of the harem. The first thing that strikes you is, that the Cashmerian women are taller and more robust than those of most other Eastern nations. There are many fine forms, which even the horrid nightgown-like dress,—entirely loose with the wives and daughters of the followers of the prophet, but confined round the waist by a red girdle amongst the Hindoo maidens, — cannot entirely hide or disfigure, and now and then a set of finely and handsomely moulded features, with large, dark, voluptuous eyes, are turned on you for a moment; but on the whole you are much disappointed with what you see of Cashmere beauty. There is also a sallow, unhealthy look in the complexion of the grown-up women, and girls that have passed childhood, which is not pleasing. As the children are generally very pretty, and free from this, it may be occasioned by the close air of the ill-ventilated city; but the most probable cause is the universal custom of carrying under the dress a small basket, in which is an earthen vessel filled with warm ashes and live charcoal, the fumes of which must be anything but conducive to blooming health.

The first excursion I made from the city was to Muttaen, to see the ruins of an ancient building, of the origin of which I heard various surmises made, but nothing put forth for fact; and I know not whether the early history of Cashmere throws any certain light on the subject, not having this, or the opinions of modern travellers to refer to. There are many of these ruinous edifices in different parts of the valley, some very much dilapidated, others almost entire, and the general impression they make on you is that they have been monasteries of some kind. There is the temple in the centre, and round it at some distance, forming a square, a massive wall, the inside face of which is portioned off into small apartments, as if intended for cloisters. No timber whatever has been used, and there have been no doors either to the large building in the centre or the apartments in the walls. The most remarkable feature is the immense size of the rough unhewn stones (rocks would be the proper term) of which these ruins are composed. It strikes one that they cannot have been lifted into their positions without more mechanical power than is used by Eastern nations at the present day. The arches are made either by laying one immense stone across, or two resting a little on each side and joining in the centre. If you question the natives about them the only answer you get is, that they were erected in former ages by a race of giants. Near the village of Muttaen I was taken to a cave full of bats, which through the whole extent were clinging to the roof like a swarm of bees. I poked my stick into the living mass, and found it upwards of a foot deep. The ruins of Muttaen are situated on some table-land a little way up one of the hills in the north-east corner of the valley.

The Maharajah gave several dinner-parties while I remained in the city. All the European visitors were invited, and nearly all went. These dinners were always followed by a nautch. Once a week he had a review of all the troops stationed in the city, numbering some eight or ten thousand, and seemed to take it as a compliment if the European visitors attended to witness the spectacle. The Maharajah, it must be confessed, omits nothing to render the residence of Europeans in Cashmere, and their travels in any part of his territories, as pleasant to them as possible, which makes it all the sadder to think he should be such a tyrant to his subjects. If the tales the Cashmerians tell be true, their condition is a thousand times worse than that of any slaves in the plantations of our friends over the Atlantic, and those who sold him this fairest portion of Hindoostan have much to answer for. One would have thought the very name of Cashmere ought to have secured it for us when once fairly our own.

One of my fellow-visitors was at the time collecting materials for a full and particular account of the present state of this unfortunate country, and his work will probably have been published long ere these rough notes see the light. A sad tale of misery and oppression it will probably unfold, and, it is to be hoped, shame the Government into expostulating with and inducing the Maharajah to relax somewhat of the severity of his iron rule over the fair country which their, or their viceroy's, short-sightedness delivered up to him. The sale of Cashmere was one of the greatest blunders ever made by our Indian statesmen, and viewed in any light, not one sound argument can be brought forward to justify the measure. In a pecuniary one, surely the money received from Goolaub Singh might have been raised by a loan which the revenues of the valley would soon have liquidated; and the guaranteed possession of his own territories was surely sufficient remuneration for anything the wily chief ever did for us. But if not, could no other place but Cashmere be found to throw away? the choicest morsel in the newly acquired provinces.

In a political view, its possession **may at some future time** be of the utmost importance to **the** well-being and even the existence of India. What an amount of blood and treasure the bare idea of the possibility of a Russian invasion cost us in the Afghan campaigns! A Russian invasion may be feasible, or it may not; I will leave **that** for our rulers **to** decide. But it is, at all events, just as feasible now as it was then. Is it likely they would be content with trying that frontier **only?** What is there to hinder one corps of **an invading** army coming from the head of the Oxus, *via* Nagyr and Iskardoo, **or, if** all that is told of Russian progress in Central **Asia** be true, *via* Yarkund and Ladak. It will be said an army could not find subsistence in such inhospitable countries. An Indian army probably would not, but any army composed of men not trammeled like our Sepoys with caste, could do so easily; so let **us not** confide in that supposition. Beef and **mutton** sufficient for half the Russian army could be drawn from the surrounding countries. Once **in** possession **of** Cashmere, from the nature of the roads to it from the plains, the passes being, on the Cashmere side, gentle slopes, and, **on** the Indian, steep ascents, 50,000 men could hold it against any Indian army, draw from it ample **supplies,** and descend when required to co-operate with their brethren attacking on the western frontier. If Russian invasion ever does turn out **to** be a fact, it will probably be at a time when England has her hands full at home, and cannot afford to send any large force to India; and to judge from what happened in the Seikh campaigns, 80,000 men, such as stood up before our guards at Inkermann, would, for anything a *Sepoy* army could do to stop them, sweep without a check from Peshawur to Calcutta. "*Un homme prévoyant donne peu au hasard;*" and if there really is any fear of a Russian invasion—and that it is thought possible, the Afghan tragedy is one proof—why not prepare for the contingency in the only sensible way, by keeping in the country a respectable European force, and not squander our resources in subsidizing wild tribes beyond our frontier, who, if the time ever comes, would be just as likely to side with the invaders as with ourselves.

It is now the end of September, and all the visitors of a sporting turn are leaving the city, allured by visions of antlered monarchs of the forest falling before their unerring rifles. Some of these, my friends, must be held straighter than they were at some of the matches and rifle practice that occasionally whiled away the time in the city, or these visions will not be realized. Nearly all, I find, are going to the hills at the north-eastern corner of the valley, or somewhere in that direction, and this is indeed by far the best ground; but as there are so many parties, I content myself with the fag-end, as it were, of the stag country, the Sinde valley, which runs up from the north-west of the city to the Buttul pass on the road to

Ladak. Wilson advised me to try it if I found a great many parties out in the other hills, as I should most probably have it all to myself, which would more than counterbalance the comparative scarcity of game. I tried to get a companion, but the other hills being thought so much more promising I could get no one to join me; so I started myself, with my two Gurwhal shikaries, and a Cashmerian who pretended to be a perfect Nimrod at stag-shooting. I was glad rather to get once more into the jungle, for now that the novelty was worn off, I began to tire of the city. In fishing I had been disappointed, the only good sport I found being near Islamabad, at the last of the rapids, where the fish, a species of trout from one to three pounds' weight, rose eagerly at the fly, and myself and a brother angler killed some fifty in one evening, on our excursion to see the old ruins of Muttaen.

Before we commence shooting, it may be as well to take a rapid glance at the game of Cashmere, or rather of the hills round it, for there is little or nothing in the valley itself. The Hungul stag is worthy of the first place. These animals are found in the hills on the north and east, and are tolerably numerous. They rarely, except in winter, come into the valley itself, and then only to the foot of the hills. In summer the stags all migrate into other countries, most of them into the Wurdwan valley, the western branch of the Chenab, behind the hills which shut up Cashmere on the northeast; the hinds all remaining. In the rutting season, the end of September, the stags return, and may be heard bellowing in the forest all day long, and it is now the shooting commences. In appearance the Hungul is not unlike the red deer of Scotland, but of a much browner colour, and the antlers are quite as large, and some probably larger. A friend sent me drawings of what were supposed to be the finest ever seen in that country, with the dimensions, and a pair I saw in Cashmere were larger every way, though not having so many tines.

The Markhoor is a wild goat, and perhaps the most majestic of the tribe yet known. It is found on the high range of hills which surround Cashmere on the south and west, but is not numerous, and very few have been killed. In habits it is not unlike the thar of Gurwhal, but much wilder and shyer of mankind. It is about the same size, of a bluish-white colour, with long shaggy hair. The horns are spiral and nearly erect, and upwards of three feet in length. This animal is said to be much more plentiful on the hills west of Cashmere. The thar, serow, and musk-deer, all described by Wilson in his notes, are also found in Cashmere; the first on the hills on the south only, with the Markhoor, the two latter on all around. The musk-deer of Cashmere, Wilson says, is a different species from that found in Gurwhal, Koonawur, Nepaul, and further eastward; the animal itself somewhat smaller, with other distinguishing traits, and the musk not nearly so good. The ibex is found on the hills on the north-side only, and in summer all the males, and many of the females, leave these and go further back into the hills of Ladak and Zanskar.

Bears, both brown and black, are very numerous, perhaps more so than in any other country under the sun. When sportsmen first began to hunt over the Cashmere hills, it was not unusual to meet with twenty or thirty in a day. The black one, which appears to be smaller and less ferocious than that found in Gurwhal and other hill countries to the eastward, is found both in the valley and the hills around, and the best time for shooting it is in the fruit season. The brown one is met with in the hills only, and is most numerous on those to the north. The best time for shooting it is in spring.

Birds of the *gallinæ* family are not numerous. There are a few moonalls and koklass pheasants, and in some places a good many chuckores. Water-fowl are plentiful, and on the approach of winter the number of ducks and geese is almost incredible; the large lake and the swampy ground near it being perfectly alive with them. Swans are said also to visit the lake in winter. Snipe are plentiful wherever the ground is adapted to their habits, but I did not hear of any woodcocks in the valley.

To return to my narrative. A march of sixteen miles took me to a small village in one of the little nooks in the Sinde valley. The Sinde river is the largest tributary of the Jhelum from the Cashmere hills. It rises in the snowy mountains, separating the valley from Ladak, and for some distance flows parallel to the valley, a range of high hills lying between; then, turning to the south-west, it joins the Jhelum some twenty miles below the city. Striking across the angle you soon get into the valley, which at first is a couple of miles broad, and full of villages and cultivation. The hills on both sides are covered with forest, and rise to an elevation of from 12,000 to 13,000 feet. Pine is the prevailing wood, and, with the exception of there being no rhododendron bushes, the hills are very much similar to those about Gangootree, in Gurwhal, and the Buspa valley, in Koonawur. The next day we commenced shooting, and I soon found Cashmere well worthy the character it bears as a first-rate sporting country, for even here, in a corner generally considered as not very promising, it was evident there was better sport than in any part of the Himalayas I had been through. A couple of hundred yards from camp, as we started in the morning, two black bears were espied in a tree; and creeping up, concealed by the bushes, to within fifty yards, I got a capital shot, knocking over one, which came down with a tremendous bump, and, rolling over a few times, expired. The other, I think, got a taste of the second barrel as it clambered down tail foremost, but we did not get it. We had gone but a little way up the hill after this when we heard the bellow of a stag, and were guided, by its repetition at frequent intervals, to the spot. The sound seemed to proceed from a strip of dense pine forest, and, waiting now and then for the bellow, I approached as noiselessly and carefully as I could, under the guidance of the Cashmere shikaree. We were, however, unsuccessful. There was a sudden crash in the bushes, about fifty yards ahead of us, and I just got a glimpse of the animal as it went off. After breakfast, and a couple of hours' rest, we went on over a ridge to another slope of the hill, finding tracks in all directions, and came across a young stag, at which I fired a bad running shot without effect. His antlers appeared to be not more than a couple of feet long, and with but two tines, so I was almost glad he had escaped. We hunted till evening, but saw no other, nor heard more bellowing; but while returning to camp we came upon another bear, which I wounded severely, and should probably have got had there been another half hour of daylight to enable us to track it up. I was half inclined to follow it next morning, for one never likes to lose a badly-wounded animal; but, as there seemed to be lots of them, I thought it more advisable to go after the stags. This day was a blank, but the third, on another hill, I managed to get a shot. Guided by the bellowing of a stag, which we heard at intervals half the day, I got up to the narrow strip of forest in which it was, and had scarcely entered when I heard the crash of the bushes as the stag rushed through; but, following as fast as I could, I was just in time to see it crossing the open hill-side in front, at not more than eighty yards, and at no very fast pace, more of a trot than anything else. I fired both barrels, and at the second it rolled over. The antlers were not very large, but particularly handsome ones, with twelve tines.

I moved the camp after this a day's march up a tributary of the Sinde, and in five days killed another stag and three bears, having besides had several unsuccessful stalks. The stag we had heard bellowing all day, in the evening we saw cross a plot of open ground into a patch of forest, in which we found him in company with several hinds. As I was creeping up to the spot they all came out into the open, a beautiful sight, and I ensconced myself behind a large stone till they came near enough for a shot. When I fired the stag dropped dead on the spot, without even a single convulsive kick, and I found I had made more a lucky than a good shot, for, though I aimed at the shoulder, the bullet had gone through his neck. His antlers were much longer and thicker than those of the first one, but not nearly so handsome, and had only nine tines. In this valley I found the remains of a similar building to that at Muttaen, but it had been on a much smaller scale, and was more dilapidated. The village, near which I was encamped, was in a very nice situation, surrounded with orchards of apricot, walnut, and other fruit trees, and, as indeed all the hill villages in Cashmere are, a perfect picture of a mountain hamlet.

The climate was perfection—a pleasanter it is impossible to conceive; and if there is a place in India intended by Providence for colonization with Europeans, that place is doubtless Cashmere. The houses in the villages are large, but ungainly-looking buildings, made for the most part of thick wooden planks. The upper story, which is partly open, is occupied in summer, and the lower in winter. The dress of the people is the same as in the city,— a long, wide, loose garment like a shirt, generally made of strong woollen cloth, but sometimes of cotton; short wide pyjamas, confined below the knee with a long band of party-coloured cloth, four or five inches wide, which is wound round the calf from the ancle; a turban or skull-cap, and grass sandals. When at work the village people sometimes confine the shirt round the waist with a rope or a long piece of cloth, but at all other times it is worn loose. The strange custom of carrying beneath the dress the little basket, with the earthen vessel full of ashes and live charcoal, is universal. When walking, one arm is withdrawn from the sleeve to carry it; and when seated, it rests on the ground beneath the dress. This singular contrivance no doubt serves to keep the body comfortably warm in the coldest weather, though one would fancy it must often be an incumbrance and injurious to health.

Coming back into the Sinde valley, and making a short march further up, I found another very good spot for stags; indeed there appeared to be some on every hill, though some places, particularly where the forest was dense and continuous, were more unfavourable for stalking than others, where the hill sides were alternate strips of forest and open ground. Bears might be found almost anywhere. While hunting myself in the forests, I sent one of my shikaries and a villager to the crest of the high ridge on the right bank, to see if there were any ibex; but they returned on the fourth day, after having examined a great portion of the range, without finding any. In the meantime I had killed two brown bears, a black one, and a stag. One of the brown bears took the most killing I ever saw any animal. I saw him feeding on a grassy bank, got up within sixty yards, and planted the first bullet, as I thought, fair behind the shoulder; but I had to follow him from place to place, and fired eleven more shots before the brute was killed outright. When the skin was dried, it appeared as if it had been used as a target at some rifle match. The stag gave me a very exciting day's tracking. The first time I went out from this camp in the evening, after having killed nothing all day but a black bear, I came across a party of shepherds, and on asking them about game, they pointed out a hill opposite, which bulged out in the middle to a sharp ridge running from top to bottom, one side of which was forest, and the other a grassy slope. Every morning and evening, they said, a stag and several hinds came out of the forest into the slope, and if I waited a little I should probably see them now. Of course I brought myself to an anchor at once, lit a cheroot, and while lolling on the grass, quietly enjoying the weed, a couple of hinds came out of the forest on to the open, and were quickly followed by a majestic old stag and two more hinds. They were too far away to go after at the time, as, there being a deep ravine to cross, it would have been dark ere I got to the place; so I sat awhile and watched them, trying to fix on my mind the advantages the hill offered for a successful stalk, on whatever part I might find them again. With the glass I could see the stag was a much finer one than either of the two I had got, and determined that, if possible, he should make the third, if I hunted him for a week. He did indeed at the distance look a noble creature, and his stack of antlers something tremendous.

The next morning I started before daylight, and when I got to the hill, and to a spot where I could look over it, had the satisfaction to find stag and hinds on the ground. It was a fair stalk, such a one as I fancy is seldom got in such a woody country; and I am ashamed to say that after all my practice I made a sad failure, though I set to work, saying inwardly, "Now I'll just show the way how to stalk deer;" and had there been any spectators I should have placed them on the opposite hill to watch proceedings, confident of being about to distinguish myself. I got up nicely to about one hundred and fifty yards, but fearful of not making a sure shot at that distance, would not fire, and lost my chance by trying to steal another fifty. The ground was broken, with here and there masses of rock, and I thought by taking advantage of the inequalities, and, where likely to be exposed for a moment, crawling in the long grass, I could manage it; but they were too sharp for me, and made themselves scarce before I had got many yards from my first hiding place. Not wishing to disturb them further I would not chance a running shot, and went at once to another part of the hill, where I found and killed a brown bear. Coming back to the slope a little before dusk I found them out again close to the ridge; and going into the forest behind it, and down to their level, when I crossed to it again, I got a capital shot at eighty yards. The stag went off with the hinds down the hill, and crossed the ridge below me into the forest; but I felt quite certain I had not missed the pot-shot—whatever I might have done with the second barrel, and the smooth gun fired as he went off down the hill—and following a little way I found blood on the tracks. Have you ever, brother sportsman, made a similar mess of two such good chances at an animal, the like of which you can hardly hope to meet again, and which you would have given almost anything to get? If you have, you may conceive how disgusted I was with myself all the rest of the evening. I don't recollect whether I dreamt about it or not, but most probably I did all night.

Taking up the tracks next morning, we followed

them for nearly a mile in the forest; sometimes guided by the drops of blood, and at others by the footprints and displacement of the underwood. A promise of five rupees reward if we found the stag, probably sharpened the eyes of the shikaries. We were tracking very carefully through a dense part of the forest, when suddenly up he jumped, apparently not much the worse for what I had given him the previous evening; and as he was disappearing through the bushes I fired a quick snap shot and hit him in the hind-quarters, and fortunately the wound, though it did not materially hurt him, bled freely, so that tracking was afterwards comparatively easy. In half an hour we came on him again, but he got off without my getting even a snap shot; indeed we did not see him at all, but only heard his crash through the bushes. Twice again we tracked him up, but I did not get a shot either time, and as the drops of blood were now only found at long intervals, and we were often at fault by coming across other tracks which it was difficult to distinguish from the right one, I was sadly afraid we had lost him; when, perceiving we had got almost to the end of the forest, I went round to the open, telling the shikaries, to whom I gave the double gun, to wait a little and then follow the track on. In a little while I heard a shot, and presently the stag came trotting out, affording me a fair cross shot which floored him. This exciting chase had occupied us nearly the whole day. I had not thought much of the other two, but when I got up to this one and surveyed his magnificent antlers, I was really delighted. He was indeed a splendid fellow, and I felt as if nothing more so exciting was left for me in Cashmere. One such animal would be compensation enough for a month's toil in the roughest hills. To enable my readers to form some idea of my prize, I give the dimensions of his antlers:—

	Inches.
Length of each from forehead to point	46
Length of brow tine	18
Circumference round the bur	10
,, ,, middle of antler	7

The tines, twelve in number, were all perfect, and this head was by far the finest trophy I brought from the hills.

I hunted for another fortnight, in various places about the valley, but only got one more stag. They had ceased almost entirely to bellow, and though their tracks were plentiful, they were very difficult to find. During the time I got five more bears, three black and two brown, and a musk-deer. The latter appear to be very rare in the Cashmere hills; though the forests seem to be very likely for them, I only saw three all the time I was out. The harvest was gathering, and plenty seemed to reign around, but the poor villagers were very badly off for food. Goolab Sing takes the revenue in kind, three-fourths of the produce being, I was told, set aside for him; and out of the remaining fourth, the kardars and other officials get something, so that there is little left for the cultivators themselves. At one village I wanted to purchase some honey, but all the hives were sealed, and the owners dare not open one without the kardar being present. When the men who carried my loads or went out with me shooting, brought breakfast with them to eat on the road, I remarked that it generally consisted of a few boiled turnips only, without either bread or rice. Often and often I was asked, "Would the British never relieve them from their cruel bondage?"

I had as yet only got one male ibex, that killed near the Mannerung pass, and as a wind-up determined to try for them a few days; so went to Soonamurg, the highest inhabited place up the valley, and took the camp up a little stream that joins the river a mile below the village. The ground was very like the burrel hills about Gangootree, but ibex I found were very scarce, and with difficulty I got two females, after four days of very hard work. I twice saw males, but they were so wild and shy I could not get a single chance; and at last, all having apparently left that portion of the range, I gave up the pursuit, and came down the valley again. At one village, just before getting into the Cashmere valley itself, bears were absurdly numerous. There was a jungle close by, of some trees not unlike blackthorn, bearing small berries, and these being ripe the bears, I suppose, had congregated at the spot. The evening I arrived I saw nine, and killed one and wounded two others; and the next morning saw seven, and killed two. They soon got frightened, for the evening of that day I saw but two, at neither of which could I get a shot, and the morning after there was not one.

I had been out six weeks, and when I got back to the city, found all the visitors except one had left for the plains. As far as I could learn, I had made the best bag of stags, no one having killed more than three; but I had been out a week longer than any other person, which of course gave me a better chance, though I might have met that by saying I had taken the worst ground. I was told, however, that one stag had been killed with antlers of fourteen tines, and much finer than the ones of mine I thought so magnificent. The person who was considered the best shot that season in the valley, and who was of course set down for the best bag, had been very unfortunate, and only killed one stag, though he had with him two men said to be the best shikaries in Cashmere. What the valley may be like in winter, I know not, but just now, the middle of November, in regard to climate, it might safely challenge any spot on the surface of the globe, uniting as it does the soft voluptuous feeling of the most favoured spots on the shores of the Mediterranean, with the sharp bracing air of a mountain country.

In whatever corner of the world Englishmen get into, if there should be any articles, not exclusively commercial, worth taking away, either for their intrinsic value, or as mementos of the place, in a few years or even months, everything of the kind doubles or trebles in price. Cashmere is no exception. A friend of mine, who had spent a summer in the valley a few years before, when it first became frequented by Europeans, had shared his purchases with me. Similar articles I found were not to be had now for less than double the amount he had then paid for them. The principal things European visitors get made or purchase in Cashmere, are, embroidered chogas, cloaks, turbans, table-cloths, bed-covers, &c., from the shawl manufactories, shawls themselves being comparatively little sought after, and papier-maché ware. The latter was formerly ridiculously cheap, and appears to have been from a remote period an article of native manufacture. My purchases were not extensive, as the price paid for the embroidered articles appeared to me to be far more than what they were really worth. A good choga could not be bought for less than fifty or sixty rupees, and a table-cloth six feet square for about the same, and shawls may be bought in Calcutta for as little, if not for less, than similar ones in Cashmere itself. The only article from the shawl manufactories I took, was a bed-cover of dark blue shawl wool-cloth embroidered with silk. It was certainly very handsome, but I paid 5*l*. for it.

Putting all my traps into a boat, I bid adieu to Serinuggur on the 20th of November, and went down the river to the Wuller Lake, having decided on going home by the Baramoola pass, and on the way trying a few days for markhoor at a place my Cashmere shikaree knew. The lake and the swampy ground near I found covered with waterfowl, but they would not let a boat come within gun-shot, so I tried the rifle, and never was more surprised in my life. I got into a small canoe with one of my boatmen, and we would get up to within perhaps 150 yards of a flock of geese which covered the water for a quarter of a mile or more further. One would have laid almost any wager that a bullet could not go through without killing at least one, and I expected indeed to see two or three struggling on the water after every shot, but I fired over and over again, and followed the flocks from place to place about the lake nearly all day without getting a single goose. I could see the ball strike, sometimes close to the foremost birds, and go on ricochetting on the surface of the water, right throught the flock as they were rising, and how it sped without coming in contact with one seemed a perfect mystery. After a few hours of such work one ceases to wonder at the small number of missiles which take effect out of the hundreds of thousands which are discharged with murderous intention, when man exerts his destructive energies against his fellow-man on the field of battle. Violent storms are at certain seasons prevalent on the Wuller Lake, and boats are sometimes lost while crossing from where the Jhelum enters to where it again leaves it.

Shortly after leaving the lake we arrived

at Shapoor, a little below which place the river enters the hills and ceases to be navigable. I had some difficulty in getting Coolies, but with the assistance of the kardars at last managed to get off, and marching along the banks of the river, in two days came to the entrance of a tributary stream, at the head of which was the markhoor ground my shikaree said he knew best, though it turned out he knew very little about it at all. On the road we had passed another old building similar in structure to the ruins of Muttaen, very perfect in all its parts, but on a small scale. Making a long march up the valley we got to the highest village, and from this made arrangements for a few days' sojourn on the hills around; taking a portion of the camp with us so as not to be obliged to return to the village every night. The ground was something similar to that I had lately been hunting over, on the other side of the valley, but the hills were steeper and more rugged, and some of the rocky faces appeared almost inaccessible. The first day was quite a blank; we went up the hill over the village, and hunted all day without seeing any animal whatever. The next, sending the few traps to another spot to which we intended coming down in the evening, we tried the adjoining hill. As far, however, as markhoor were concerned we were equally unsuccessful, but came across a flock of tahr, out of which I killed a fine male: they are exactly the same as those in Gurwhal. A musk-deer was the only other animal seen. There had been a little snow on the hills, which still lay on the north and west sides of all the ravines, so that we could tell pretty well what animals had lately been on the ground, and though game was apparently very scarce, it was evident from the traces a flock of markhoor were somewhere near. The shikaree pointed out to me the difference between the footprints of these and those of the tahr, very trifling certainly, but plainly distinguishable when the prints were perfect in the snow. Directing the camp to be moved to another spot we tried a third hill, hunting upwards to the rocky crest, and down another side, over some lovely ground, alternate strips of forest, rock, and grassy slopes and ravines, and a perfect place for stalking. There was, however, nothing to be seen in the shape of game, and I began to think my shikaree had brought me into the only corner of Cashmere where there was nothing to be got, but I could not feel the least angry with him, for there was already more mortification expressed in his countenance than any words of mine could occasion. It was getting towards evening, and we had got nearly half way down the hill, when we came across the track of a single markhoor in the snow; it led towards the bottom, and as luck would have it, in the direction of our camp, but the ground was something frightful to walk over, and it was not without some hesitation I ventured to follow. It was a succession of narrow gullies and sharp ridges running from the middle of the hill, which above, though steep and rocky in many parts, was good walking ground; one side of the gullies being covered with forest trees and low jungle; and the other composed of rocks and open ground, which, though covered with short grass, was so steep, that the footing was very precarious, and a single false step would have precipitated one to the bottom. It was, however, a splendid place for a shot, and the freshness of the footprints, showing the markhoor had passed not many hours before, encouraged me to venture over it. We had gone over several of the little ridges, examining each fresh gully very carefully before showing ourselves, and had got into one rather wider than the rest, where the forest on the shady side was rather thick, when suddenly out of it jumped the markhoor, sprung on to the opposite rocky face, crossed it, and disappeared over the next ridge, all so instantaneously, that, though the rifle was pushed into my hands at once, I did not get a shot. I went on, almost disgusted with markhoor-hunting, and got to camp without seeing anything else. Here I found my servant had got hold of a village shikaree, who, with two more men was returning from a few days' shooting with a matchlock and a couple of female tahr he had killed. He offered to take me to a hill where they had seen a flock of markhoor, and a bargain was soon concluded, the conditions of which were, he was to receive five rupees if we found them, and nothing if we did not, the proposition being his own and gladly acceeded to on my part. He sent his companions home, and giving directions to the villagers, who carried my traps, where to take the tent to, we started early the following morning and got to the ground about noon. My new friend, I soon found, was an acquisition; he knew every inch of the hills around, and appeared very intelligent. He gave me to understand that markhoor were very difficult animals to get at, very wary, wandered about a great deal, and when once disturbed on any hill, left it entirely, giving no chance of a successful pursuit; also that there were very few of them, and a person might be considered very fortunate if on one range of hills he found more than one lot. We had now got to the extreme head of the valley, and the forest only extended a little way up the hill-sides, which were everywhere steep and rocky.

Instead of proceeding to hunt we went a little way up one of the hills, and, getting on a favourable spot, where we had a good view around, sat down to watch. After sitting some hours, my new guide went, with one of the other shikaries, a mile further, to look out from another spot, and in a little while I saw this man coming back alone, which gave me hopes they had seen something; nor was I disappointed. He beckoned me to come on, and when I joined him, he told me a flock of markhoor had just come out of the forest on to a ledge of rock and grass, on which they were now feeding. I soon got to the spot, and there, sure enough, they were, about 500 yards off, and the Cashmeree behind the ridge watching them. The stalk was a rather difficult one, for there was a deep ravine between, and the only possible way of getting nearer was by going up the hill behind the ridge on which we were till out of their sight, and then crossing the ravine on to their hill, and coming down on them from above, all which it appeared difficult to do without being seen. Leaving all the men but the new shikaree, I went nearly a mile up the hill, crossed the ravine, and came down the opposite slope towards the spot where the markhoor were feeding, the swell of the ground concealing our advance much better than we anticipated. I felt this would probably be my only chance of getting a markhoor, and though determined to be as cool and collected as possible, the thought made me feel very nervous, and I could feel, and I think even hear, my heart beat as we got near. What an easy thing, when away from the actual scene, it appears to be to knock over an animal offering a pot-shot at eighty or a hundred yards, and having in your hands a rifle with which you can smash a bottle at that distance almost every shot! How very easy it seems to be to keep as cool and collected when firing at wild animals, as when firing at a mark! You determine over and over again to be so, yet how often does the determination prove of no avail at the critical moment, and your heart beats to that degree that you miss the shot, or make a mess of the whole affair! This is, indeed, the one reason why so few of the many sportsmen who ramble in the Himalayas turn out successful deer-stalkers, particularly young hands. They walk perseveringly enough, no hill is too steep, no peak too high, no toil too severe, if they do but find game; and when it is found, and they get within shot, after perhaps an excellent stalk, their coolness leaves them just when most needed, and they become so excited that the result is almost a farce; several shots have probably been fired, and the animals are gone without one having been hit. I have known first-rate shots at a target, or such a mark as a bird perched in a tree, who could not hit a deer or a wild goat once in half-a-dozen times; and have seen beginners get so excited that they scarcely seemed to know what they were doing, as ramming a ball down the rifle without powder, or reloading in some such strange fashion, abundantly testified. In imagination it seems quite as easy to shoot at animals in the forest, with just as much coolness as at a card stuck against the trunk of a tree from your tent-door, yet nevertheless, when it comes to practice, not one in ten of those who turn to the rifle for amusement or excitement can do so in their noviciate; many acquire but a moderate share of this coolness, and but few become perfect masters of the art.

To return to our markhoor; —the village Nimrod to whose guidance in the stalk I had entirely surrendered myself, took me up beautifully, and finished his share of the work by pointing out from behind a little ridge the flock of markhoor on the opposite rocky face of the hill, the nearest being not more than eighty yards distant. With the greatest caution I rested the rifle on the rock, having singled out one of the longest horned fellows that offered a favourable shoulder shot, and holding my breath, took a deliberate aim and fired. There was a grand rush, the whole flock, consisting of nearly a score of males and females, going helter-skelter over the rocks at such a pace that the second barrel and the smooth gun were fired almost at random, it being impossible to take any certain aim as they leaped from crag to crag without halting a single moment. But where is the one first fired at? I felt certain he was hit, and with some difficulty getting to the spot where he stood, we found a few hairs cut off by the ball, and a few paces further drops of blood on the track. A little way behind the next ridge we found him lying at the foot of a steep rock, in a cave formed by its hollowing a little at the base, and another bullet in the neck finished him. He was a noble animal, and the other shikaries coming up we skinned him carefully, and he made the last addition to my now magnificent collection.

I hunted the following day in hopes of getting a female, but saw no more, and the shikaree said there was not much probability of finding another flock in the valley. This finished my shooting.

We went down the valley again to the road where I had left my heavy baggage, made another march along the banks of the Jhelum, then leaving it and crossing the Baramoola pass, in six more marches through low hills and well cultivated valleys reached Bimber, at the foot of the hills. From this place I marched to Umritsir, one of the chief towns of the Punjaub, where I took dak to Meerut, putting all my traps and servants on the government bullock train; and so ended my summer ramble in the Himalayas.

THE END.

LONDON
PRINTED BY SPOTTISWOODE AND CO.
NEW-STREET SQUARE.

www.ingramcontent.com/pod-product-compliance
Lightning Source LLC
Chambersburg PA
CBHW020226240426

43672CB00006B/434